COLLECTED WORKS OF CHARLES BERG

Volume 8

I0083723

MADKIND

MADKIND

The Origin and Development of the Mind

CHARLES BERG

R Routledge
Taylor & Francis Group

LONDON AND NEW YORK

First published in 1962 by George Allen & Unwin Ltd

This edition first published in 2022
by Routledge
4 Park Square, Milton Park, Abingdon, Oxon OX14 4RN

and by Routledge
605 Third Avenue, New York, NY 10158

Routledge is an imprint of the Taylor & Francis Group, an informa business

British Library Cataloguing in Publication Data
A catalogue record for this book is available from the British Library

ISBN: 978-1-032-16970-5 (Set)
ISBN: 978-1-003-25348-8 (Set) (ebk)
ISBN: 978-1-032-17248-4 (Volume 8) (hbk)
ISBN: 978-1-032-18036-6 (Volume 8) (pbk)
ISBN: 978-1-003-25257-3 (Volume 8) (ebk)

DOI: 10.4324/9781003252573

Publisher's Note
The publisher has gone to great lengths to ensure the quality of this reprint but points out that some imperfections in the original copies may be apparent.

Disclaimer
The publisher has made every effort to trace copyright holders and would welcome correspondence from those they have been unable to trace.

This book is a re-issue originally published in 1948. The language used is a reflection of its era and no offence is meant by the Publishers to any reader by this re-publication.

CHARLES BERG

MADKIND

THE ORIGIN AND DEVELOPMENT
OF THE MIND

London

GEORGE ALLEN & UNWIN LTD

RUSKIN HOUSE MUSEUM STREET

PREFACE

Although Charles Berg wrote many books, he was always gathering material and making notes of what he hoped would one day be his *magnum opus*. The book as he conceived it was on a much grander scale than the present work and would have run to three volumes. The first volume consisted of a detailed anthropological 'Symptomatology' or 'Family History'; the second was a modern cosmogony and modern cosmological theory, and the third contained clinical material, based on his vast experience in the field of psycho-analysis, and an examination of present-day civilization to show how the mind acts in accordance with emotionally determined beliefs.

Unfortunately, fatal illness overtook him while he was still finishing the work.

For practical purposes it has been necessary to reduce the manuscript very considerably, and while some of the overwhelming clinical evidence has had to be sacrificed the main argument has in no way been invalidated. I would like to thank all the many friends who have helped and encouraged me in this work, in particular Dr Leo Pincherle for kindly checking the later scientific chapters.

RUTH BERG

CONTENTS

I.	General Introduction	page	1
II.	Symptomatology: Delusions of Primitive Man		7
III.	Mythology, Cosmogony and Comparative Religion		20
IV.	Current Behaviour: Libido Expressed in Social Customs		37
V.	The Social Neurosis of Modern Man		50
VI.	Marriage		58
VII.	Growing Up		71
VIII.	Education		81
IX.	Sport, Games and Social Expressions of Aggression		95
X.	Fear		102
XI.	War		108
XII.	Politics and Punishment		122
XIII.	Culture and the Psychology of Authoritarian Institutions		137
XIV.	Belief in God		145
XV.	Religion, an Emotionally Determined Belief		156
XVI.	'Treatment' and Ego Development		173
XVII.	The Mind is Primarily a Physiological Organ		181
XVIII.	A Modern Cosmogony		189
XIX	The Macrocosm		199
XX.	Protein Synthesis and the Origin of Life		205
XXI.	The Origin of Living Forms and the Development of Nerve Tissue		216
XXII.	Outline of Evolution		230
XXIII.	Growth and Structure of the Mind		240
XXIV.	Treatment, Prognosis, Untruth and Truth and the Feeling-Tone of Life		255

NOTE

All reference numbers in the text refer to the
Bibliography listed on pages 269-270.

CHAPTER I

GENERAL INTRODUCTION

This book is an attempt to understand the Mind of Man—to understand its relation to the Universe, its origin and development, its capacity (if any) for objective observation, its capacity for assessment of truth, its function and its future. *Madkind* is the case history of a psychosis.

The 'Case' that I have in mind is the 'Patient' of today, the 'normal', 'mentally healthy' man of today. His history, including family history, extends back to the primitive ages of man, in which the morbid diathesis will be strikingly apparent. Aetiology, the science of causation, will go back even further, very much further, to show that the primal causes and physical contributions could hardly be expected to make for a reality sense uncontaminated by psychosis.

Our emotions will be regarded as appropriate for consideration in this book—as a study of the *subject*, by which I mean mind. In the meantime, there is much of an objective nature to be considered before we shall be ready to study the instrument (mind) which is engaged upon this study.

The matters for our consideration, however necessarily limited, will include an objective study of the beliefs and behaviour of primitive man, then we shall consider the instrument, our mind, and how well-equipped or how ill-equipped it is for reality appreciation and assessment, in contradistinction to mere emotional reaction. Emotional reactions will be shown to give us no true basis for any reality assessment. Finally, there is a scientific assessment of how our minds came into existence.

The subject matter of this book is more than that of a mass-psychosis. The illness has practically no beginning, and as far as we can see, no end. Is it all pervading in human space and time? Compared with an individual psychotic, the patient is enormous. This surely is a 'case' worth studying, describing and analysing.

Professionally for forty years I have been listening to the private equivalents of these same emotionally determined beliefs and behaviours which comprise our history, and it has been borne home to me that the whole of our lives, our thoughts and behaviour are founded upon delusions. However, it is obvious that these matters are relative, and if we are going to make so bold as to describe the average person as suffering from delusion, we must look for a special yard-stick for comparison. This is provided by comparing the beliefs of one age with those of another. For instance, it is easy for us to see that primitive man, with his life ruled almost completely by innumerable spirits and vexatious superstitions was, by our standards, deluded; but it is not so easy for us to see delusions of the present day, except perhaps where one can demonstrate the fact *that so many of the old systems die hard and permeate the new.* It would seem that mankind is too immersed in the emotional or symptomatic experience of his present illness to be able to answer it by the yardstick of anything in his current life. But if we present to him the emotional or symptomatic behaviours that belong elsewhere in time or place, the slight divergence from his current behaviour enables him to measure those psychoses, at least in relation to his own, and thereby to see how mad *they* were.

In this book an attempt will be made to trace in broad outline the development of the human mind up to the present day. It will be shown that it is largely a legacy of the past, physically, chemically, biologically and psychologically, and I have felt it most important to give examples of two varieties of knowledge, historical and scientific, in order to justify the conclusions that I have reached.

Primitive societies, and even more so, highly cultured societies, are hiding their repressed psychological struggles under masks which are their cultural patterns. Society, like the individual, has illnesses, small ones and large ones (e.g. war), and it may therefore not be an idle study to strip these behaviouristic manifestations of their disguises, to trace them to their sources in hidden conflict, and, so far as possible, to lay bare the psychopathology of social ills.

One extraordinary lesson the practice of psychotherapy has taught me is that, the one thing the patient is most keen about is clinging to his psychosis. He resists most violently the slightest attempt to alter it, in any of its aspects, delusion or behaviour. This is because it enables him to live emotionally, which relieves tension and is gratifying, rather than rationally, which does not relieve tension and is not gratifying. Probably in most cases this is an understatement. He would probably have this psychosis only if he really needed it in order to feel tolerably comfortable inside, in order not to have more tension or anxiety than his system could hold without illness or death. Anyway, he clings to it as though his life depended upon doing so, and in dozens of obvious ways, from rigidity of custom to rigidity of belief, we are no doubt all doing the same sort of thing. Sanity comes very slowly in psychological evolution.

In this book I have sketched the psychopathology of the process which is responsible for the manifestations of life, which we call culture, civilization, customs and social institutions. Only thus will we be in a position to see them in their true light, in spite of being so accustomed to them and in the habit of regarding them all as basic, inevitable phenomena.

Human beings, with their long animal instinct-based history, have for many thousands of years been basically in conflict with the demands of the society or social group in which they live. The current conflict can be expressed simply, perhaps over-simply, in the following terms: we have a heritage of instinctual impulses which have long since become the pattern of the life process, as in all animals. The instincts in us, as in them, are forever pressing their demands for immediate gratification.

If that was all there was to it, we would be no madder than any other wild beast, but probably mad enough in this society of ours to be speedily put away. The id, or reservoir of the instincts, is sometimes said to be mad on this very account. This may be true if we define it as a level of mind which has no cognizance of environmental reality; in this sense it is largely a theoretical abstraction. Even the most primitive animal has some cognizance of reality, if only a sense of smell that takes it to its food.

But the degree of reality sense possessed by the animal, even the higher animal short of man, would hardly be enough to fit us into the wheels of our social structure. When we do meet the occasional person, inside or outside a mental hospital, who appears to behave too much in keeping with his instinctual demands, and with too little regard for reality, particularly for social reality, we unhesitatingly regard him as at least a bit 'mad'. His inner world is too much with him at the expense of appropriate reality adjustment. Whether he seems to us too sexual or too aggressive, he is likely to arouse a reactive aggression in us, which collectively would tend to have the effect of segregating him at least. Nevertheless, instincts, whether we divide them into life and death instincts, sexual and aggressive instincts, or any other specification we wish, have been our heritage for millions of years, and have been responsible for our survival so far.

But not so long since—perhaps during the last fifty or five hundred thousand years—another factor has arisen. This other factor is due to family and social organization. There is no doubt that the individual, in uniting with his fellows to form a social group, a tribe, clan, a society or a nation, has to control or suppress to some degree at any rate his instinctual desires, his omnipotence, in order to avoid conflict, battle, and probably extermination. To gain the benefits of communal life, a certain amount of omnipotence and the pressure of desire for immediate instinct gratification, must at least be under some degree of control.

The balance of these two forces within the psyche, instinct

pressure on the one hand and social demands on the other, calls for a continued delicacy of adjustment. Ideally of course this should be the work of the ego or reality principle. If this were so, a greater degree of sanity than we possess might be the result. The truth is that this struggle or intra-psychic conflict has a long history, much longer than our knowledge of primitive cultures would indicate. We know that ontogeny is largely an abbreviated repetition of phylogeny, and therefore these considerations would be conducive to the belief that something equivalent to what happened in the baby's mind was beginning to take place in the mind of prehistoric man, or the pre-human animal. Emotional reactions in adult life all have their infantile equivalents. In the light of psychoanalytical discovery, it may not be too much to say that it is impossible for an adult to get a really new sort of emotional reaction. His reaction patterns, apart from the inherited ones called instincts, were all laid down during his earliest weeks, months and years of extra-uterine life, and anything he experiences can only be a reactivation of some earlier or instinctual reaction pattern.

The 'reality' environment which the infant first encounters in its life, is supplied by parents or parent substitutes. Quite early in its life it begins to learn that attempts to facilitate instinct gratifications are not enough. Parents exercise their prohibitions and their demands, and they are stronger than the child.

Conflict is in a sense mitigated by revolutionary changes within the psyche, such changes as introjecting the parent figures and their demands and building up a department of the mind which operates intra-psychically in the same way as parents operate environmentally. Instincts are not allowed to have everything their own way. The parents will not allow it, and the introjected parents, now in the form of the infant's superego, also will not allow it. What is more, the introjected parents, or superego, is inside and there is no escaping its watchful eye, indeed it can detect even the thought or phantasy in the absence of the deed and withdraw love, or institute persecutions and punishments inside the mind itself. In other words, this conflict between instinct and environment has now led to revolutionary changes within the mind itself, and has paved the way for the subsequent instinct control, suppression and repression which will continue when the child leaves parent domination to take his place in society.

Perhaps it is the discomfort of life and the force of the discomfiture that drives us into a hundred and one complicated and inadequately successful attempts to alleviate the otherwise intolerable internal distress. We have nevertheless attempted to solve this problem, either theoretically or practically, and there is evidence for the theory that all our behaviour, activities and beliefs are due to an anxiety-driven compulsion causing us to cast about trying to get a modicum of relief.

There are curious features about this internal mental structure, features which are variously responsible for the different manifestations which our activities and beliefs assume. All symptoms, behaviouristic or otherwise, individual or cultural, are composed of elements or energies taken from the opposing sides of unconscious conflicts. What we may be expressing, symptomatically or in any other way, is a complex structure compounded of two or more opposites in conflict with one another. This for instance is how symptoms, complexes, patterns of behaviour and patterns of culture originate.

It will be seen that the mind becomes the victim of inhibiting and early acquired conflicting forces within itself long before it has time to make an accurate assessment of reality or the balance of merits between instinct gratification and reality adjustment. In other words, it grows up 'ill', with an over-riding need to get rid of, to assuage or to mitigate its uncomfortable distressing state by hook or by crook. It chooses both ways, indeed every way that it can, as it were, lay its hands upon, and it is from this that we get the development of culture, symptomatic behaviour and beliefs, some of them institutionalized, which comprises our civilization.

If our ego, reason or capacity for reality appreciation were adequate to the task, which it is not, we would discover, one, that the world in which we live has been created by our own internal psychosis and, two, that it is not in any way necessary that this structure is inevitable (except for our psychosis) and that if our reason came more into the picture, and was competent to rule our psychosis, we would envisage and create a state of affairs which could maintain and increase all the gratifying advantages, and discover that most of the ills from which we suffer are not in the nature of things at all, but merely expressions of our internal pain or conflict of our psychosis. It is a question of cause and effect. We are too ready to assume that the external situation, sociological or otherwise, is the cause of our internal state. So far as social situations are concerned, although there is some reciprocity, in other words, although they can and do influence the individual, they are not primary causes. This can be deduced from the very fact that they came second. The'internal state of the mind has the developmental priority. This fact alone proves that the external or sociological situation is secondary to the internal or psychological situation.

If there is one thing I am more convinced of than another, it is this. If our internal state, particularly our unconscious phantasy, changed, our external state or pattern of culture would follow suit. If all babies and infants were brought up in keeping with modern psychological enlightenment, within a generation or two there would be world-wide changes in the social and international order. The individual, each and every individual is absolutely set upon living in a childhood repetition of a most fantastic pleasure world, a world closely related to his period in the womb, to his period on the breast, to his subsequent emotional attachment to his parents, to fantastic conceptions of security and love and emotional gratification. Romance and imagination rule the day to the exclusion of everything that is true and real. The important thing about all this is that indulgence in this process is his life, his very life, his whole life, and nothing but his life.

I have not spent all these years countering the resistance of individuals, even of those with positive transference, to nurse the illusion that the average reader, singly or collectively, will change his views or attitudes, or surrender more than one iota of his resistances. He may surrender to propaganda if it is sufficiently rewarding emotionally, but hardly to factual and scientific reality. As I have said, the one thing people are keen about is clinging to their psychosis. Why then, am I attempting to write this book at all? It is because I believe that incorporated in the evolutionary process there is a tendency for more primitive mechanisms (originally physical and chemical, and subsequently emotional) to give place to or rather to evolve to greater and greater reality adjustment. To ignore reality is to perish. There is no doubt that life survives only in proportion to its capacity for reality adjustment and in my opinion the era is approaching, however far away it may still be, when adjustment of life to environment will necessitate the aid of the newly developing and still very embryonic faculty of reality appreciation and reason. In any case it is obvious that universal changes will meet with resistance, and at the best can be only slow in their achievements.

CHAPTER II

SYMPTOMATOLOGY

DELUSIONS OF PRIMITIVE MAN

I propose first to confine myself briefly to a history of the early symptoms of madkind. To understand the workings of the primitive mind, we need to know something about anthropology, mythology and religion, all of which provide us with an abundance of material. There are such subjects as animism, superstition, mythology, folklore and religion or comparative religion on the speculative side. There is also the concept of *mana*. On the behaviouristic side, we have such subjects as magic (with its spells, its rites, and its sorcerers), cannibalism, incest, regicide and parricide. Perhaps most of these could be grouped as positive or gratifying expressions. Negative or restricting expressions include taboos, totems, initiation ceremonies such as circumcision, and sacrifice.

In the well-known book *General Anthropology*, edited by Franz Boas,[1] Benedict says: 'In animistic belief and practice, man created the universe in his own image. He extended his human attitudes toward his fellows to an anthropomorphic universe.' Primitive man regarded 'the external world, the tree, the sea, the pot, the corn . . . as persons', and therefore felt that he had obligations towards them as though they were living beings. A major function of his religion was to discharge these obligations. Thus his religious behaviour was a sort of mixture of behaviour towards things and persons.

Magic according to Money-Kyrle[2] is associated with animism and animatism. 'Animism is concerned with the belief in spirits, which inhabit things or persons, and animatism with the belief in impersonal but supernatural forces, which often emanate from them. Now in animism and animatism may be found . . . the core of human irrationality, the source from which nearly all irrationality may be derived. For, as analysis has shown, in particular the work of Mrs Klein, it is not only the savage who believes himself to be aided or persecuted by spirits and supernatural forces. Every child passes through a stage of similar belief; and in later life even the sanest of us show traces of the neurotic and psychotic disorders which are one of the legacies of this stage.'

Frazer's distinction between magic and religion is that magic consists in the direct control by man of the forces of nature, while religion relies upon the propitiation of these and other higher powers. Another distinction is that magic is usually an executive procedure, while the term religion includes, besides its executive activities, such as prayer, spells and ritual, a system of beliefs.[3] In antiquity priest and sorcerer were one and the same person, but it would seem that as religion went in more for propitiation of the powers that be, and magic more for coercion, the two parted company, and even became rivals. However, Frazer affirms that religion has everywhere been preceded by magic.

According to Benedict[1] 'science deals with cause and effect . . . in the natural world', while 'magic deals with cause and effect . . . in the supernatural world, *and these are fabrications of the human mind.*' (My italics).

Prayer also was commonly used as a magical formula, and could even be, like magic, compelling to the god. To the savage, words have a very special magical significance. This is specifically the case when they are used in the form of spells at a magical rite, but even apart from this, words appear to have a magical power of their own. This is familiar to us even at the present day in the form of blessings and curses.

The life of primitive man is full of restrictions. For instance, one of the many tabood objects or things is, as one might expect, blood. There are a million and one taboos connected with blood. Royal blood apparently has some special quality in this respect, and in some tribes it must never be shed upon the ground. This does not mean that the life of a king is necessarily safeguarded. Frazer tells us that about the year 1688 the King of Siam was put to death 'after the manner of royal criminals, or as princes of the blood are treated when convicted of capital crimes, which is by putting them into a large iron cauldron, and pounding them to pieces with wooden pestles, because none of their royal blood must be spilt on the ground, it being, by their religion, thought great impiety to contaminate the divine blood by mixing it with earth'.

There are a lot of taboos connected with the head and particularly with the hair and hair cutting. The hair should not fall into the hands of malicious persons who might work magic on the man it came from to his detriment or death. Sometimes a precaution is taken not to cut the hair at all, otherwise the thing is hedged about by a lot of ceremony. It seems that a man may be bewitched by means of the clippings of his hair, the parings of his nails, or any other severed portion of his person. This superstition is almost worldwide. Apparently an Australian aborigine can dispose of his wife by taking some of her hair, tying it to his spear-thrower, and getting a friend of his to stick the spear-thrower up every night in front of the camp fire. When it falls down his wife will be dead.

Like blood, spittle is also subject to various superstitions and taboos. We have almost instinctual reactions to blood and to spittle, for example, which are in no sense reality based. It would seem that the primitives rationalized such reactions and built practically a religion out of them whereas we just accept them as part of our instinctual heritage. Sometimes we leave it at that, but sometimes we are not immune from some additional elaboration or rationalization of such instincts of ours. Secretion from the body, excrement in particular, is obviously the subject of very pronounced instinctual reactions, all of which have at some time or place been rationalized into superstitions and delusions.

Food naturally comes in for a good deal of superstitious taboo; probably all the food fads of today are relics of this emotionally based superstition and delusion.

But where superstition and taboo really come into their own, is with anything and everything connected with the two basic ingredients of the unconscious mind, and those are sexuality and murder. We of today are certainly very far from free from superstitious and magical attitudes towards these primary instincts and their associations. It has been said that no person is capable of a reality attitude towards sexuality. I have no doubt that the same applies to murder. In both instincts the quantity of emotional reaction aroused forces the ego or reason out of court, as it does with the savage in everything connected with *mana*. Amongst savages also as we might expect, the strongest reactions and therefore the firmest taboos are encountered the nearer we approach to the core of these basic instincts. Therefore it should not be surprising to learn that the physiological function of reproduction and of fertility and childbirth also comes in for special superstitious, magical and religious attention. In some places this 'takes the specific form of the fear of *menstrual blood*, which is believed to make fields barren (New Guinea), make cows go dry (Africa), or rob men of their power in war and hunting.'[1]

Anyone who handles things which have been touched by a menstruating woman is killed. Australian aborigine women at these times are forbidden under pain of death to touch anything that men use, or even to walk on a path that any man frequents. They are also secluded at childbirth, and all vessels used by them during their seclusion are burned. In Uganda the pots which a woman touches, while the impurity of childbirth or of menstruation is on her should be destroyed. 'Among the Ot Danoms of Borneo girls at the age of eight or ten years, that is before puberty, are shut up in a little room or cell of the house, and cut off from all intercourse with the world for a long time . . . the girl is in almost total darkness. She may not leave the room on any pretext whatever, not even for the most necessary purposes. None of her family may see her all the time she is shut up, but a

single slave woman is appointed to wait on her. . . . Her bodily
growth is stunted by the long want of exercise, and when, on attaining
womanhood, she is brought out, her complexion is pale and wax-
like. She is now shown the sun, the earth, the water, the trees, and
the flowers as if she were newly born. Then a great feast is made, a
slave is killed, and the girl is smeared with his blood.'[3]

An immigrant from Russia tells me that even today amongst the
very orthodox in the country, no Jew ever shakes hands with a woman
for fear that she may be menstruating, and he will have touched
something unclean. After each menstruation the woman must go to
a bath especially provided for the purpose, and be totally submerged
three times by an attendant, before she can go near her husband.

Thus we see that menstrual blood, completely harmless in every
reality aspect, is endowed by primitives and by modern man with
fictitious attributes borrowed from genital (and anal) complexes connected with sexual conflict. The result, delusionary and behaviouristic, reveals a psychosis, as well as a neurosis, which inflicts a host of
senseless restrictions and miseries of a completely unnecessary
nature. This is madness whichever way one looks at it, and is abundantly illustrated by the obsessional neurotic who practises negative
magic in his system of taboos. The actions he taboos symbolize, to
him, the satisfaction of a repressed desire. Money-Kyrle says[2] 'But
obsessional neurotics also practise positive magic; they have compulsive rituals as well as compulsive avoidances. . . . At one extreme,
the repressed desire is symbolically dramatized in the ritual; at the
other, it is repudiated by the ritual, which has therefore the same
intention as a taboo and is often, as it were, an expiatory or purifi-
catory act after the accidental breaking of a taboo.'

As we might expect, the horrors of menstruation are exceeded by
the horrors connected with the phenomenon of childbirth.

It would seem that when superstition rather than common sense
or science dictates one's behaviour, there is no limit to the absurdity
and the barbarity of the practices that can and sometimes do ensue.
For instance, Father Dupeyrat, a Roman Catholic missionary writing
in modern times of his experiences in New Guinea, describes a childbirth ceremony which appears to us almost incredible in its barbarity.
To explain the mother's behaviour he says: 'Inexorable ancestral
laws force her to accomplish one of the most revolting acts'imaginable.'[4]

The mother bearing her first child is beaten and even jumped
upon during childbirth. Having given birth to the child, 'the mother
is left strictly alone, . . . she is regarded as unclean, and cannot be
touched.' Therefore she washes herself, and leaves no trace of her
ordeal, otherwise 'the spirits of death . . . could . . . cast evil spells over
the mother or her future offspring. This done, the young mother

takes up the new-born child . . . by one leg . . . then, with a vigorous gesture, she dashes it against a rock.' Thereupon a number of sows which have young litters eat the corpse, and a piglet from the most pushing sow, a boar if the victim is a boy or a young sow if the victim is a girl, is handed to the mother 'who immediately starts feeding it at the breast.' This animal she takes, suckles it at her breast, and rears it in every way as though it were the child she has been forced to kill. When it becomes a really large pig, it is slaughtered as a feast for neighbouring tribes, but nobody of the tribe to which it belonged may consume any portion of it, but look for reciprocal invitations. Apparently all this is necessary because otherwise the worst calamities would befall the tribe 'as the spirits of the ancients would be angry'. Father Dupeyrat says that such 'a repulsive ritual is reminiscent of certain customs mentioned in the Bible, and more especially of the sacrifices offered by Carthaginian notables to propitiate the terrible god Moloch.'

This brings us to the many rites connected with fertility. It seems that 'our rude forefathers personified the powers of vegetation as male and female, and attempted, on the principle of imitative magic, to quicken the growth of trees and plants by representing the marriage of the sylvan deities in the persons of a King and Queen of May' (we still celebrate the Queen of the May) 'a Whitsun Bridegroom and Bride, and so forth'. Today in modern Europe the seasons of the year are worshipped with the appropriate ceremonial in the various Churches (e.g. Easter, Whitsun, St John's Day, Hallowe'en, Christmas).

'In central America certain persons are even said to have been appointed to perform the sexual act at the very moment when the first seeds were deposited in the ground. The use of their wives at that time was indeed enjoined upon the people by the priests as a religious duty, in default of which it was not lawful to sow the seed.'[3]

'In Ambyna, when . . . the crop is likely to be scanty, the men go naked to the plantations by night, and there seek to fertilize the trees precisely as they would impregnate women. . . . This is supposed to make the trees bear fruit more abundantly.'[3]

If all this strikes us as a bit crazy—as it undoubtedly is in that it substitutes 'magic' for science—we shall not be allowed to get away with our superiority-dissociation from it, ('They are savages so what can you expect of them? We of course are civilized and sane'), for our attitude to sexuality contains barely a grain of reason or reality sense and an abundance of unscientific superstition.

'Among the Eskimo the idea of hospitality as a moral obligation is so highly developed that a man is willing to lend his wife to a lone stranger visiting his village for any length of time. A refusal to do so attaches to him a moral stigma. In connection with a particular ceremony held to drive off evil spirits the same tribe require extra-marital relations for a day and a night. . . . Sexual licence is indulged in at mourning feasts.

'In Australia (amongst the aborigines) minutely defined restrictions are placed on formal marriages, but during the period of the tribal assemblies or corroborees all these restrictions break down—men, regardless of their class, totem, or kinship, provided they are not father, brother, or sons of the women, may have access to them. . . . Ordinarily a man must avoid his mother-in-law most carefully, but at such times he may even have intercourse with her should she be assigned to him by the council of old men.'[1]

Circumcision is another most widely distributed custom. 'In Australia subincision is practised, which consists in slitting open the urethra. Excision of the clitoris, sometimes connected with infibulation, is practised in Africa.'[1]

African boys are not considered adult members of the tribe until they have gone through the circumcision school. 'For three months they are isolated from the rest of the community. During that time they are subjected to a number of tests which purport to make them brave and to teach them endurance. Suffering is one of the important features of the instruction. The boys are subjected to blows from the attendants:' (I am sure that our 'civilized' treatment of children, especially about puberty—for instance in our Public Schools—is a homologue of this, with identical causes in our unconscious.) 'Any infringement of the rules or any disobedience is a cause for severe punishment. Formerly those who divulged the secrets to the uninitiated or who tried to escape were hanged,' (c.f. floggings at our public schools.)[1]

Camara Laye, who spent the whole of his childhood in darkest Africa behind Sierra Leone and Liberia, belongs to the Malinke tribe. He is a negro who benefited from French education, and he migrated to Paris in adult life to study. He describes frankly the terror and ordeal he had to undergo when he, at the age of fifteen, with all the other youths of the tribe, had to be circumcised. He says that: 'The public ceremony differs completely from the secret one. The public ceremony is one of rejoicing. It is the occasion of a great festival, a very noisy festival in which the whole town participates and which lasts several days. And it is almost as if by dint of noise and activity and dancing and merry-making people were trying to make us forget our anxiety about the coming ordeal, and its very real physical pain. . . .

'That year, I danced for a whole week in the main square. . . . My boubou . . . was of a brownish-red colour, a colour on which blood-stains would not show too clearly.' All this merry-making ended up with an enormous public banquet, and on the final day of the celebrations 'we were all worked up into a strange kind of excitement. The men who perform this initiation . . . shaved our heads' and then after more dancing, which lasted right through the night, 'we went immediately into the bush. . . . We were lined up, each of us in front of a stone . . . and we took off our clothes. I was afraid, terribly afraid . . . suddenly the operator appeared. . . . I had hardly realized he was there before I saw him standing in front of me . . . I felt something, like a burn, and I closed my eyes . . . when I opened my eyes, the operator was bent over my neighbour.'[5]

'The haemorrhage that follows the operation is abundant, very long, and disturbing', but the healer finally puts on the bandage. In the village the celebrations begin again, but the circumcised boys have lost too much blood, and probably have fever in addition, to take very much interest in the proceedings. Their convalescence lasts for about five weeks, and they are eventually allowed to return to their families. They have become men, but as Laye says 'What a price to pay.'

Every surgeon and medical man knows that the actual operation, injury or mutilation can hardly give an adequate picture of the inflammation, swelling and pain, and of the severity of the general febrile condition which ensues several days later, and all too frequently ends in death. The 'punishment is a measure of parental authority for his displacement (unconsciously murder) by the younger generation—another example of morbid unconscious and insane mechanisms.

I personally can bear witness to the objective and subjective truth of these accounts of circumcision in primitive cultures, as a friend of mine, who is a resident of central East Africa, brought home a large selection of the most interesting cinematograph films of the entire ceremony. Apparently he had won the confidence of the local natives and by becoming an 'uncle' or 'guardian' of the cult had managed to insinuate himself into all their ceremonies. What is more, he had employed a trained African servant to take the films, including the most vivid and detailed close-ups of a succession of operations.

In spite of everything I had read about the subject, I must say that I was amazed at the unnecessarily drastic nature of the operation. I said to a doctor friend beside me at the time: 'This is not circumcision, it is mutilation.'

As the accounts here recorded describe, there was the usual frenzied dancing, the initiates being distinguished from the rest by having the most elaborate headdresses of feathers which were jerked in every direction as they danced. Apparently this went on for an extraordinarily long time, day after day, until the criticial moment when each youth stood, holding his hands in the air and looking towards heaven, while the native operator or operators appeared to remove strip after strip of skin from his penis. The impression was that they were skinning it from the glans upwards, in strips. One could see the blood pouring out as the films were in colour, and the telescopic lens showed a close-up as though one's eyes were only a foot or two away. The camera shifted from the seat of the operation to the face, and one could see the agony being endured by the youth who had been forced by tribal custom to allow himself to be victimized like this. Indeed one saw on this film one youth, but only one, whose fear exceeded his fear of the elders, and who made a bolt for it. Naturally he was caught and dragged forcibly back to his symbolical execution.

One knows that the condition of the boy will become worse and worse, possibly for many weeks, and I have had confirmation that a certain percentage of them actually die. My European friend told me that the British hospitals are full subsequent to the ceremony, but unfortunately the patients are not allowed to apply until sepsis is well established and it is almost too late.

The most unusual film of this series was one which depicted the same ceremony being performed on females. Here the brutality appears to be even worse. The technique is to excise an area of skin or mucous membrane, with a radius of at least one inch, from the vaginal opening; clitoris and labis minor all are removed. I heard that one tribe was rewarded by fifty per cent of the girls and young women victims actually dying of it.

Circumcision is a symbolical castration, mutilation or murder, of the adolescent by the parent or of the id by its antagonist, the superego (introjected parent). As such, like all equivalents and all restrictions which are not reality-based, it is a symptomatic expression of conflict, emotionally determined. Its sources are irrational and morbid, and in this case plainly psychotic.

Another extraordinary cult is Totemism. A Totem is an object, commonly a particular animal, adopted as the emblem of a clan and assumed to be an ancestor or relation. A psychological explanation of totemism is given by Money-Kyrle[2] He tells us: 'A totem clan is a group of people, usually related matrilinially, who identify themselves with, and believe themselves to be descended from, some species of animal or plant. . . . Freud, in the course of his work, had occasion to study the *animal phobias* of children . . . the 'totem' of the civilized child invariably turned out to be unconsciously identified with, that is, to be a symbol of, some member of his own family, usually his father. Here again, it was natural to suppose that similar results have similar causes, that primitive totemism is an institutionalized form of the animal phobias and obsessions of our own children, and that the totem of a savage clan is a parental, most often a father, symbol.'

Leading anthropologists believe totemism to have been once universal, and an early stage in the development of all religions. Freud, who published *Totem and Taboo* in 1913, says:[6] 'Psychoanalytic investigation of the individual teaches with especial emphasis that god is in every case modelled after the father and that our personal relation to god is dependent upon our relation to our physical father, fluctuating and changing with him, and that god at bottom is nothing but an exalted father. . . . The faithful called the totem their ancestor . . . then the father would be represented twice in primitive sacrifice, first as god, and secondly as the totem-animal-sacrifice. . . . That a man should become a god and that a god should die, which today seems to us an outrageous presumption, was still by no means offensive to the conceptions of classical antiquity. But the deification of the murdered father from whom the tribe now derived its origin, was a much more serious attempt at expiation than the former covenant with the totem.' . . . 'The original animal sacrifice was already a substitute for a human sacrifice, for the solemn killing of the father, and when the father substitute regained its human form, the animal substitute could also be retransformed into a human sacrifice. . . . Thus in the Christian doctrine mankind most unreservedly acknowledges the guilty deed of primordial times, because it now has found the most complete expiation for this deed in the sacrificial death of the son. . . . Through the ages we see the identity of the totem feast with the animal sacrifice, the theanthropic human sacrifice, and the Christian eucharist. . . . At bottom, however, the Christian communion is a new setting aside of the father, a repetition of the crime that must be expiated. We see how well justified is Frazer's dictum that "the Christian communion has absorbed within itself a sacrament which is doubtless far older than Christianity".'

Thus the nuclear conflict in the unconscious mind of man, which Freud called the Oedipus Complex, is the basic source not only of recognized neurotic and psychotic symptomatology, but is similarly the aetiological explanation of our social and religious beliefs and practices throughout the ages.

Freud, in the first chapter of *Totem and Taboo*, which he calls the 'Savage's Dread of Incest'. after enumerating the complicated systems and strong prohibitions (punishable by death) of sexual relations between people of the same totem, gives the psychological explanation of this remarkable institution.

'We must say that savages are even more sensitive to incest than we, perhaps because they are more subject to temptations than we are, and hence require more extensive protection against it. . . . In the Fiji Islands a father will not remain alone in the house with his daughter any more than the mother with her son. . . . It is assumed without question by these races that a man and a woman left alone together will indulge in . . . intimacy, and as they expect all kinds of punishments and evil consquences from consanguinous intercourse, they do quite right to avoid all temptations by means of such prohibitions.'

The existence of this very extensive incest taboo on the one hand, and on the other hand the licence allowed at sacred orgies, depict in turn the two opposite solutions of a conflict between id and superego. As we have indicated, id or primary instinct would have intimacy with just these forbidden persons, the most intimate persons of infancy and childhood, mother, sisters and so on. The id must not have its way, for it would also remove or destroy the frustrating aspects of the parents, particularly the parent of the opposite sex, that is to say, like Oedipus, it would 'murder' the father. Therefore the introjected parent figures (the superego) forbids most drastically the freedom of the id in these respects. With civilized races, the superego is a larger intra-psychic entity, and even goes so far as to repress utterly from consciousness any such incestuous desires, in fact they are substituted in consciousness by their opposite as an added precaution.

To my mind, the prohibition is proportionate to the strength of the desire in the same way that the bars of a cage are proportionate to the strength of the animal within. In ourselves, it shows itself by an inadmissability to consciousness of such desires, and also by legal and religious prohibitions, not only of incest but an extension of this to family-relatives-by marriage.

We still victimize ourselves, or rather one another, by an illogical and unnecessary extension of the (already illogical) incest taboo to non-consanguinous marital relations. The last page of the Book of Common Prayer contains a list of them, almost as numerous as the list of consanguinous relations. Recently there was a public outcry at the Act permitting a man to marry his deceased wife's sister—so powerful is the indoctrinated hold of 'incest' superstition even in these 'enlightened' times.

Incest is abhorred, and is punished differently by various tribes. In parts of Australia the punishment is death. 'Among many peoples it (incest taboo) is believed to come through supernatural means. Where that is the case any ill luck incurred by the participants for years after will be ascribed to the breaking of the taboo.'[1] Recently, in London, there was a television programme called 'Is this Your Problem?' A woman said she was unhappy with her second husband as he was inclined to be jealous. A clergyman on the panel interrogated her and at last she admitted that she had had sexual relations with him before she was free of her first husband. The clergyman then persuaded the woman that she must expect great unhappiness as she had sinned—she had broken a modern taboo. He said that this was cause and effect.

There is, of course, abundant psychoanalytical evidence that the earliest sexual desires were incestuous, and developed naturally out of such biological phenomena as the mouth-breast relationship. It seems that the accompanying phantasies soon included rebellious or mutinous elements directed against the edicts of parents. To mutiny is to murder. Thus arose the early conflict between desire and authority; subsequently, when repressed, to become the basic unconscious conflict between id and superego. The desire for incest is in great part relegated to the unconscious but is sufficiently dynamic to give rise to the ever-present intensity of the taboos (or expression of parental authority and resistance to being murdered), which form the unconscious basis of morality and the structure of society, ancient and modern. This is just another instance of the fact that mankind's attitudes past and present are nothing more or less than an unreasoning and unreasonable expression in symptomatic form of morbid, unconscious conflict formed at a primitive (infantile) level of mental development.

Indeed, it is quite obvious that we are by no means free from the sexual absurdities which are so conspicuous in savages.

Human sacrifice, as well as parricide, regicide, incest and cannibalism, are real enough to primitive races. There are equivalents of such ideas and practices in our religions, for instant Christ on the Cross, and even in such current practices as entering the priesthood or taking the veil. Human sacrifices were offered to the Earth Goddess by tribes, branches of tribes, or villages, both at periodical festivals and on extraordinary occasions.

'The mode of performing tribal sacrifices was as follows. Ten or twelve days before the sacrifice, the victim was devoted by cutting off his hair, which, until then, had been kept unshorn.' (Cf. the ceremony of shaving the hair of novice nuns and priests in Catholic ritual. This is a castration symbol, vide my book *The Unconscious Significance of Hair*.) 'Crowds of men and women assembled to witness the sacrifice; none might be excluded, since the sacrifice was declared to be for all mankind. It was preceded by several days of wild revelry and gross debauchery. On the day before the sacrifice the victim, dressed in a new garment, was led forth from the village in solemn procession, with music and dancing, to the Meriah grove, a clump of high forest trees standing a little way from the village and untouched by the axe. There they tied him to a post, which was sometimes placed between two plants of the sankissar shrub. He was then anointed with oil, ghee, and turmeric, and adorned with flowers; and "a species of reverence, which it is not easy to distinguish from adoration", was paid to him throughout the day. A great struggle now arose to obtain the smallest relic from his person; a particle of the turmeric paste with which he was smeared, or a drop of his spittle, was esteemed of sovereign virtue, especially by the women. The crowd danced round the post to music, and, addressing the earth, said: "O God, we offer this sacrifice to you; give us good crops, seasons, and health"; then speaking to the victim they said, "We bought you with a price, and did not seize you; now we sacrifice you according to custom, and no sin rests with us".

'In some places they took the victim in procession round the village, from door to door, where some plucked hair from his head, and others begged for a drop of his spittle, with which they anointed their heads. As the victim might not be bound nor make any show of resistance, the bones of his arms and, if necessary, his legs were broken;' (Cf. the custom of breaking the bones of the legs at crucifixions, as was suffered by the two thieves at Calvary, Christ only just escaping.) 'but often this precaution was rendered unnecessary by stupefying him with opium. The mode of putting him to death varied in different places.'

The similarity between the psychological pattern of some of these histories and that of Christianity is to my mind inescapable, and certainly comparable in the emotions of horror and sympathy involved. Nevertheless human sacrifice and cannibalism do not always or necessarily have the sanction of religious or god-propitiating or corn-growing purposes. It appears that they are sometimes indulged in by primitives without pretext or excuse, simply for the joy of the thing and are extant in the present day.

Even in 1930, Father Dupeyrat, whom I have previously mentioned, penetrated deep into New Guinea where no white man had ever been before, and he found 'a race of humanity which . . . has remained for centuries sunk in unimaginable ignorance and degradation. For here are people who cannot even count up to four, who have no conception of time and cannot tell their own ages. Cannibalism is practised on all sides; The villagers' naked bodies are unspeakably filthy, and often covered with sores'.

Frazer says 'The flesh and blood of dead men are commonly eaten and drunk to inspire bravery, wisdom or other qualities for which the men themselves were remarkable, or which are supposed to have their special seat in the particular part eaten.'[3]

Mythology as practised in Greece demanded that human sacrifice should be made to the gods who 'were seized with a fierce longing to partake of human flesh.'[3]

It is pretty clear to a psychiatrist that the idea that the gods 'were seized with a fierce longing to partake of human flesh' can be nothing more or less than something originally felt by human beings who projected their feelings on to their gods, and so originated and nursed this delusion. In other words, it suggests that people, or some of them, must themselves have been 'seized with a fierce longing to partake of human flesh' and projected this idea on to the gods in the same way as they projected all the other attributes of their gods.

It would seem not always easy to judge how much hunger and oral lust inspired the superstitions connected with cannibalism—as a sort of rationalization and justification for the behaviour—or how much the superstition and belief determined the behaviour. In spite of some anthropological bias in favour of the latter idea, I am sure that the instinct is the primary determinant and the superstition a secondary elaboration and excuse. In Belsen and other German concentration camps during the 1939–45 War, there are accounts of starving prisoners eating portions of their dead or dying companions without invoking any cannibalistic religion or ideal to prompt them or excuse. Superstitious and religious concepts are secondary elaborations of processes which have more primitive (e.g. instinctual) determinants.

Our own superegos (introjected parents, mentors and moralists) cause us to look upon these activities of our forebears more with horror than with objectivity, but considered from a scientific or pyschological point of view they should not surprise us, for they are essentially no more or less than the natural expression of basic instincts which lie in the nuclear core of the unconscious of all of us, namely oral libido (hunger) with its destructive accompaniment. With genital organization these may become the instincts of rape and murder, the former typically represented as incest and the latter as parricide.

In the light of this, perhaps it is small wonder that taboos have been urgently and violently instituted. It is not these basic instincts, nor their expression, which justified me in the title of this book, in describing mankind as madkind, and in alleging that he is a victim of a protracted and still uncured psychosis.

What characterizes behaviour as psychotic is not so much that it emanates directly from the id or instinct reservoir—(in a sense that is psychotic in so far as it does not take account of reality)—but rather the peculiar effects upon this behaviour resulting from the institution of anxiety-driven, and excessive taboos, restrictions, diversions and perversions forced upon it. Perhaps it is when these forces are incorporated into the psyche in the form of some ill-formed or over-grown superego that psychosis, characterized by behaviour inappropriate to reality, emerges.

CHAPTER III

MYTHOLOGY, COSMOGONY AND
COMPARATIVE RELIGION

After a most extensive study of anthropology, mythology and folk-lore, Franz Boas[1] came to the conclusion that: 'It is impossible to draw a sharp line between myths and folk tales, because the same tales which occur as myths appear also in the form of folk tales'. It has also been said that all cosmogonies are myths and thus it may be difficult to hold a hard and fast line between cosmogonies, cosmologies and mythology in general. Boas goes on to say 'It is fairly clear that stories are unhesitatingly classed as myths if they account for the origin of the world and if they may be said to have happened in a mythical period, different from the one in which we live now. . . .

'*The most important characteristic of mythology concepts is personification.* It is not difficult to understand why animals should be personified, for their behaviour resembles in many ways that of man. Their actions are easily understood as motivated by hunger, fear, anger and love. When their strength is superior to that of man and he succumbs to their attack, it is proof of their greater power that is pitted against him.

'These personified animals appear everywhere in tales. In striking contrast to the human actors, they are sharply characterized according to their observed habits. The cunning fox and the greedy, stupid wolf of European folk tales, the monkey of India, the coyote, raven, and rabbit of North America, the jaguar of South America, the turtle and spider of Africa, are types whose mental characteristics reappear in every tale. . . .

'The extension of the belief that will-power exists in natural phenomena that interfere in the life of man is also perfectly intelligible. Destructive floods, gales, thunder storms, rock slides, are not considered as due to natural causes, but are believed to be endowed with the will to destroy. All moving objects that have any influence upon human life are thus easily viewed as endowed with human passions and human will-power. Sun, moon, stars, clouds, are included in this group. If the phenomena of nature are once endowed with human qualities, it is not hard to understand why imagination should not also endow them with human form. . . .'

The conceptions of the Greeks are of course well known and

remind us of the imaginative spirit evidently founded upon the mythology and the moral concepts of those days. There are numerous tales
and legends, including of course the famous one of Oedipus Rex.
The Romans were so taken with the Greek cosmogony and mythology that they adopted it and adapted it, adding numerous comparable elaborations, though mostly changing the names of the rapidly
multiplying deities.

Naturally, the Greeks and Romans were not the only pre-scientific
peoples who endeavoured to explain the universe and the existence
of man. It is said that these attempts contrast with modern scientific
cosmogony particularly by containing no conception of gradual or
evolutionary change; but I feel that the successive generations
amongst the creative gods employs some anthropological equivalent
of an evolutionary or progressive movement, put in the form of what
people were familiar with, namely, reproduction and the growth of
families. Overtly at least all these primitive theories postulate a
simple creative act. In the more thoughtful races, for instance of
India, the act is accomplished by the mere thought of the creator
(cf. the Old Testament), and according to Frazer[7] 'In Egyptian
mythology, Khnoumou, the father of the gods, is said to have moulded
men out of clay on his potter's wheel' (cf. the Old Testament). The
Babylonians also had this conception.

In Persia teachings associated with the name of Zoroaster became
the dominant religion of Western Asia (550 B.C.), and continued to
be so for some hundreds of years until the conquest of Persia by
Alexander the Great in about 331 B.C. He taught the existence of a
supreme being, who created two other supernatural beings, one of
whom was good and the other bad, thus perhaps anticipating the
later Christian mythology of God and the Devil. His priests were
called Magi, who worshipped fire, light and the sun as the emblems of
good. The religion of Zoroaster continued to flourish even after the
introduction of Christianity, and in the third century was the dominant faith of the East, till the rise of the Mahometan power and the
conquest of Persia by the Arabs in the seventh century, who compelled the greater number of the Persians to renounce their ancient
faith. Those who refused to abandon the religion of their ancestors
fled to the deserts of Kerman and to Hindustan, where they still
exist under the name of Parsees, a name derived from Pars, the
ancient name of Persia.

There appears to be a narrative link between this religion and that
of Christianity, in so far as the Wise Men from the East who had seen
a star and thereby found their way to Bethlehem are known as the
Magi.

'The religion of the Hindus is professedly founded on the Vedas
which undoubtedly teach the belief of one supreme God. The name

of this deity is Brahma.' The division of the Hindus into classes or
castes, with fixed occupations, apparently existed from the earliest
times and are well known, but it is not without interest to the psychoanalyst that the Pariahs, who are employed in the lowest services are
according to Bulfinch[8] 'not only considered unclean themselves, but
they render unclean everything they touch.' The persistence in this
social attitude right up to modern times serves to remind us that
cosmological beliefs, however fantastic, are not harmless. They have
repercussions in customs and behaviour right through the community
and can affect individual happiness and survival in an equally fantastic and insane way. In other words, irrational beliefs are inevitably
related to irrational customs and behaviour.

Buddha is said by his followers to have been a mortal sage, named
Gautama. The Buddhists reject entirely the authority of the Vedas,
and the religious observances prescribed in them and kept by the
Hindus. They also reject the distinction of castes, and prohibit all
bloody sacrifices. Their priests are chosen from all classes and they
are expected to procure their maintenance by begging.

Buddhism in Tibet is described most interestingly by Heinrich
Harrer in his book, *Seven Years in Tibet.*[9]

'The daily life of Tibetans is ordered by religious belief. Pious
texts are constantly on their lips; prayer wheels turn without ceasing;
prayer flags wave on the roofs of houses and the summits of the moun-
tain passes; the rain, the wind, all the phenomena of nature, bear
witness to the universal presence of the gods whose anger is manifested by hailstorm, and whose benevolence is displayed by the fruit-
fulness and fertility of the land. The life of the people is regulated by
the divine will, whose interpreters the Lamas (priests) are. Before
anything is undertaken, they must test the omens. The gods must be
unceasingly entreated, placated or thanked. Prayer-lamps burn
everywhere, in the houses of the noble and in the tent of the nomad.
. . . Earthly existence is of little worth in Tibet and death has no
terrors. Men know that they will be born again and hope for a higher
form of existence in the next life, earned by pious conduct in this
one . . .' and no one expresses 'the slightest doubt about the truth
of Buddha's teaching.' The Tibetans never kill an insect, and 'It is a
catastrophe when a fly falls into a cup of tea. It must at all costs be
saved from drowning as it may be the reincarnation of one's dead
grandmother.' Anyone doing such things has done something for
the good of his own soul. 'The more life one can save the happier one
is.'

There is therefore 'no capital punishment in Tibet. Murder is
regarded as the most heinous of crimes, but the murderer is only
flogged and has iron fetters forged on to his ankles. It is true that the
floggings are in fact less humane than the death penalty as it is

carried out in Western hands. The victim often dies an agonizing death after the penalty has been inflicted, but the religious principle has not been infringed. . . .'

Throughout the long history of religions, and throughout the long history of punishment, it is curious how the most diabolical aspects of the id (i.e. sadism) invariably reveal themselves masquerading in the guise of ego-ideal or superego. The spontaneous id has never devised such refinements of protracted torture as has the moral indignation of the superego (e.g. witness the witch trials and trials of heretics.)

The religion founded by Mahomet is essentially sadistic and Forsyth comments[10] that 'it expresses the male attitude to life, to the detriment of the female. Its appeal is to men rather than to women.' It claims to be divine revelation communicated to the world through Mahomet, who was the last of a succession of inspired prophets, beginning with Adam. . . . Around the throne of God are the angels, pure, sexless beings, some of whom bear the throne, while others praise Him continually; they are also His messengers and are sent to help the faithful in their fight with unbelievers.

The similarity between Northern Mythology (founded on the Eddas) and Hebrew or Christian mythology is patent, though it has certainly undergone some fantastic elaborations of its own, and it is apparent that though the common elements seem to be universal cosmogonies tend to be affected by the actual physical environment of the peoples who invent them.

The Druids who were the priests of the ancient Celtic nations 'taught the existence of one god, to whom they gave a name "Be'al", which Celtic antiquaries tell us means "The life of everything", or "the source of all beings", and which seems to have affinity with the Phoenician Baal. What renders this affinity more striking is that the Druids as well as the Phoenicians identified this, their supreme deity, with the sun. Fire was regarded as a symbol of the divinity. The Latin writers assert that the Druids also worshipped numerous inferior gods.

'The Druids observed two festivals in each year. The former took place in the beginning of May, and was called Beltane or "fire of God". On this occasion a large fire was kindled on some elevated spot, in honour of the sun, whose returning beneficence they thus welcomed after the gloom and desolation of winter. Of this custom a trace remains in the name given to Whitsunday in parts of Scotland to this day. . . .

'The other great festival of the Druids was called "samh'in", or "fire of peace", and was held on Hallow-eve (31st of October), which still retains this designation. On this occasion the Druids assembled in solemn conclave, in the most central part of the district,

MK—C

to discharge the judicial functions of their order. All questions, whether public or private, all crimes against person or property, were at this time brought before them for adjudication. With these judicial acts were combined certain superstitious usages, especially the kindling of the sacred fire, from which all the fires in the district, which had been beforehand scrupulously extinguished, might be relighted.'[8]

The Bards were a part of the Druidical hierarchy. The sessions of the Bards and minstrels were called Eisteddfods, which are still celebrated in Wales.

The basic similarity between all the cosmogonies cannot be too greatly stressed. For instance the Japanese believed that the world appears as nebulous, moving chaos and Divine beings develop in it by spontaneous generation.[11] In Central Celebes the maker transferred a portion of the male to the female figure and the Creator then allowed the common wind to blow on the figures and they drew breath and life from it. The North American tribe, the Muskhogeans, believed that before the creation a great body of water was visible and over this waste, two pigeons flew to and fro, until they saw a blade of grass rising above the surface, when dry land gradually followed. The similarity between this and the story of the Flood and other stories in the Old Testament is inescapable. Both the Australian aborigines and the New Zealand Maoris have a cosmogony which includes the idea of moulding man of clay, and the Burmese and the Bedel Tartars of Siberia have the tradition that woman was created from a rib of man (cf. Genesis).[7]

If the innumerable episodes in mythology and folk-lore can be held in any way to support the theory of psychosis in our family history, it is partly in so far as they reveal an immaturity which precluded people from restraint in putting their feelings into practice, irrespective of any sense of objective justice. The ego was no match for the impulses and desires, revengeful or otherwise, which broke through into consciousness. Powers of judgment, if they existed at all, were easily swept aside, and behaviour in accordance with the impulses, destructive or otherwise, came into play. We might in a sense call this a 'natural' psychosis, contrasting it perhaps with irrational behaviour instituted by the taboos and superego or contra-instinctual forces. The latter are commonly more elaborate, indeed they can reach any degree of absurdity in elaboration, and therefore in a sense are more interesting as morbid psychological phenomena. The former, like cruelty, destruction and cannibalism, horrify us, the latter intrigue. The point I wish to make is that we are all so much the victims of the latter psychosis, namely irrational behaviour instigated by anti-instinctual or superego forces, that we are today accepting it and mistaking it for rational custom even necessity. We can detect the frank expression of id forces very easily, and have no difficulty in denying that we are like that, that we are not like our brutal ancestors, the cannibals. But what we fail to see is that our superego obsession can be just as psychotic and commonly provides an even better outlet for the very sadism which we repudiate.

Apart from indoctrination and emotional processes at work from infancy and childhood onwards, there is no reason why the mythology of the Hebrews and Christians should be immune from the same objective or even critical attitude that we have adopted in describing all other similarly determined histories, folk-stories, mythologies, religions, beliefs and associated activities. Many people, including even non-Christians, believe that the greatest value of Christianity is its ethics, and it was certainly a revolution in ethical standards at the time when it came into being.

The dogma of Christianity can be traced to the pre-Christian worship of the old Persian God Mithra, and the Mithraic religion proved a formidable rival to Christianity. Indeed the issue of the conflict between the two faiths appears for a time to have hung in the balance. A relic of the long struggle is preserved in our festival of Christmas, which the Church seems to have borrowed directly from its rival. In the Julian calendar the twenty-fifth of December was reckoned the winter solstice, and it was regarded as the Nativity of the Sun, because the day begins to lengthen. Mithra, who was identified with the Sun, also had his birth celebrated on the twenty-fifth of December. The Gospels say nothing as to the day of Christ's birth, and accordingly the early Church did not celebrate it. It was only at about the end of the third century that the Western Church adopted the twenty-fifth of December as the true date. It therefore appears that the Christian Church chose to celebrate the birthday of its Founder on the twenty-fifth of December in order to transfer the devotion of the heathen from the Sun to one who was called the Sun of Righteousness.

Frazer says: 'When we reflect how often the Church has skilfully contrived to plant the seeds of the new faith on the old stock of paganism, we may surmise that the Easter celebration of the dead and risen Christ was grafted upon a similar celebration of the dead and risen Adonis'. . . . 'Now the death and resurrection of Attis were officially celebrated at Rome on the twenty-fourth and twenty-fifth of March, the latter being regarded as the spring equinox, and therefore as the most appropriate day for the revival of a god of vegetation who had been dead or sleeping throughout the winter. But according to an ancient and widespread tradition Christ suffered on the twenty-fifth of March, and accordingly some Christians regularly celebrated the Crucifixion on that day without any regard to the state of the moon. . . . The inference appears to be inevitable that the passion of Christ must have been arbitrarily referred to that date in order to harmonize with an older festival of the spring equinox. . . . When we remember that the festival of St George in April has replaced the ancient pagan festival of the Parilia; that the festival of St John the Baptist in June has succeeded to a heathen Midsummer festival of water; that the festival of the Assumption of the Virgin in August has ousted the festival of Diana; that the feast of All Souls in November is a continuation of an old heathen feast of the dead; and that the Nativity of Christ himself was assigned to the winter solstice in December because that day was deemed the Nativity of the Sun; we can hardly be thought rash or unreasonable in conjecturing that the other cardinal festival of the Christian church, the solemnization of Easter—may have been in like manner, and from like motives of edification, adapted to a similar celebration of the Phrygian god Attis at the vernal equinox.'

Frazer has further remarks to make about the nativity; 'The ritual of the nativity, as it appears to have been celebrated in Syria and Egypt, was remarkable. The celebrants retired into certain inner shrines, from which at midnight they issued with a loud cry, "The Virgin has brought forth: The light is waxing!" The Egyptians even represented the new-born sun by the image of an infant which on his birthday, the winter solstice, they brought forth and exhibited to his worshippers. No doubt the Virgin who thus conceived and bore a son on the Twenty-fifth of December was the great Oriental goddess whom the Semites called the Heavenly Virgin or simply the Heavenly Goddess; in Semitic lands she was a form of Astarte.'

'The custom of eating bread sacramentally as the body of a god was practised by the Aztecs before the discovery and conquest of Mexico by the Spaniards. Twice a year, in May and December, an image of the Great Mexican god Huitzilopochtli or Vitzilipuztli was made of dough, then broken in pieces and solemnly eaten by his worshippers.'[3]

As we know, there are many instances in mythology and religion where a god is represented by some other object such as a human being, an animal, or even bread, and symbolically eaten. For instance, in Greek mythology: 'Dionysus was turned into a goat. Hence when his worshippers rent in pieces a live goat and devoured it raw, they must have believed that they were eating the body and blood of the god.'[3]

Perhaps enough has been said to suggest at least that many mythologies and religions, not excluding Christianity, may have certain features and origins in common with one another.

Forsyth says:[10] 'The comparative study of religions has shown how much Christianity shares with pagan religions and the primitive religions of savages. At its inception it borrowed largely from earlier pagan sources. Most of the miracles recorded in the Bible are to be found also in pre-Christian religions. Even the fundamental miracles of the Resurrection and the Ascension were taken over by Christianity in this way.

'Many gods besides Christ have been supposed to die, be resurrected and ascend to heaven. This idea has now been traced back to its origin among primitive people in the annual death and resurrection of crops and plant life generally. This explains the world-wide prevalence of the notion.'[10]

'The Christian sacrament of the Eucharist carries a vastly different significance now that we know that the custom of men eating their god is one of the commonest in religions of all kinds, and especially among savages.'

The idea of the virgin birth is also by no means peculiar to Christianity, and several pagan religions represent their Saviour as born of a virgin, dying for the sins of mankind, rising from the dead and ascending into heaven.

The ideas of a Trinity, an Incarnate Saviour, the Second Advent, and the Conversion of Saints are duplicated in other mythologies and religions.

In the light of these considerations, we may get the impression that one religion may well be a sort of precipitate of those which have preceded it. They may continue to live side by side, as it were competing for popularity, six or seven of the greatest still surviving, whereas some have had their day and given place to others which may still embody some of their basic concepts and dogmas. For some centuries after its birth, Christianity itself was still a fairly delicate growth, until Constantine the Great made it the official religion of the Roman Empire. However, by the Middle Ages the Church controlled practically every aspect of contemporary society.

Apart from its retarding effects upon scientific emancipation and progress, this control by the Church was not always a helpful state of affairs, even in the realms where one would expect it to be most beneficial, socially and from a humanitarian point of view, for instance in the realm of child welfare. This is far from a criticism of the spirit and ethics of Christianity, and of the One who said 'suffer the little children to come unto me', but rather an indication how the basic psychology of man representing his particular stage of development at that time, emerges in spite of any consciously expressed principles.

Perhaps the population, with all its Christianity, had really not progressed very far beyond the mental level of being more concerned with magic than with reality. Professor Malinowski says: 'no people however primitive is without it',[10] and in my opinion, no people, however civilized, is without it. 'Magic is especially obvious in

religious ritual, since this is based on the belief of the religious celebrant
that his ritual actions possess the power of altering the outside world.
This belief is seen in many religious ceremonies, from that in which
the priest sprinkles holy water over the people to the dread act of
excommunication which is supposed to have the power of determining
even the future life of an offender. Another religious example is
found in the use of church bells. These were originally rung, not, as
many suppose, as a summons to service, but to scare away the Devil
while folk were on the way to church. A special instance of this is
the "passing bell", which was tolled when anyone was dying; this
was to frighten away the evil spirits waiting to pounce on the soul
while it was "passing" from the body.'[10]

'Until a century or two ago astrological notions were widely
prevalent in medicine, and illnesses were believed to be influenced
by the phases of the moon, by tides and eclipses. . . . Other medical
associations of magic are the use of charms and spells to cure illness—
this still survives among us, and not only in country parts—and the
cure of mental disorders, for which the only treatment throughout
the centuries was the magic of exorcisers. Indeed, so recently has
medicine become scientific that many of the laity still expect doctors
to effect cures by some magical process.'[10]

Whether a population was pagan or Christian in its religious
beliefs appears to have made very little difference to its behaviour
and practices, whether in the name of religion or not. Indeed religion, whatever it may have been (pagan or Christian), seems to have
been a force for increasing intolerance and its 'Punishment of heresy
by death'. The Roman Church first resorted to the general and
systematic slaughter of heretics in the eleventh century. Perhaps the
bloodiest instance of the suppression of heresy is that in Mexico and
Peru in the sixteenth century, when, according to the estimate of the
Spanish priest Las Casas, twelve million natives were killed as heretics.

According to Llorente,[12] the psychosis of the Inquisition reduced
the population of Spain from twenty million to six million. The
persecution of unorthodoxy, and heresy, both general and individual,
is well known in history.

The superstitious persecution of witchcraft (1484–1793) with its
indescribable cruelties, continued until the end of the eighteenth
century. It has been referred to as a mass-hysteria not limited to
nations, but extending right across the Christian world. At one time
a woman had only to be accused by some spiteful neighbour to be
liable to indescribable indignities, obscenities, cruelties and torture,
rationalized as investigation. For example, the Hoskins test consisted of thrusting long pins or bodkins (especially made for the purpose) into various parts of the accused woman's naked body, until
she had reached such a state of exhaustion that she ceased to feel

the torture. It was then claimed that the 'witch's mark' had been found, proving her guilt and justifying her burning.

Lowie tells us[13] that as late as 1737 at Zug in Switzerland, a seventeen year old girl confessed to witchcraft, to riding with others 'stark naked on sticks to the witches' gathering-place', to seeing the devil and to taking the form of 'dog, cat, owl, mouse or black pigeon'. She named some half-dozen accessories, and all of these poor women were tortured.

Lowie also gives an account of a French priest being lynched less than ten years ago for bewitching a peasant in his village. 'We may press electric buttons to switch on lights and drive automobiles, but the supernatural that baffled the reindeer-hunters of France, 20,000 years ago, is still floating about.' In evidence of this today there are slot machines in the USA from which for a small coin one can obtain a charm printed with the Lord's Prayer to be worn around the neck.

These witch atrocities did not cease until 1793, the last being burnt in that year. Thus it is only too evident that religious or any other beliefs do not begin and end simply as harmless, mythological or delusional conceptions, but inevitably tend to have their counter-part in similarly incalculable behaviour. This was as late as the end of the eighteenth century, and it may well be asked if it was any advance on the human sacrifices to fertility gods described by Frazer, and the cannibalism of New Guinea described by Father Dupeyrat. One can imagine that the public of 'civilized' countries of the witch-baiting time would have been horrified at the suggestion of canni-balism, but from the victim's point of view it may be questionable whether it is better or worse to be eaten by cannibals, wolves or id instincts, or to be burnt alive by the superego in the name of religious orthodoxy? I am inclined to think that if anything, the latter is worse as it has added a mental torture to the physical, namely the mental torture of alleged guilt, often believed and accepted by the victim. Devoured by cannibals we may still be on the side of the gods, but castigated by witch allegations we are more likely to be driven to feel that our 'soul' is destroyed as well.

In general, when sadism is taken over by the superego, it has deeper and more cruel effects than in its original form. From an ego point of view, perhaps both are as far removed from reality valuations and therefore comparably mad.

From the massacre of the Huguenots on St Bartholomew's Day (1572), the burning of Giordana Bruno, the ex-Catholic priest for venturing to promulgate the scientific teaching of Copernicus, and his revolt from ecclesiastical teaching, and the imprisonment and torture of Galileo for denying that the sun moved round the earth, we see that: 'The Church demanded an unqualified acceptance of

all its teachings, and these alone were to be accepted as true. . . .
And yet freedom of thought is the breath of life to science. . . .
The Roman Church has not abated its claim that beliefs must agree,
not with facts but with religious dogma, and it has continued to
resist practically every scientific discovery, with the exception of
those in mathematics, physics and chemistry—sciences which do not
trespass on the theological field.'[10]

'The most outstanding instance of this was in the middle of last
century, when Darwin published his work on the origin of species
and the descent of man. The Catholic Church placed his books on
the Index, where they still remain, the reading of them forbidden to
its followers. The Church of England attacked them violently and
bitterly.'[10] Some states in the USA have made the teaching of
them a punishable offence. 'Darwin's work assailed what was regarded by Christians as a vital part of the religious position. Christianity had firmly held to the story of the creation of the world as given
in the Book of Genesis. . . .

'At a Vatican Council in 1870, a declaration was made of papal
infallibility, that is, the dogma that the Pope speaking *ex cathedra* is
free from error. . . .'[10]

For many centuries the Church 'had the almost sole care of the
sick . . . the prevention and treatment of most diseases, including
pestilences which used to decimate peoples, have been made more
effective in the last fifty years than in the previous fifteen hundred.
None of this amelioration of the conditions of human life could have
ensued except by first rejecting as false the religious belief that disease
is God-sent as a punishment for sin, and is therefore best treated by
prayer.'[10]

Prayer is based upon 'The magical belief that thoughts and words
in themselves possess a potency in the outside world. Praying, therefore, would seem to be one of the many survivals of magic in modern
religion. . . . A Christian community will pray to God for rain, but
will have no opinion of an African tribe that prays to the new moon
to give good hunting. . . .'[10]

Forsyth is of the opinion that a lot of the dynamic energy that
vitalizes religious beliefs, particularly religious conversion, has some
libidinal or sexual source. He attempts to substantiate this by pointing out that in religious conversion 'the mean age among young
women is fourteen and among youths sixteen. Psychologically, the
phenomenon is none other than the new strong tide of sexual feeling
that accompanies puberty, being checked in its usual course and
deflected into religion. The check comes from an undue sense of
guilt about sexual matters; and this is the outcome of a correspondingly undue strictness in the child's earler training. . . .' Similarly
with mysticism: 'It is eroticism that seeks communion with another.

. . . In view of this, it is instructive that mystics attach great importance to a period of sexual abstinence as a preliminary and aid to getting themselves into the mystic state. . . .'[10]

Forsyth claims that an understanding of the psychology of religion has been completely transformed by psychoanalytical investigation. To clarify this he stresses that Freud pointed out 'that all thinking activities come into one of two categories: some essentially pleasure-giving—dreams and daydreams; others concerned with adapting our individual wants to the conditions of our environment. . . . To these two kinds of thinking Freud gave the names of pleasure thinking and reality thinking; and underlying them are the pleasure principle and the reality principle, as the two main tendencies of mental action. It was the distinction between these two that gave the first clue to understanding the supernatural.'[10]

'. . . with infants this power of discrimination has not yet been acquired. They regularly confuse the two, and for some time after birth are quite unable to distinguish between what is psychic and imaginary (hallucinatory), and what is objective and real. All through early childhood they see these mental images, not as in their mind's eye, but as outside themselves; they must regard, therefore, both the psychic and the real as equally real. . . . It seems to it (the child) that the (unknown) forces of nature can be influenced by its desires; and this, as we have seen, is the essence of magic. . . . A belief in magic is, therefore, inescapable by children, and is entirely outgrown by so few adults that no surprise need be felt on occasions when it is found mixed with religion or science. At all ages it is an expression of pleasure thinking, and in no way the product of the reality principle. . . .'

In a recent psychoanalytical chapter, Joan Riviere writes: 'The beliefs, activities and rituals, etc., of primitive tribes appear to be very largely representations both of taking in to the body or expelling from it good and bad objects respectively, and of fears of the converse and defensive measures against that. What to the savage is comparatively conscious, however, and a normal part of life, has become increasingly taboo and repressed to Western civilized man, though it has played a large part in the Christian religion, e.g. in the Communion rite.'[14]

Fenichel says:[15] 'The complement of creating worlds by magic is the "wishing away" of an undesired piece of the world, the strange ability to deny reality at the point where it opposes the patient's wishes. A true loss of capacity for testing reality is a characteristic feature of psychoses . . . a turning away from real objects toward the images of infantile objects. In this respect, the compulsion neurotic, because of his "omnipotence", stands a step nearer to psychosis than does the hysteric. An unconscious part of the ego may repudiate parts of reality, while the conscious personality at the same time really knows what is true and what is false. . . .

'Children who, convinced by reality, have to give up their belief in their omnipotence believe instead that the grownups around them are omnipotent.'[15]

A belief in our own omnipotence, with which apparently we all start life, is surely synonymous with a belief in our own magical powers. As reality disillusions us in this respect, we transfer the magical power to the grownups around us and this is the *first step* towards creating an omnipotent God.

To outline the possible psychopathology of the origin of superstition, and the manifold forms and elaborations into which it can develop, it would be necessary to begin with instincts or inherited reactive patterns. To do this would be to open up far too large a theoretical subject for the present work. We must be content to begin with the difficulties at the dawn of exta-uterine life, when the baby is not distinguishing between hallucination and phantasy on the one hand, and objective reality on the other. There is much evidence that this type of difficulty is never fully overcome, and in its extreme form it may be regarded as a characteristic of immaturity. We tacitly recognize this when we encourage children to play their games, particularly their games of make-believe. We recognize that infants and children do not really *want* our reality. It would be too great a hardship for them to abandon their pleasure-giving phantasies, imaginings and games, except in the course of the gradual process of maturation.

Obviously in the uterus there is little environmental reality. The organism reacts entirely to physiological processes based upon the natural laws of physics and chemistry. It may be surmised that the same generalization is largely true immediately after its birth. There is evidence that it *feels something* in consequence of physiological processes within it, and reacts accordingly in keeping with its instincts or inherited reactive pattern. It breathes air in and out. If it feels full, it evacuates. If it feels empty it makes noises until it has something (e.g. the nipple) on which to exercise its instinctual sucking movements. It would be very natural if it believed that its crying or screaming magically caused the appropriate object (nipple or teat) to come into existence, and that, by its own potency in sucking, it itself omnipotently removed the preceding discomfort. It may well be that ideas of omnipotence and of magic are inseparably associated at this stage of life. The reflection may occur to us how curious it is that an organism or individual should harbour ideas of omnipotence when it is obviously at its most helpless stage of existence. Philosophically we may wonder whether our own helplessness in the face of the cosmos and its natural laws, which we do not understand in absolute, may foster the continuation of this reactive illusion, or even make it necessary or inescapable in order to compensate us for helplessness, precisely in the same manner as that which is characteristic of the helpless baby.

Nevertheless, even in babyhood, the situation has arisen when reality, that is to say, something apart from the internal physiological functions of the organism itself, has come into relationship with it. Sooner or later it must inevitably begin to recognize this external reality. For instance, the appearance or feel in its mouth of the nipple. It must also sooner or later recognize that this object can be removed without its specific or magical wish. In other words, it must sooner or later painfully discover that there is something which is not completely subject to its omnipotence. My suggestion is that that is a painful discovery, and one which would tend to be resisted. I would suggest further that the mind does not basically alter from that point. It naturally prefers its pleasure-thinking, however illusionary, to the painful recognition of a reality over which it has not omnipotent control, a reality which can deny its pleasure, and, torture it unendurably and deny it its very life. Perhaps babies and children could not bear to face up to such a truth. Perhaps all living creatures have never been able to face up to full recognition of such a situation, neither in the past nor in the present. Nevertheless, minor aspects of this truth implacably intrude themselves into our would-be pleasure life, with its would-be omnipotence and freedom from anxiety.

Perhaps the baby finds that with or without its screamings, it cannot be more than momentarily satisfied with a hallucinatory breast or mother. The uncomfortable empty feelings return or persist until the *real* object relieves them, and if the real object is not entirely subject to the baby's will or omnipotence, anxiety is unavoidable . . . until the baby is assured not only that mother is omnipotent, but that she is also reliably benevolent. Thus, if it cannot retain the illusion of omnipotence itself, it may eventually sidestep anxiety by transferring the magical quality of omnipotence on to a benovelent godlike successor. Indeed, there is much evidence that the infant must feel the security of being wanted and loved. There is also evidence to show that like the infant, the adult also (having grown from the infant), if he is unable to retain these illusions about his ageing parents, tends to transfer them to someone chosen for the purpose, such as elder, chieftain, leader or king. *Mana*, magic or omnipotence there must be in the hands of some person or figure benevolent towards himself. Therefore he will cling for all he is worth to the idea that if he himself has not got it, someone else such as his king has got it.

If, owing to a clinging reality sense, the transference of this magic (omnipotence) is no longer possible on to other specimens of humanity, owing to their being recognized to have limitations such as ourselves, then it is not a very great step to transfer these qualities on to some mythological being, even if we cannot actually see him. Early in the history of mankind, these mythological beings were more clearly anthopomorphized, built in the image of ourselves, than they are in later religions, but perhaps they never depart very far from anthropomorphism, which clearly indicates their source, and the source of omnipotence in ourselves and in our parents.

Thus we may see the origin of phantasy in our original unreality or pleasure-thinking, with its reassuring quality of omnipotence. The truth, which is not incapable of being painfully borne home to us in small degrees, is that our real power only increases in so far as we abandon the delusion of omnipotence and appreciate and understand the nature and power of the reality around us. In so far as we withdraw from this reality, and enjoy our phantasies and delusions, our consolation can only be transient, and our actuality impotence. In so far as we turn our attention to the interfering 'devils' around us, and learn their nature, we gain potency to make them our servants rather than our inhuman masters. The impinging of reality upon our pleasure-seeking minds has, as I have said, not been without effect. The effect is a matter of degree and tends to increase with maturation in the course of development and evolution. Indeed, it is the stuff of which is made not only our common-sense dealings with nature and the real world, but even of science, faith in its inception and in its highest stages of development.

Anxiety, like hunger or pain, is intolerable. If we cannot find an explanation for natural phenomena in reality, and thereby be re-assured, we must when the first process fails, immediately fly to our anxiety-relieving illusions, just as we did as infants, placing the omnipotence upon some anthropomorphized or otherwise benevolent or powerful figure or force. This has always been a very easy process, since we became expert at it at the very dawn of our individual and collective culture. In fact, probably the earliest mental process was to project our mental image as we do in dreams and think it real. As children and savages this was our favourite pastime and we do it now. We project our mental image and think it real. Thus we come to believe that God made the world by an identical process, that is to say, it was in his mind, and then it became real. He thought it, and it was.

Of course, what actually happened in our minds is that we saw what it was and then projected our mental operation as it were the other way round. The whole course of progress is the history of un-learning this simple 'solution', and it is mainly because we reached the stage we did, it failed adequately to relieve our anxiety, but we have not yet learnt to do without it. Perhaps because we have not yet learnt enough (if we ever shall) to feel confidence in an impersonal

cosmos and the impersonal natural laws of its behaviour. The function of the psyche is to avoid discomfort or anxiety by one means or
another.

The object of these pages is to remind us that throughout the ages,
as today, mankind has, one, been the victim of an intra-psychic
phantasy life which has not necessarily any relationship to reality or
truth, and two, that his behaviour, customs and religious beliefs and
rituals have throughout been nothing more or less than the expressions, often in symbols, of this irrational, emotionally determined
unconscious phantasy life with its conflicts and generally fantastic
and imaginary struggles. That is why I call these phenomena
'symptoms'.

It may be asked why, having recognized this, I am not content
simply to accept it and leave the matter there. The answer, perhaps
the curse or blessing of the life process, at least in its mental aspects,
is that we can never leave the matter there. A residue of anxiety
drives us everlastingly to further efforts to reduce it, or to progressive
attempts to adjustment. I may attempt to rationalize this, for instance by asking could any of us remain content with the mythological
beliefs or superstitions of savages, if we saw the behaviouristic
equivalents of these, such as human sacrifice and cannibalism.
Could any of us be content with mediaeval catholicism if we had to
partake actively or passively in inquisitions and witch baitings.

I may add to this by declaring that a compromise between science
and superstition is no compromise at all. It is a perennial conflict
which enters into every aspect of our life, international, national,
social, intra-psychic and even physiological. For instance, it is certain aspects of this conflict which are responsible for all the ills that
man is heir to, not excluding gastric ulcer. The one thing I am sure
about is that delusion cannot cure conflict. To withdraw from reality
or to encourage its withdrawal, however seductive, spells death . . . ,
and all the diseases on the way to death, including a form of schizophrenia from which we all suffer.

In the course of my professional work, I see this conflict at every
level, for instance between a patient's idealism or religious beliefs on
the one hand, and her instincts on the other—instincts the recognition of which at least is a necessity for health, but the damage or
suffering caused by the visible levels of this conflict are small in
comparison to its invisible repercussions. It is this conflict in its various
forms and levels which makes people ill and keeps them ill, which
makes society ill and keeps it ill, which is the source of all ills, physical,
mental, social, national and international.

In short, the attempts to 'cure' our anxiety, particularly in so far
as these attempts include withdrawal from reality into the consolation of illusion, lead to a situation where the cure appears to be as

bad as the disease. Life consists in projecting our intra-psychic state and acting it out, often at the expense of our own well-being and that of others. In so far as we do this by projecting our delusional symptoms and their consequent behaviour, we are not moving towards any possible betterment of the situation. In so far as we endeavour, however inadequately, to cope with reality, the facts and natural laws of the environment around us, as well as within us, so far we may be attempting a movement towards a progressively improving adjustment.

CHAPTER IV

CURRENT BEHAVIOUR

LIBIDO EXPRESSED IN SOCIAL CUSTOMS

The mind of modern man can be divided into various theoretical components, some of which, or some groups of which, are perpetually more or less in conflict with one another. Roughly speaking these components are divided into the id, or instinct group, on the one hand, and the ego group, comprising mainly the superego, on the other. The id group is theoretically divided into life instinct and death instinct, or libido and aggression.

Anxiety can be provoked by conflict even at the lowest level, such as between the instincts themselves, but more conspicuously as a result of the conflict between the two main structural levels, id and superego, usually superego plus ego, for our ego, generally speaking (unless we are criminals), comes down on the side of the superego. I would qualify this by suggesting that it is not entirely true. In my opinion, the ego invariably suffers some degree, minor or major, of split, at least a portion of it as it were going over to the enemy. Thus conflict is generally not so clear-cut as we like to suppose.

Now the point is, having theoretically divided the mind into these functional entities or components, what would be our best method of examining the manifestation in the form of social symptoms of these various forces, their combinations and their conflicts? I would repeat first that the theory is that our social as well as our individual manifestations, behaviours and beliefs are nothing more or less than modes of expression of these ingredients of the psyche, whether the ingredients are free to discharge their energy, as it were, directly (which is never the case), or whether they are tied up in unison or conflict with other intra-psychic components (which is always more or less the case). In other words, in the same way that the individual expresses symptoms, which when unmasked show causal ingredients arising both from his instinct levels and from his repressing superego forces, so society in its behaviour, customs, institutions and principles, is revealing the symptomatic expression embodying components from various usually conflicting levels of the mass-mind, past or present, usually past *and* present. It is generally conflict and the energies of the conflict which emerge to cause a symptom, a custom, a delusion, or a belief.

All these things have, of course, a developmental aspect which must sooner or later be taken into consideration. The developmental aspect itself may be regarded as having two phases, one being phylogenetical, the history of evolution and of the race, and the other being ontogenetical, the development of the individual and his conflicts from birth onwards.

Morbid conflict manifests itself in many ways. For instance, whether or not the individual suffers from unconscious superego-induced constipation, he will commonly make a fetish of removing excretory productions from the surface of his skin, and indeed removing any foreign material which may have arrived there by contact with his environment. In short, his first activities on awakening consist largely, if not exclusively, of the removal of dirt or dirt equivalents. Unlike the natural animal, he does not appear to be content with the expulsion of internal bad substances. He follows this physiological compulsive process up with a thorough eradication of external or surface 'badnesses'.

The elements responsible for this concentration on the utmost cleanliness are brought into vivid perspective by the study of obsessional neurotics, with their handwashings and similar compulsions. One knows of cases in which the hands, though quite clean by ordinary standards, have to be washed and rewashed at such frequent intervals that the sufferer is prevented from pursuing any other occupation in life. Is the average cultured person with, for instance, his habitual daily bath, suffering from a minor degree of a similar neurosis? It does not prevent him from pursuing his ordinary occupation, but may well take away ten minutes or more of his otherwise useful working day, and disadvantages include not only the expenditure of time but also of energy and expense (heating, soap, towels), to a degree probably unjustified by reality considerations. On occasions the disadvantages to health of depriving the skin of its natural fats and superficial oils may outweigh the advantages.

That this is not a purely theoretical consideration was brought to my notice by an old lady patient who complained of such insistent itching of her whole skin surface that she was unable to sleep at night and had in consequence become nervously ill. With tears in her eyes she explained how she had increased her bath to twice daily, on each occasion changing her underwear as she feared that such insistent itching must be due to an animal parasite. The remedy had, however, greatly aggravated the disease. She had no parasites and no skin or other complaint. The irritation of her skin was due chiefly to soap and water, and the consequent deprivation of its natural fats. The remedy, entirely successful, consisted of the daily rubbing in of lanoline.

A skin specialist of extensive experience has informed me that the majority of skin troubles originate in a symptom of itching, and are the physical expression of what he calls a 'mental itch'. If a physical itch all over the skin can be psychogenic, so too can be our semi-obsessional toilet activities. It would seem that there is something which we have to get rid of, and no doubt that feeling, however habitually expressed physically, has its source in unconscious guilt feelings. Perhaps this is made more apparent not only by the obsessional neurotic, but even more conspicuously by religious rituals which, not content to use the expression 'washing away sin', put it into symbolical operation by the actual use of water at baptism and other ritual ceremonies.

A middle-aged lady who came for analysis with the apparently trivial symptom of fidgeting, soon revealed that she had spent the whole of her adult life in a constant war against dirt and dust, but had nevertheless been regarded as a perfectly normal, though commendably particular, housewife. Analysis revealed as was to be expected that her war against dirt was merely a symbol of her unconscious war against certain reprehensible (or dirty) addiction tendencies, albeit repressed and unconscious.

We who feel better after our daily bath are similar, though less severe cases. Every person of this civilization has some feelings of guilt which have arisen in the course of the superego battle against primitive instinct desires. Apparently we relieve some modicum of the uncomfortable feeling by washing away the badness of sin—if we cannot succeed in washing away the whole body—in our ablutions. Would we fidget if we did not bath, or would we at least experience some sense of unrelieved tension?

To show the close relationship of sex, guilt (anxiety) and washing or bathing, it may be as well to quote the case of the sixteen year old girl at a party who, having experienced some sexual pleasure with a man in the garden shelter, was discovered four hours later in a hysterical condition in a bath. She explained that she had felt guilty and dirty, and had locked herself in the bathroom to wash her hands. Repeated handwashing did not remove the guilt (or dirt). She still felt uncomfortable, so proceeded to extend the area of her ablutions. Eventually she tried complete immersion and when discovered after a search was in an exhausted condition, having been vigorously bathing herself for about two hours. This evokes the thought that we do not feel as guilty as all that, but that we can do with a comparatively mild wastage of our time and energy.

It should be mentioned here that there is an alternative, an opposite method of symbolically dealing with guilt, which has been practised by holy men throughout the world. Whereas bathing eradicates something (dirt-guilt), which should not be there, this other method 'gets rid of' by ignoring its existence, *by turning it out of consciousness*, thereby as it were exterminating it by the reverse process to washing.

The disadvantages of a symbolical method of dealing with our unconscious conflicts or complexes is that it is never quite adequate. As in the case of the girl and her bathing, no amount of such symbolical activities can remove the whole thing, perhaps the entire body would have to be removed and even then in the life hereafter we would apparently go about driven by the discomfort of the same conflict (we can see how the ideas of everlasting torment have arisen from man's unconscious). Although perhaps slightly comforted (very slightly) we are so far from cured by our symbolical act or ritual, that we go on from one more or less compulsive activity to another throughout our lives, trying symbolically but never succeeding to eradicate our mental discomfort.

Now the dynamic energy the mind initiates and continues in psychological (and physical) movement is generally encountered in the form produced by the evolutionary process which we call instinct. In short, it is usually some instinct drive which sets the ball rolling. Then all the other factors, including superego, taboos, prohibitions and so on, enter into the struggle and the net result may not look so virile, aggressive, forceful or healthy. Now, of the instincts which are the legacy of our normal anestry, the libidinal one encounters social and superego prohibitions only when its direction happens to be towards its fellow beings. In so far as libido operates on an infantile or baby level in the form of oral or eating desires, there is, generally speaking, no very strong social or religious prohibition placed upon it, though even here I should qualify this remark by saying that there certainly would be in some circumstances, and we do get individual instances where through some unconscious regression to forbidden forms of eating, such as cannibalism or coprophilia, strong unconscious prohibitions come into play and the individual suffers from eating difficulties which may range from rationalized dietetics to the exteme and sometimes fatal psychoneurotic illness called *anorexia nervosa*, where the sufferer cannot allow anything to pass her lips.

There are many other ways in which the unconscious phantasy connected with libido on an oral level reveals its presence in our social activities. The obsessional ritual connected with our eating habits, such as the emphasis on cleanliness, on tablecloth as well as plates, on using instruments such as knives and forks, on eating in a particular way, not talking with the mouth full and so on, and so on, are all indicative of elements of a conflict in connection with oral lusts. On the other hand, such social institutions as banquets, feasts, political and otherwise, are expressions of this conflict involving an emphasis on the libidinal or pleasure-giving aspects thereof, not to mention an abundance of unconscious phantasy connected with mutual pleasure-giving, helping one another to food and drink, or at least partaking of the pleasure together so that pleasure is increased through mutual encouragement; while guilt is shared and therefore diminished. This was very conspicuously the case in cannibal feasts recorded in anthropology, for instance when the community or the brothers ate the sacrificed body of king or father. It was essential that they all ate together and were all implicated, like the conspirators who stabbed Caesar.

The social expressions of libido on an oral level have many ramifications which we are naturally more concerned to enjoy than to analyse. For example, the convention of Christmas dinner, when all the relatives (cf. the band of brothers who must all participate in the totem feast) gather together, and the essential ingredient of the banquet is some large bird, turkey or goose, a symbol, as our analysed dreams reveal to us almost daily, of a portion of the father's person, namely his phallus, the eating of which provides the conviviality of sharing and enjoying the unconscious introjection of the enormous potency attributed to the great ancestor. In short, we are still doing out totem feasting, safe under what we feel to be its heavy disguise, the unvarying object being, of course, pleasure with as little guilt or conflict as possible. Of course it is a jolly occasion coupled as it is with implications of the old human sacrifice, which assuages the guilt, washes away our sins, and enables us to enjoy libidinal satisfaction on many levels without prohibitions, guilt or castration threats. What a lot of trouble and elaboration society has to go to to extract enjoyment from living.

Another eating ceremony, where the sexual accompaniments are more conspicuous, is of course that of the wedding reception. There the bride is the main 'totem' figure, and the uncut wedding cake the main symbol of the purity of her body and of her virginity. The cake is cut in front of the guests voluntarily by the bride, with the assistance of the bridegroom using, if he be a soldier, his sword for the purpose! To the analyst nothing could be more clearly symbolical of the unconscious phantasies and their meaning. The guests at the reception must all partake of the bridal cake, small pieces of this cake are placed in little boxes and distributed to the bride's friends who were not present to partake at the time. Thus does she voluntarily share her person symbolically with all those she loves and who love her. Perhaps eating ceremonies are only different in the strength of their disguise and the more hidden nature of symbolism from what they were in the ancient days of totems, taboos and cannibalism.

Most of our activities, customs, or patterns of behaviour show a certain interesting characteristic of expressing either simultaneously or, more clearly, in turn, some aspect of the two principal antithetical ingredients of our main structural conflict. For instance, we go to church first and sin afterwards . . . and then perhaps confess and go to church again. I do not mean this quite literally, but we see equivalents in a good many patterns of our behaviour, as though the superego dominates for a time, and after we have 'been good' we have, as it were, a licence to let the id out. The child sits at its desk in class, then the bell rings and it runs round the playground shouting. Primitive man was, or his id was, cabined, cribbed and confined by his taboos and restrictions, and then periodically had a wonderful orgy of head-hunting, murder, and cannibalistic feasting. The same pattern shows signs of survival today. This should not be surprising, as it is an outward expression or dramatization in the appropriate two parts of the basic structural conflict within. It can be seen in our alternation of work and play, of being 'good' and being 'bad', in fasting and feasting. It also prevails in our general habits of having periodic holidays after periods of work, corresponding in primitive life to the long period of taboo and the short period of relaxation from taboo, or orgy. We organize our lives in general according to this pattern, in so far as we have terms of work and vacations.

In looking for the determinants of this system in the psyche, one is not surprised to find that work is largely determined by superego and ego pressure, and vacation by a release from our taskmasters when we have more or less satisfied them. This release can be detected to be a licence for the id. What sort of a licence, and how far does it take us? With many people, there is too much unconscious conflict to enable them to enjoy this licence unless they partly anaesthetize their superego by an undue consumption of alcohol. The first witticism mentioned by Freud in his book *Wit and the Unconscious* is the condensation of ideas producing the neologism alcoholiday, of which this phenomenon had reminded me. But I do not think it is generally recognized how difficult it is for some people, perhaps for the average person, to throw off the accustomed superego restriction adequately to enjoy himself libidinally, even in the displaced or symbolical manner which is socially permitted.

A patient of mine whilst he was in the throes of his current holiday struggle illustrated this. The holiday island which he planned to visit, getting to it and being there, represented the consummation of all his desires. It was identified with phantasies of relaxation and happiness. Although he had booked his passage and there was no reality hindrance in the way, things were not so simple any more than they had been simple before his marriage, when more than one girl-friend had tried unsuccessfully to seduce him. There was his wretched lumbago which threatened to become worse as the time for departure on holiday approached. He was in a frantic state of anxiety. Which would win—desire or the unconscious forces which were mobilizing themselves to prevent the gratification of his desire, by striking him down with a physical incapacity in the form of lumbago?

With the help of dreams, free association of thought, and other material, it eventually became apparent that the holiday island symbolized the woman, in the last analysis the mother of his Oedipus complex. That is what accounted for its fantastic over-valuation. It was on this very account, connected with over-valuation, that anxiety reached a climax, threatening to prevent the beginning of the incestuous act. The form in which he was expressing this anxiety was merely part of the defensive system, defensive against insight which presumably would have been more frightening. The essence of such a situation is the struggle between libidinal desire on the one hand and anxiety on the other. We are familiar with the manoeuvre of the defensive forces in reversing the situation on a conscious plane, so that the patient's conscious mind tells him that he is afraid of *not* being able to do the desired acts.

However, the ingredients of the conflict between id versus super-ego and ego are not always expressed in such a separated or distinct form. More often each ingredient infiltrates the territory of the other, so that we get conflict at work and conflict at play, conflict to do with any and every activity which we shoulder or in which we indulge.

The pattern of conflict between being 'good' and being 'bad' shows itself rather more clearly in some banqueting ceremonies. For instance, it is a usual masonic practice, having first eradicated all guilt by, one, debarring women and two, dressing very formally, usually even with white cotton gloves, putting a symbolic apron over the genital region, to attend a chapel service, in which ridigity, formality and ritual are most firm and conspicuous, and perfection is the watchword. Immediately this superego ceremony is over, the 'brothers' rush into the bar, where they toast one another excitedly with sherries and cocktails. This is merely a curtain-raiser to the enormous banquet or feast where, in the pre-war days at least, every imaginable oral gratification was provided, including a succession of wines, champagnes, ports and brandy, finishing with cigars. In contrast to the chapel service, conviviality prevails. Practically every-one is toasted and drunk to by practically everyone. It is not lost upon the analyst that the success of every speech, small or long, depends entirely upon the appropriateness of the little sexual joke which is practically always introduced. If anything were needed to reveal that feasting and banqueting is a symbolical, mutual, libidinal pleasure, the masonic feast, no less than the orgy of old, should help to reveal it. Drinking together, like eating together, is a symbolical form of encouraging one another's libidinal pleasure.

Eating can be more than an oral pleasure, it can and commonly does symbolize genital sexual relationship. The point I am here try-ing to make is that these social customs, even such ordinary ones as eating and banqueting are, like everything else we do, not so much an adjustment to reality relationship or environment, as an expression of the dynamic energy of the ingredients of various unconscious conflicts, which go on unbeknown to us in our unconscious phantasy. These exist because they help to relieve or express the inner tensions, and they have commonly nothing to do with any reality except the 'reality' of these conflicting tensions within us.

Psychoanalysis points out that the whole structure of mature adult sexuality begins with the oral pleasures which the child achieves in its sucking activities. Perhaps this is the first manifestation of libido that is thrust upon our attention, because to my mind there is every reason to suppose that pleasures have been achieved within the cells and within the developing psyche throughout the whole process of cellular nutrition, growth and cell-division.

But there is little doubt that this oral achievement of pleasure is a definite step towards the even more clearly describable sexual pleasures on a genital level. But even on this oral level the process of sexuality is more complicated than would at first appear. In the course of development the stage arises when the impulse to suck is not the only one which the mouth displays. With the development of the teeth, the biting stage arises. This ushers in what analysts call the second oral phase of libidinal (or sexual) development. It too has its relationship with later stages of sexual development. Some lovers, not content with kissing, even include biting as one of their fore-pleasures, or perhaps more frequently as an orgastic accompaniment. Either or both of these oral levels are capable of development into a sexual perversion. The former, in the form of kissing, is unwittingly encouraged in our civilization by the very much stronger taboos placed upon more overt and more natural sexuality.

I may add here that curiously enough I did not intend to embark at the moment upon socialized libidinal expressions at an *oral* level, but it may be that none of these levels can be justifiably separated. I was going to suggest that at an oral level, taboos and prohibitions are not so conspicuously operative, but it is only too apparent that when libido develops to its mature form of genital desire, where the object with which it seeks gratification is some other person of the social community, that we see all the anxiety and prohibitions of the old totem days ranging themselves in the guise of the most powerful social, legal and religious forms. Restrictions of every variety abound, and of course reinforce the restricting factor already present within the intra-psychic conflict; there is an enormous degree of disturbance, individual and social, a disturbance which is only held within measurable or controllable proportions by the superabundance and intensity of prohibiting and sanctioning forces. However 'natural' you may be on every other plane, society ethics and religion, not to speak of economics, insist that in this form no suffering is too great to be endured to keep the peace and ensure that the fabric of society shall remain intact.

It is chiefly on this account that the strength of the forces constrained within the almost adequate strength of the prohibitions are responsible for so many of the phenomena, both individual and social, which manifest themselves in the doctor's consulting room, and in the attitudes and institutions of the social structure.

But we do not have to turn to obvious sexual behaviour to detect the expression of conflict between id and superego in every fabric of our social life. In a broad way, this is revealed by the general antithesis which we draw between the sexes. For instance, in appearance we are not content with the differences that nature has made, but we must proceed to emphasize these out of all proportion by a difference in detail from the head to the feet. Though nature has made the heads alike, we ornament them with strikingly different headgear. We dress the hair differently. We ornament or cosmetic the face differently. Admittedly we go out of our way here to strike a similarity by removing the male facial hair, but this exception perhaps merely proves the rule, for it needs a troublesome and painstaking application of our conscious mind to the subject.

Every article of dress is antithetically different, right down to and including the structure and appearance of our footwear, although nature made the feet in both sexes identical. A detailed history of fashions in dress and even in footwear would make this subject very much more interesting and more convincing. Even with regard to footwear, I believe there was a time in English history, about the period of Elizabeth I, when men wore footgear not according to the size of their feet, but according to their rank or station, so that in consequence the long, pointed toes of their boots had to be brought round and tied to the leg. Subsequently the fashion became one of showing one's rank by the width instead of the length of the footwear, until Elizabeth I had to pass a law prohibiting anyone, no matter what his rank, to wear footwear more than nine inches in width.

On first sight it would seem that the sexual implications are absent from these particular footwear fashions, until analysis reminds us that in dreams and symptoms, footwear is commonly a sexual, genital symbol, the size of which therefore symbolizes degree of potency. The difference between the footwear in the sexes, particularly the high heel to the woman's shoe, is revealed analytically as compensation for unconscious genital inferiority feelings, the symbol being as usual much over-determined. For instance, in one respect it is a phallic symbol, but it has more general effects, such as increasing the apparent height and lending an appearance of erection to the stance, all connected with subjective and objective sexual stimulation.

Apart from clothing, even articles carried in the hand have their sexual connotation or significance. Not long ago, no gentleman was complete without his stick (or umbrella) and gloves, (both of interesting psychological significance, particularly when associated together), whereas a lady carried her important appendage in the shape of a handbag, as feminine a symbol as the former are masculine.

Thus it would seem that even in our presentation of ourselves socially we, in this civilization, have gone to endless trouble to tell the world that sex is here and that it is the most important thing in our minds, but we confine our telling to these mute actions, while we would hotly deny the whole thing in theory and in words.

When we consider such phenomena as transvestism, wearing the clothes of the opposite sex, we may ask in passing what our body itself symbolizes, that we should be at such pains to play out our conflict in connection with it.

Freud stated that the ego is primarily a bodily thing, that is, the perception of one's own body.[16] According to Fenichel the 'body image' is the nucleus of the ego. 'An exaggerated reaction to clothing means generally an exaggerated reaction to body sensations.'[15]

According to psychoanalysis, the transvestite act (putting on the clothes of the opposite sex) has two unconscious meanings: '(a) an object-erotic and fetishistic one; the person cohabits not with a woman but with her clothes, the clothes representing, symbolically, her penis; (b) a narcissistic one: the transvestite himself represents the phallic woman under whose clothes a penis is hidden. Transvestites who are exhibitionistic about displaying their female attire show their symbolic penis in the same manner and for the same reason as true exhibitionists actually show their penis.'[15]

With regard to female transvestites, Fenichel says: 'Making believe that one possesses a penis and playing father are the unconscious meanings of female transvestitism.'[15]

The analyst is in the special position of having the symbolical significance of these symbols, and of all the other gadgets of civilization, thrust upon his attention during his scientific work, so that he cannot afford to have the popular quantity of defensive resistance. For instance, the significance of the lady's handbag might not have struck me so forcefully had I not had a woman patient who, early in analysis, brought me a dream to the effect, to use her words, 'I found that my handbag had been slit open so that all my valuables had been lost'. She, like everyone else, had no idea what her handbag might symbolize, but it is of significance that she confessed at the end of the session something which she had hoped to hide from her analyst, and that was that she had lost her virginity, which she had highly valued (cf. 'valuables') the previous evening. It was only at this point that she fully appreciated the meaning of her dream and the significance of the handbag.

The sticks and gloves similarly often appeared in the dreams of male analysands. They were commonly being lost, both in dreams and in actuality, in accordance with the analysand's unconscious castration phantasy. From this it was easy to see why the male, or at least the gentleman, felt more complete with them. But now the fashion has changed somewhat. Sticks and gloves as a symbolical potency reinforcement have given place perhaps to cars, albeit the symbolism of clothes is always with us. Commonly it seems to indicate that socially we are more concerned to make a display of our potency or to pretend to a potency, as though that were more important than the truth.

I have written a book (*The Unconscious Significance of Hair*) to indicate how even such an apparently minor feature of our cultural life as the hair we display, has ramifications emanating from the basic struggle of our unconscious conflict, and has no reality justification, but is merely like our physiological functions, nothing more or less than a mode of trying to deal with our internal struggle and attempts to externalize it and make it less uncomfortable. This is not necessarily psychosis but it certainly has nothing to do with sanity. Similarly the psychology of dress and the changing fashions is an equal expression of these internal irrational needs.

But I have no intention of writing a thesis on this subject. The late J. C. Flugel has already done so in his book on the psychology of clothes. In this, his general summary is that the primary determinant of the wearing of clothes is not a utility one, in fact all other determinants are completely over-shadowed by the main determinant, which he declares is that of display or exhibitionism. This may be more credible for us if we reflect that most of the shops up and down the country, or at any rate in the principal towns, seem to be full of various apparel, particularly ladies' apparel, as though the main objective in our lives, or at least in the lives of women, was some sort of exhibition of our clothed bodies, in order presumably to achieve some unconscious satisfaction or titillation of satisfaction, perhaps both in ourselves and in the other members of our social group, or in all persons who see us. Thus we might suggest that this aspect of civilization at least reveals a way of getting back some substitutive or attenuated sexuality, which social organization has denied us in a more primitive form.

Flugel's other determinants of clothes and fashion he relegates to relatively insignificant importance, the one of keeping out the cold, for example, is perhaps shown in its true light in the specially social occasions of women's evening wear. Here it is clearly shown that clothing is designed to display the body attractively and at the same time perhaps denying the existence of anything that may not be attractive.

The third, and only other motive, according to Flugel, comes in here, namely that of modesty. Havelock Ellis tells us that modesty exists even amongst the female animals and is presumably designed to avoid repulsing the male when he is desired.

I am not alleging that these social customs of ours, or habits of eating and dressing, are necessarily psychotic. On the contrary, in so far as they titillate our sexuality, and prompt us to keep alive the pleasure which in its more natural form is socially prohibited, they are probably the best we can do in regard to maintaining our potential sexual health . . . and happiness. In short it may be said that the greater part of our activities and mental preoccupations from the cradle to the grave are engaged upon *symbolical* attempts to relieve the tensions (especially guilt feelings) arising from intrapsychic conflict inaugurated during the period of infancy and childhood. Apparently this experience of growing up has given us enough internal disturbance to occupy us for the rest of our days. This is what the careful examination of human activity and the construction of culture or civilization reveals. The point is that we are unconscious of the true nature and source of the conflict. We are repressing it all, but nevertheless the leakage of its affects on to the conscious level gives us so much discomfort that we are, as it were, compelled to do what we can in our blindness to alleviate our intrapsychic pains. The basic source of these pains being inaccessible to us, we play out the unconscious phantasy by the use of symbols. We create for this purpose the customs of civilization and use all the gadgets and paraphernalia we can lay our hands on to keep ourselves busy in the pursuit of this mistaken 'therapeutic' activity. This is what our daily life, including its institutionalized forms, consists of, and this is why I consider it all symptomatic behaviour.

But this is not all. Those emotionally charged conflicts of ours do not only determine our lifelong activities, they also determine the nature of our thoughts and beliefs. It is not only our bodies that are held in this vice, or thrown upon this treadmill, it is our minds also, and that perhaps is the principal justification for the title of this book. Nevertheless the nature of mind, especially of its deeper levels, is not easy to see and generally speaking it is the activities, customs and institutions which it produces that most vividly reveal something of its nature. If we can understand the meaning of the symbols with which we are acting out our conflicts, whether they be hair, clothes and everything else that composes our individual and social world, we can get a little nearer to understanding the hidden matters which they symbolize. I would suggest however, that the very fact of ignoring the real source of our compulsions and acting them out with irrelevant or symbolical substitutions is itself a childish and somewhat insane phenomenon, especially when we all so readily fly to these symbols and accept them as though they had some intrinsic value, obtaining thereby some illusionary modicum of temporary relief, which is prone to disappear almost as soon as we experience it, and leaving our problem without even the beginnings of understanding or lasting solutions.

We assume that our behaviour is rational. Indeed the usual argument in support of this, is the fact that 'everyone else does it, and one has to conform'. This is true enough as far as it goes, but the matter of psychological interest is why have these customs or institutions come into being, and the psychological answer is that they have gradually been created and developed as a symptomatic expression of the unconscious conflict within the mind of their creator, man. We are reviewing them because, like all symptoms, they are the clue to the hidden or unconscious psychopathology which they express. The fact that they are not individual symptoms but embrace the behaviour of the entire social group makes them (especially when institutionalized) of outstanding importance for our purpose. This is because we are not studying the psychosis of any particular individual, but of humanity as a whole, of mankind or madkind, whose psychopathology as a whole gives rise to these massive group phenomena. Of course we do not escape these emotionally charged impulses and phantasies by dint of repression, they emerge through the cracks nevertheless. Thus in Victorian times even the sight of my lady's ankle might well serve as an erotic stimulus, whereas in these days, having become accustomed to seeing ladies in bikinis, we are probably less erotically moved.

The point I wish to emphasize is that these customs even in so far as they have become socialized, are not essentially reality adaptations, their determinants are the psychopathological conflicts within the unconscious mind. These repressed conflicts create certain conscious-level tensions. Not knowing the source of these tensions, we are prompted or compelled to act out the phantasies from which they arise in a symbolical form. The particular symbolical form which we have devised or found around us is the particular form of culture or civilization which we mistake for the essence of our reality life.

CHAPTER V

THE SOCIAL NEUROSIS OF MODERN MAN

It is encouraging to my work to learn that a well-known sociologist, Burrows,[17] uses this expression 'the social neurosis' for what he calls 'The common condition of disorder and conflict which exists throughout its structure, though generally unrecognized by society'. He goes on to say: 'It is expressed symptomatically in the nervous and mental disorder of the individual, and also in man's so-called normal inter-relations—in his peaceful social institutions, in economic conflict, crime and war. Viewed phylobiologically, this general social condition is the primary and essential disorder of which the individual manifestation of neurosis is an arbitrarily isolated expression'.

He goes on to speak of 'beliefs and prejudices which are deeply ingrained in the individual and in society but for which there is no objective demonstrable correspondence in actuality. These emotionally toned impressions have no direct relation to the object or situation upon which they are projected. The social image is wishfully determined and is not based upon demonstrable reality'.

I feel that this is more than a hint that the authentic ethnologist does at least sometimes recognize that society, its habits, customs and institutions, are a psychopathological structure. The popular illusion that the social structure with its division of labour and so on came about through some ego-like operation of one man going to another and saying, 'I will make your footwear if you will make my coats, or supply me with food', and that type of transaction, is not the cause of the knitting together, but probably a relatively late result of it. Like every other activity of man, we would be safer to pursue our investigations on the hypothesis that his behaviour was determined by emotional trends emanating from his unconscious, and not necessarily of a logical or reasonable nature.

According to Weston la Barre, in *Family and Symbol:* 'sound social scientists have given up the task of seeking to explain man's gregariousness and now accept it as a basic datum of social science'.[18] In view of the psychoanalytical explanation of gregariousness, I think we can readily excuse them! But it is interesting to learn this from La Barre as justifying attempts to seek an explanation in man's unconscious psychopathology.

Freud says: 'In the light of psychoanalysis we are accustomed to regard social feelings as a sublimation of homosexual attitudes towards objects'. According to this view the psychological mechanisms would be comparable to those previously detailed, which lead to an over-estimation of the loved object. The aim of the sexual instinct is inhibited and repressed. In consequence of this the unrelieved libidinal energy causes an idealization of the object just as it did in infancy when the aim-inhibited love of the child led to idealization of the mother. In the social equivalent of this, the individual projects his ego ideal on to some leader or outstanding personage. His contemporaries who choose the same projected ego ideal are then felt by him to share the same highly estimated all-important thing in common. Hence we get social groups, political parties, religious denominations etc., clinging together as social units. In other words it is this emotional over-valuation, formation and projection of ego ideal, all having its inception in frustrated libido, that brings about the coherence of society.

The emphasis here is laid upon *sublimation*. This in turn results from inhibition of libidinal aim, consequent over-valuation, and the creation of an ego ideal. In short, the cohesion of individuals into a social unit is primarily due to unconscious emotional sources, according to Freud sublimated homosexual attitudes. It may be that the homosexual attitudes are those which are most subject to inhibition of aim and repression, leaving no alternative but the formation of the process above detailed. Presumably this is because in the heterosexual equivalent, the aim would not be so prone to inhibition, and the libido would flow in a more realizable and gratifiable direction. That is why perhaps in some groups an introduction of the opposite sex has the reputation of having a disruptive and disastrous effect upon the social cohesion. This is notably the case in certain religious orders, e.g. monks and nuns, freemasonry, specially built up male units such as the army or the fighting forces, or indeed in any group where it is of understanding importance that the males should be united and not in conflict with one another.

Freud goes on to tell us that the overt homsexual is a person who has 'not fully detached his special development of social instincts from sexual object choice'. The aim of some portion of his homsexual instinct has escaped from inhibition and repression to some degree, and moved sexually towards the object, so it would appear that we can have sex as well as society, but in so far as libido comes into the former, the latter is relatively impoverished. That is why so many societies encourage the inhibition of sex or at least of the sexual aim. Thus it would appear that whatever the mechanisms involved, it is frustrated and aim-inhibited libido that becomes sublimated and leads to the promotion of the social unit.

So it would seem that gregariousness or union with a group can

give the individual inspirational courage, both to forego his id gratification and in certain circumstances courage to give them freer outlet
than he would dare to do as an individual. The former process is
apparent in our peaceful and constructive social endeavours as well
as in religious activities, and the latter not only in mob activities,
hooliganism, riots and disorders, but also in the phenomenon of war,
or at least as an important undercurrent as well as determinant of it.
The point I wish to make is that even the 'best' aspects of the social
group are to be seen as the products of irrational unconscious forces,
whereas the worst aspects are manifestly irrational, disruptive and
destructive, obviously emanating from pathological sources and
mechanisms.

Whatever the psychopathology and mechanisms that go to unite
the social group, there can be little doubt that biologically this group
begins with the family group. In primates and other mammals this
stage of development has already been reached, and in some cases
passed. We can see the little families sticking together, and the children playing together. Primates have definitely gone further than
this stage. The entire horde will extend a vociferous welcome to any
previous member of the group which has been away and then returns.
I believe that the essential difference between their welcoming
gestures and ours is that we take man by his hand, whereas, according
to Zuckermann, the primate welcomer affectionately grasps his
genitals. Perhaps this gesture alone indicates that we have specialized
in more displacement and symbolization, to express our affective
state socially or at least publically.

Not every individual of the social group feels the same enthusiasm
for this cultural development. The analyst has a large clientele of
persons who feel they have been maimed, castrated or psychologically
exterminated by the insistence of society to make them fit. Most of
these seem to accept their ill or impotent fate, but we occasionally
get rebels, some of whom seem ready to destroy the world to get back
the potency or life of which it has allegedly robbed them. I have a
patient who described himself as a castrated and harnessed horse,
restricted, and with a bit in his mouth. He said also that they had
endeavoured to further harness him with blindfolding or permanent
blinkers. This was his reference to what he regarded as indoctrination, but he claimed that he had managed to shake it off. His attitude
to society was something like that of a man seeking revenge for terrible
wrongs. Most people with an emotionally charged complex of this
nature have long since become so terrified of it that they have repressed it deep into their unconscious, and may well present the
symptoms of an Anxiety State, including perhaps a fear of meeting
people or mixing with people, and certainly a fear of letting themselves go, or perhaps of even opening their mouths.

Such a one told me that in the long walks he had had as a boy with his father, there was always a silent understanding that certain subjects must on no account be broached. The patient said: 'It is as though there was a chalk line drawn between what was permitted and what was not permitted. One was so terrified of inadvertently overstepping the line, which would certainly have happened if one had become relaxed or natural, that most of our walk passed in silence. The most awkward moment would be when some acquaintance accosted us. I am sure we both walked with our hearts in our mouths, because he might not know the rules, and might blunder over the chalk line, and perhaps we would be in danger of being dragged over it by him.'

Our social behaviour, like all our other reactive patterns, has its source or origin in phantasy, in the reactive patterns formed in relation to parents and siblings. The usual practice is that the child (id) accepts the parent's (superego) ruling. For instance, the child may like dirty hands, but if the parent says clean hands, finally the child accepts the good parent, introjects her and adopts the clean hands idea.

Our relationships to other people are not necessarily or primarily ego-determined, or rational. Every scrap of psychoanalytical evidence tells us that certain reactive patterns were created in our earliest years of infancy, and have become almost like instincts, acting themselves out more or less compulsively, whether or not the actual situation even of our adult life fifty years later is appropriate for the acting out or not. It is only in the case of some striking deviation from the normal that the mechanism of our social relationships and the source of it can be vividly brought home to us.

When we consider the psychopathology of the social neurosis, and indeed of the social life in general, we will see that the individual organisms have been moulded to fit the multicellular social structure. Perhaps they have lost something in the moulding but it seems they may have acquired something also, if only the impression of the mould. The emotional forces involved are the dynamic forces of life and death, and are much too powerful to be superseded as determinants of our life and behaviour by such a new and immature and feeble new growth as the reality ego, or reason. That is why La Barre and the ethnologists could find no explanation for gregariousness. They were looking in the wrong direction, towards the ego, presumably having assumed that mankind was sane. And that is why I have detailed the psychoanalytical theories as the only explanation of these social phenomena, despite their nonconformity with rationality.

Patients under analysis, particularly those with definite individual characteristics, are commonly people who have still retained some of their inherited primitive nature in visible form. Some of them have been not so thoroughly modified or so thoroughly bowed down by the yoke of the superego, as has the more usual or more 'normal' person. Thus the outlook, attitude and material which they supply often provide one with an insight into something which is common to all, only too covered up and hidden to be apparent or vivid enough for exposition. Apart from his unusually natural and outspoken ways, I have a patient who would be regarded as normal in all respects. Although a bachelor, he is well-adjusted to a heterosexual life, well within normal limits. In the course of an analytical session following his experiences at a party, a social function in which he seldom indulges, he clearly revealed to me the secret of the unconscious forces at work in such circumstances, forces which to my mind determine this social phenomenon of indulging in parties and enjoying them, albeit sometimes with a modicum of conflict.

He was there with his girl-friend, and while he had to be as careful as possible not to give her cause for doubts of his loyalty, or stimulate her jealousy, which might well have made her miserable and spoilt the evening, he could not help at the same time being attracted by at least one previously unknown female. There he was amongst all these people, pretty well ignoring the males and anything but ignoring a proportion of the females, and on top of all this pretending most of the time to an equal interest in both sexes. Perhaps he found some of the women unusually stimulating and in some little ways he fell to the temptation of pursuing his impulse as far as the social situation would allow. Perhaps he would make remarks a bit out of turn when a particular person was involved, or go into the kitchen when she was there, whisper something in her ear, touch her, and so on, all the time hoping but not really believing that his girl-friend did not notice these little manoeuvres. He himself was well aware of a state of suppressed excitement, conflicting forces and phantasies were very active inside him. It was our business to sort them out and bring them to consciousness during his session.

Perhaps he had not been quite so discreet in his behaviour at the party as the average mature person should have been. Here his superego, however allegedly diminutive, showed itself as something to be reckoned with, for if not at the party, certainly the morning after, it had caused him to subject his conduct to some critical scrutiny. What was plainest of all was that left to his id or instinctual impulses, he would without undue delay have proceeded to coitus with at least half a dozen of the women present. Indeed it became quite evident to him that his suppressed excitement during the party was nothing more or less than a blind anticipation of this exciting happening with many of those present. The id and its impulses take little cognizance of the inappropriateness of the reality situation. At his session he recognized clearly that the anticipation of intercourse was his main preoccupation during the party, although his ego knew it was impracticable, and that despite this knowledge his reaction when the party ended was just as though he had in fact been interrupted in the middle of an incompleted intercourse. He said: 'I cannot imagine subjecting myself to the practice of coitus reservatus. It would be utterly foreign to my nature, in fact impossible for me to carry out. And yet I go to a party and the fact of it is that that is exactly what I do.'

It may well be that people who have achieved more successful maturity do not allow their subconscious excitements to reach such a pitch that they feel so high and dry when the party ends, but nevertheless the revelations from this, and other patients under analysis, convince the analyst that the aptitudes are there, whether they are allowed to exercise themselves or not. In fact it is well known that at less conventional parties these more or less hidden or even denied tendencies reveal themselves pretty openly in the form of flirtings and pettings, and show ample evidence of the direction of the normal trend, and thus justifies the conclusion that the determinant of this particular item of social behaviour must be the sexual urge, or rather a compromise between sexual desires and the taboos of the superego in the form of convention and public sanction.

Thus we must regard the party as a form of symptomatic behaviour, which like all symptoms shows the characteristics of conflicting antagonists embodied in the same behaviour. It may be that it is not unusual, especially in adolescence, that half a loaf is better than no bread, and that it is a good thing to obtain considerable pleasure or fore-pleasure within the confines of the social practices permitted within one's own group. Therefore it would be suggested that the symptom here displayed, in so far as it is more gratifying than frustrating (as it was in the case of the patient mentioned) may be regarded as a normal neurosis rather than a minor psychosis. However, if we look at it from the purely reality point of view, for instance that nowadays there is not any reality need why such instinctual conduct should not reach its full gratification, we may regard the social structure which prevents this as being comparable to an unnecessarily interfering parent figure, or of psychotic construction.

When dancing is included in the proceedings, enormous facilities are offered for the very sort of thing which my patient found so difficult to achieve at his party, namely for an actual physical approach to the desired female or to each desired female in turn. Thus he may, albeit only symbolically, dramatize his phantasy of coitus with everyone of them in turn, the only sacrifice demanded is that he should pretend to some pleasure with some of those he does not want, and of course that all participants should pretend that the whole proceedings are purely social and have nothing whatever to do with sex. Naturally of course this pretence is extended to oneself most of the time, or in the majority of instances. There are occasions, however, when pretence is not so successful, or when something reveals the true unconscious source or determinant of the social custom.

I am reminded of a patient of mine, a 'youth' of twenty-five, advisedly so-called, whose plump, rosy-cheeked, attractive mother brought him to the psychiatrist on account of various phobias, including a claustrophobia which prevented his travelling in trains. Having got rid of mother, I was surprised to find that this not-too-young young man not only had never had a girl-friend, or so much as broached any sort of physical contact with any female, but could genuinely not remember when he had last had a seminal emission.

As I did not feel that he or the situation were very suitable for long treatment, I supplemented analysis with some advice regarding social contacts. He was an obedient young fellow and at my suggestion took up dancing. We were both rather surprised to find that this 'sexless' male suffered an involuntary ejaculation immediately he stepped on a dance floor with his arm round an unknown young woman. Perhaps equally surprising to his analyst was the fact that his involuntary phenomenon did not appear to worry him in the least! The explanation must be that he had succeeded in dissociating sexuality so completely from consciousness that it carried out its functions as it were in a separate department. I am glad to be able to say that within the short period of three or four months, phenomena like this that had at first persisted, had completely disappeared, and his heterosexual relationships, as well as his sexual functions, became absolutely normal and speedily led to engagement and marriage. He had proceeded to the normal undoing of the mother fixation.

The case is mentioned here as a revelation of the unconscious meaning of such pleasure-giving social habits as ballroom dancing, but before leaving the subject of dancing I should mention that many modern dances concentrate chiefly on muscular rather than genital eroticism, and in that sense represent a regression of libido to a more infantile component instinct, the eroticism of muscular activity and movements, whether or not associated with heterosexual or homosexual interest.

Such minor indulgences as the pleasures of television, cinemas, theatres and books, may represent an attempt to retreat from the too stimulating and unmanageable situations of parties and emotionally charged relationships to other persons, in favour of experiencing these vicariously. We can look at or read about other people having these emotional experiences, respond so much as we desire—and not more—and have the satisfaction of knowing that in reality we are onlookers, however much emotion we have succeeded in experiencing, and that nothing has happened in reality to interfere with the even tenor of our ways.

When it comes to such social functions as dinner parties and cocktail parties, we have of course a combination of all the unconscious elements detailed earlier in this chapter under 'Party', added to by the pleasures of eating and drinking. It is as though we said: 'Well, let's have everything while we are at it', which may seem to be more sensible. One of the chief concerns is to avoid undue conflict or anxiety, and if the party should proceed a little further than the superego will sanction in the direction of, for instance, flirtings and pettings, then conflict is liable to arise, if not at the time then subsequently. So our ego and its institutionalized social equivalent, convention, in steering a difficult course between pleasure (perhaps the greatest possible pleasure) on the one hand and superego watchfulness on the other.

Some of my patients are apt to find that in endeavouring to navigate these straits, they are liable to be wrecked if not on Scylla, then on Charybdis, but the miraculous feat which many perform appears to be to get themselves wrecked on both. Perhaps this is what our social civilization turns out to be, a symbolical playing out of our conflict without the certainty of avoiding psychological disaster.

Perhaps it is by dint of these experiences, particularly in adolescence, that an attempt is made to find a situation less frustrating and more gratifying and ego-syntonic, something that will fit not only our instinctual and superego demands, but also our ego or reality principle. This 'solution' is of course being dangled in front of us all the time by society. It is so important that it has been institutionalized. I am of course referring to marriage.

CHAPTER VI

MARRIAGE

Naturally the subject of matrimony is not, and cannot be, dealt with compendiously or exhaustively here, for no book or library would be large enough to house the material. We have to be content with a few passing examples. I fancy they could be added to indefinitely.

The marriage system differs very much from one country to another. In China, for example, it was until recently, dominated by certain family rules and traditions. In Hindustan, parents of the same social class arrange a child or infant marriage, the choice of the parties being brought into no consideration whatsoever. Nevertheless, most of these marriages turn out 'well enough' to remain established, and the social order is not threatened. May it be that peoples', or at least civilized peoples', ids have become so inured with restraint that any mate is gratefully accepted as an almost unexpected favour and liberation from what would otherwise be merely a prison to which all have grown accustomed and expect to be lifelong. All animals and humans accept what is allowed them if they have little or no hope of anything at all. All living creatures adjust to circumstances as best they can. The only question that may arise from a scientific point of view is the question of at what cost do they adjust? Is the framework or outer wall of the prison absolutely necessary? Anyhow, it is better than being confined in a solitary cell, so most of us accept it gratefully and may even be particularly glad that our mate is similarly confined. Indeed, if the institution of matrimony suits both sides of our repressed conflict, endows us with the degree of libidinal liberty which we are capable of without undue anxiety or without undue castration threats from the opposing superego, then there is no doubt that it was made for us and in a sense us for it, and everything is perfect . . . provided we are not unlucky in our partner.

Generally speaking the social order is such that those who cannot fit themselves into it fall by the wayside. Is the social order above reproach, or should it go unchallenged without criticism? Can three hundred million Roman Catholics be wrong? Or two hundred million Hindus or fifty million Mussulmen? Or might the whole lot be wrong? Or is man, in the light of our study of primitive cultures, more likely to be wrong than nature? As Montaigne said: 'Man cannot even make a flea, yet he presumes to create gods without number'. Similarly, he cannot make health, yet he presumes to make laws and taboos to interfere, very often ignorantly, with nature and to make illness. We survive in spite of it, perhaps in the same way that animals survive in spite of their innumerable difficulties, including the hosts of parasites which usually infest every part of their bodies, externally and internally.

Fortunately for the survival of the species, the sexual instinct of physically uncastrated man is in most cases so strong and healthy that it persists in some degree in spite of its psychological and apparent castrations—the institution of matrimony and others. But there is an increasing proportion of men, particularly in more civilized (castrated) white races, upon whom the sexually inhibiting or castrating forces are reaching their cumulative effects. Man, particularly white man, and even more especially white woman, are becoming increasingly more impotent or frigid. With our institutions and laws, they succeed sufficiently in controlling or mutilating a law of nature. They will seek in vain to undo their handiwork. Although most institutionalized interference with nature has not yet succeeded to the extent of a physical extinction of the species, it has already succeeded to a considerable extent in psychic mutilation, perhaps in partial extinction.

The function of man's handiwork reaches its eventual expression in the phenomenon of suicide. Though one in every seventy deaths is legally established as suicide, there is still a large proportion of direct suicides which are classed as 'accidents'. In addition, in the light of the revelations of medical psychology, we are probably not far wrong if we assess all deaths other than those from old age, as suicide with a more complicated psychological mechanism than that of overt suicide. Though it has been said that the effect of man's handiwork reaches its full expression in the phenomenon of suicide, I would add that its lesser expressions permeate every walk of society, and every civilized individual carries a multitude of resulting *psychic* mutilations. Here we are concerned with its effect on his or her sexual function, but medical psychology reveals that you cannot have grave flaws like this in the foundation of the psyche without every part of the structure being affected and endangered. In practice, it is man's happiness and his will to live which are interfered with by his destructive superego. He is not content to limit the activity of this superego to his individual psychical organization, but he has externalized it in the form of powerful institutions, so that those fortunate members of the community who should not be destroyed by too harsh a superego, are subjected to the destructive effects of this externalized superego—such as the institution of matrimony—and beaten and mutilated by it.

As we cannot be happy in our inner psychic life, we have arranged a world in which we cannot be happy in our outer social life. Freedom, nature, God, is denied. Prison and destruction are apparently a part of our external world, created by their internal equivalents. Under the guise of something very pleasant we have built ourselves a prison of prisons, which we call marriage. The psychological conflict between libido and superego has its sociological (i.e. symptomatic) expression in:

1. The popular pleasure and approval manifested towards marriages and the doings of married couples, their pregnancies, their children, and so on. This pleasure has its mechanism in sympathetic libidinal release.

2. In contrast to this we have the popular social condemnation and often horror manifested towards sexual irregularities of any and every description. Here the superego is showing its hand and raging against the libido.

Like neurotic symptoms, these sociological expressions have no necessary corresondence to reality-values. It might be argued that the 'reality' they support is the stability of our social code, necessary for social stability. But would not that serve to indicate that our social stability depends upon an adjustment between two forces (libido and superego) which are both dissociated from reality, which have no reality-appreciation . . . any more than the social code of the old totem and taboo and cannibalism days had a reality-appreciation. A social code can be regarded as sane only in so far as it is founded upon an appreciation of reality-values.

So in considering man's more recognized or institutionalized social life of today we are apt, like the bad politician, to turn our back upon its historical development and its teeming mass of glaring inconsistencies, inanities and insanities, and glibly to assume that the present social order is a marvellous construction of the reason and intellect. We are rather like the narrow-minded anatomist who describes the marvellous structure of the anatomical systems and concludes that the body is perfect, and assumes that it is a recent creation of an omniscient Mind. Having shut his eyes to embryology, comparative anatomy and evolution, he has overlooked the key to the understanding of it, and in his bewildered admiration he fails to reflect upon what he would think of an electrical engineer who laid some of his wires on a tortuous course twice as long as need be, or a plumber who left old and disused pipes still connected with the system and a potential danger to it.

This analogy is more than a mere analogy, for I have hoped to show that the proper study of contemporary social life and its institutions, such as marriage, should lead us not only to a consideration of its historical development, but consistently and logically far beyond that to a study of the actual anatomy and physiology of the individual organisms that conglomerate to form this social organism or organization.

It is *because* in our earliest months we sucked a breast or a teat that we later suck our thumb, suck sweets, admire breasts, kiss our lover, smoke cigarettes or a pipe, practice oral 'perversions' of eating, drinking or love-making—or speak of the person we fancy as our 'cup of tea', and it is *because* we are taught to control these and similar or subsequent desires that we still impose various conditions and restrictions upon our kissings and upon our eatings. We may indulge our oral pleasures pretty freely and that even publically, provided we submit to certain conditions such as polite manners.

The explanation of our social system (e.g. marriage) lies in the following fact: though we started life by eating our mother (nipple sucking) she did not mind this, but on the contrary liked it and gave to us freely—therefore this oral lust, being approved by God (mother), remained guiltless (we can still even kiss on the public stage), but it was when lusts deriving from other zones and orifices of our infantile body were similarly directed to mother—lusts which she was not prepared to gratify, lusts or desires disapproved by God (mother)—that guilt arose. For, shameful to relate, we still directed these lusts towards mother, in fact we could not help it, and freely and constantly indulged in this wickedness (*in phantasy*), so no wonder we grew up full of guilt and fear and illness. For if the truth is to be known, we not only investigated the interior of mother's body (subsequently to our nipple sucking period) and secretly enjoyed its smells, but we also, in secret phantasy, performed our excretory acts therein, (as we had actually done *in utero*) and in every way were enormously potent or omnipotent.

Our conduct emerged more upon a 'social' (or anti-social) level when we began to recognize mother as an 'individual', and simultaneously became aware that we had a rival in the field—or so it seems from our clinical experience that these recognitions laid the more obvious foundations to our subsequent social life and to the emergence of our social institutions of today. Our bodies had increased in weight and our lusts had become proportionately stronger, more varied, more violent and insistent. But now a relationship to the parents had arisen, we had to retain their love, avoid their hostility, *in spite of these lusts which we could not adequately control.*

Here we have Conflict, and amongst our early resources we included the expediences of, one, gratifying these not-to-be-denied lusts in phantasy at the same time hiding them from their victims (the parents) and feeling guilt-ridden, and, two, enlisting the aid of the parents to help us to combat these enemies to what we now preferred to think was our true selves, but which was really the parents (or society) beginning to be introjected into the superficial levels of our mind.

Out of this dangerous situation where we (our lusts) do hidden battle against the parents, society, god (or in brief *other* people's lusts) arises and develops on the one hand adult sexual intercourse, and on the other hand those restrictions against it which we find canalized in the institution and laws of matrimony. If proof were needed we have it in the especial prohibitive tendency of these laws in regard to incest. In fact, so strong is this prohibition that it radiates from its central figure (the mother) originally most desired, to include even ridiculous pseudo-relationships. The process is reminiscent of the exogamous laws of the totem and taboo period of primitive culture—or savagery.

Thus in the institution and laws of matrimony we see a compromise formation between an instinct urge on the one hand and a conglomeration of prohibitions or restricting forces on the other hand. Neither have necessarily anything whatsoever to do with reason or logic. In their essential nature of compromise between id and superego forces they show the characteristic mark of every neurotic (and psychotic) symptom. If then the institution of matrimony *does* fit the social order, it is not necessarily because either institution is sane, but rather because the social order itself and everything in it (like matrimony) is a compromise formation of irrational id and superego struggles. However hidden their previous stages, these institutionalized products of the struggle between id and superego have a vivid stage, if not origin, in what is known to psychoanalysts as the Oedipus situation.

We know that individual life began with a libidinal incestuous relationship to the parents and to the family. At the sucking stage this was all-sufficient. It continued to be at least tolerable, if not indispensable, throughout childhood, indicating that however strong the increasing libidinal frustrations may have been the incestuous libidinal gratifications exceeded them and over-compensated for them—or at least that no better world containing less frustration and more gratification could be found at that time.

With the increasing primacy of the genital organization of the libido, frustration (since actual incest was taboo) came more and more to exceed gratification until an intolerable situation increasingly developed. In short, we may state with confidence that the reason (or cause) why the individual finally abandons the family and seeks a mate is because the family (through the incest taboo and castration fear) fail to gratify his sexual needs.

That those needs were primarily directed towards the members of his family is obvious even from extra-clinical observations, not only of infants and children where they are patent, but negatively in adults. What young man has not noticed that the actual physical proximity or presence of his doting mother is a source of 'unaccount-able' *irritation* to him. For instance, if she sits too near him he is uncomfortable. This irritation is an outward sign of the old conflict (now unconscious), repressed incest urges inducing their intolerable frustration from taboos and inhibition. The conflict tends to be reactivated by the physical presence. He cannot bear it, so he leaves home—gets as far as possible away from his mother—and as near as possible to some substitutive female whom he loves and to whom he clings for the rest of his life—perhaps. What was once the breast is now the vagina and it has been found—or refound. Thus all this phenomenon of marriage is the result of mother's refusal (with threats) to gratify his *genital* sexuality.

The corollary also may be detected extra-clinically. If we see a young woman who should have reached maturity, who nevertheless is not irritated by her father's physical proximity—who likes to sit on his knee and be kissed by him, this woman has sacrificed (repressed) her normal sexual development in favour of maintaining an uncon-scious sexual relationship to her father. She is living in a sort of infantile (but nevertheless genital) relationship to Daddy, and her husband, if any man should be so unfortunate, will be merely a part of the neglig-ible superstructure called civilization or society. She is almost cer-tain to be psychosexually frigid, and if not it will be by virtue of incestuous phantasy, conscious or unconscious.

So again we see that the frustration of incest is the one thing that leads to 'exogamous' marriage. Nature—incest-nature—has been frustrated and we are forced to look outside our first choice, mother, or our second choice, sister, for a substitute to gratify our increasing genital demands.

In the light of all this we need not jump to the hasty conclusion that our horror of incest, which horror by the way has quite other (namely castration phantasy) sources, is therefore amply justified. The contrary may be the case; sufficient experiments in guilt-free incest have certainly not been tried to justify a conclusion on social-scientific data of observation. The popular horror is an emotional reaction, derived not from the pleasure of the idea of gratification of early desires, but on the contrary, from its opposite, namely fear and horror of castration if the impulses were to express themselves. Therefore we endure the minor castration of frustration—but do not escape the horror.

Again we have a striking instance of a normal human opinion, conviction or judgement, being founded upon fancy and independent of fact. And what a phantastical fancy—an infantile delusion of castration! Is this indeed the sort of ego (reason) we have—for judge-ment is an ego attitude? Is delusion responsible for our judgement, our exogamy, our institution of matrimony? And have we no insight—not even a suspicion of all this? Surely then we 'have nothing on' those we call mad. We are quite sure of their madness—based upon delusions no more fantastic than our own. Cannot we have the same confidence about our madness?

Analysis gives us a much deeper knowledge of this madness within us, and therefore a greater confidence in it, and less condemnation for the madness we see so clearly in others. Analysis of every person, normal or abnormal, reveals what may be called the universal sex-conflict. By 'conflict' is meant a battle between opposites. The antagonists here are on the one hand the natural primitive sexual impulse, urging towards sexual gratification, and on the other hand the struggle of more recently developed tendencies (superego and ego) against this urge.

Seeing that this mechanism, this sex-conflict, is not only wide-spread but universal, one would expect to find it 'externalized' in the great social institutions of mankind. Nowhere, perhaps, is it more clearly (and disastrously) expressed than in that human institution the avowed purpose of which is to cater for the needs of the sexual urge, namely to the Institution of Matrimony.

One might be tempted hastily to assume that matrimony being the avowed handmaid of the sexual urge, the latter's dictates would here, if anywhere, rule absolutely, unfettered and unhampered by the restraints and restrictions of its enemies. Are not husband and wife joined together by the 'Holy Bonds' and permitted, nay enjoined, with full social sanction to allow their sexual urges a healthful mutual freedom. The term 'Holy' and the term 'Bonds' should, but do not as a rule, give us a clue to the real situation. Indeed the psychological would be surprised if the other antagonist in the psychological situation had not crept in to assert himself in the institution of matrimony. Even the psychologist, however, would hardly expect to see the overwhelming extent to which these antagonists (the forces of the superego and ego) have really won the day in spite of their professed beneficence towards the sexual urges. That their beneficence is only apparent the data, on close examination, abundantly reveal. In fact, the data reveals the shabbiest trick played upon the sexual urges, and the most 'holy' victory for their oppressors. Here more than anywhere are the primitive life forces within us castrated by reality and superego elements.

This may be illustrated by considering the physiology of the female sexual function: what is it that best prepares the female sexual organs and nervous reflexes for gratification? Probably the first essential here is something which is independent of the male or of his desire. I refer to the sexual periodicity of women. Put briefly, one may say that there are periods (e.g. immediately before and shortly after menstruation) when these organs and this nervous reflex are ready, 'keyed up', for their normal function and gratification. This nervous-physical state of affairs may be apparent to the woman in the form of desire or easily arousable desire—a psychical predisposition to give her consent. Does the institution of matrimony take this matter into consideration? It frankly does not. It tacitly denies its existence. Without matrimony, left to itself, this factor would assert itself to the benefit and gratification of the woman. She would have intercourse when she desired it, like any other female mammal, when her desire was at its height; and thereby she would gain gratification and nervous-physical health.

Matrimony, on the other hand, ignoring this, is tacitly or practically ignoring the existence of the sexual urges and needs as such; it is as much as saying that they do not exist or are of no importance. This is a castrating function of the superego. Here we see matrimony is in part at least an institution erected by the superego rather than by the id demands. Matrimony indeed rides roughshod over this physiological basis of the woman's sexual desires, and taking his cue therefrom many possessive husbands likewise ride roughshod over their spouses' emotions. This is but one of the factors that fills our civilization with neurotic or unhappy women and perplexed and equally unhappy men. Were it not for this castrating (i.e. opposite to gratifying) institution, the man would woo in vain when he wooed at a period unhealthful (undesire-ful) for the woman, and he would have to look for another to gratify and make healthful and happy instead of satisfying himself at the expense of a long-suffering wife.

The woman in this situation is disposed by the institution of matrimony to give her superficial and conscious consent to the *organically* unwelcome attentions of her husband. What is the result to her? Local pain instead of pleasure. The organs and reflexes do not adequately respond—or they show a negative reaction. Instead of the normal secretions there is a dry and contracted vagina. There is on her part a complete failure of sexual relief and gratification. This may superficially seem a light matter, but analysis reveals that the effects of such experiences are far-reaching and cumulative, and that they react throughout a person's emotional, physical, intellectual and psychical life.

Thus we see marriage as a thwarter rather than a liberator of the id's healthful demands for freedom. The superego has won again—even on the id's ground.

This argument, based upon the physiological elements in the sexual function, may be stated in another form, thus: there are circumstances in the life of all creatures, animal or human, which lead to a physiological readiness of the sexual organs (secretion, moisture, etc.) for intercourse. This state of affairs should be normally present in consciousness in the form of sexual desire. Now the human institution

of matrimony, avowedly made to cater for this, actually ignores
desires or refused gratification based upon these instinctive (and
therefore healthful) id demands. Instead, it bases permission for
intercourse upon ego considerations relatively independent of the
actual instinctive desire—and thereby it greatly robs the instinct of
its normal demands and its normal gratification.

Thus ego conditions and ego considerations not only have nothing
to do with id desires, but are commonly antagonistic to them—
enemies from the opposite camp—and include the weightiest matters
with which the ego is concerned. A woman's life-long economic
security or ego-level luxury, superiority over her competitors in the
social struggle, and a hundred and one other things of the highest
ego-valuation are explicitly at stake . . . if she will only sacrifice the
reflex contractions of her uterus . . . and the health life of her germ-
plasm (whose immortality she has learnt progressively to devalue)
in favour of this, which life-long exhortation to be *reasonable* have
told her is the highest aim of her life.

The all-too-frequent sequel is that she discovers too late that not
only is her germplasm (or immortality) sacrificed, but that to her and
to everybody's else's astonishment, including her doctor's, her nervous, that is to say her somatic health, is also impaired. Together
with her germplasm, she has begun the path towards racial extinction, if not towards individual demise. Thus is it that thirty-three and
a third per cent of British married women are already psychosexually frigid—and nervously ill.

The psychologist commonly encounters cases where the reactive
patterns of at least one partner make him or her totally unsuited
for the other partner, and sometimes totally unsuited for any partner.
We see instances of the submissive angle of a man being bullied
through his life by a termagant of a woman. No doubt she is acting
out her reactive patterns, but in some instances one wonders if what
she is so cross about is the 'impotence' of her husband, and even if
he is not sexually impotent one wonders if she is so cross because he
is aggressively impotent, or whether his absence of aggression
allows her too much free rein for the unrepression and expression of
her own aggression. Of course things can be the other way round. The
husband may be the impossible bully and his wife the victim.
Marriage may be a case of putting up with each other. Fortunately
it is only sometimes as bad as this. What is usually not appreciated
even by analysts in spite of a repetitive experience with every long
case of analysis in turn, is that it is usually only a question of time
before repressed aggression and hate take courage under the umbrella of the transference situation to emerge and display themselves
more and more freely. In my opinion this is what commonly happens
to one or other or both of the parties to a marriage. Sooner or later

the man or the woman is astonished to find his angel of a spouse becoming nagging, bullying, vituperative and full of hostile feelings or
hate directed against him. It is only too natural to react to hate with
hate, and it is the destructive instinct which was originally so
thoroughly repressed before the relationship between the parties
became too poor and too free which at last emerges sometimes with
disastrous effects. It is as though something comparable to mutual
psychoanalysis had at last reached its negative transference stage—
only there is no competent analyst present to stand outside the dog
fight and analyse it.

It may surprise some people to learn that the majority of marriages
that fail badly enough to result in divorce do not do so on account
of the sort of factors I have drawn attention to. The surprising fact
is that the majority of divorces come about owing to economic
causes. A study of such cases brings it to our notice that on the reality
plane economics can be more important than the sufferings of the
soul. No doubt the next most frequent cause for divorce is some sexual
incompatibility such as total impotence on the part of the man and
more rarely total frigidity on the part of the woman. It may surprise
us that psychological incompatibility does not more often lead to
divorce, unless it is connected with or results in one or other of the
above sources of disruption. Of course all sorts of foolishness, such
as pride, superego indignation, anger, jealousy and so on may be a
starting point of avoidable miseries and even of partings.

Practically all women who are psychoneurotically unwell suffer
from some degree of psychosexual frigidity, and practically all men
who are psychoneurotically unwell suffer from some degree of disturbance, usually impotence, of their sexual function. There is, however, the occasional exception, such as the man who, instead of like
the majority being too 'castrated' to fit in tolerably with the social
order (including the institution of matrimony), appears to be too
little castrated to fit in tolerably with the social order. There is a
tendancy to call him a psychopath or an aggressive psychopath,
rather than a neurotic.

Indeed, the distinction has some justification, for his conflict is not
one between his id and superego in which, as in the case of neurotics,
the id has been worsted, but the conflict is rather between him
(including his id) and society at large, in which, unfortunately for
him, but perhaps fortunately for society, he is hardly strong enough
or big enough to get the better of it, and suffers as it were by banging
his head against a stone wall. He might be described psychologically
as refusing to accept the fact that father is stronger than he is, and
everlastingly rushing at the great man, getting hurt, but refusing to
capitulate or to cease battling. The condition need not be very marked
or apparent. He need not necessarily be a criminal, overtly at least,

or even very apparently psychopathic, but it is certainly not easy
for anybody to deal with him. Perhaps it is unusual for him to come
voluntarily for psychotherapy.

Now such a man, unlike the majority of those suffering from
psychoneurosis, far from having his sexuality diminished or impaired
in the ordinary sense, sometimes displays more of the Don Juan
characteristics, but nevertheless may show a peculiarity of not subjecting himself to the same sort of criticisms that one would expect
the ordinary socially-adjusted person to subject himself to in such
circumstances. In other words, he regards what most of us might call
his asocial and antisocial conduct as absolutely normal and justifiable.
Otherwise he can be quite an intelligent person, and as much able
to make objective judgements as most of us.

Such a man, during his analysis, summed up his unusually extensive experiences of the opposite sex in the following words: 'I have
come to the conclusion that all women's sexuality is completely
warped. It is a truly dreadful position that they are in, and that a man
like me who is natural and healthy is in. I have a theory as to why it
is. It is because they (women) are trying, for reality ends, to make their
sexuality into something that it wasn't meant by nature to be. If they
are ordinary, 'respectable' women, the reality end they are aiming
at is usually marriage, with the economic and social advantages of it.
Even if you let them make love to you, they are not doing it to enjoy
it naturally, they are daring to treat you (i.e. the man) as though
you were some little boy, or abnormal creature who wanted such
excitements, which they of course are too mature to want, or too
superior. They are not concerned to get anything like orgasm or even
pleasure, though they may want to give you pleasure in the hope, it
seems to me, that you will marry them.

'The whole treatment one gets from such women is a damnable
insult. They think I am abnormal, but I know that they are. They
have sold their natural sexual response for reality ends, money,
marriage and position. I think the worst of them for not being open
about this. The prostitute is at least open about it. She just demands
the money and that at least is frank. I would rather have the prostitute, although I know a good deal about her disadvantages too. They
are all abnormal, whether respectable or prostitute. If they have a
capacity for sexual warmth, they try all the harder to suppress it.
Why, I have met even prostitutes who had vaginismus, because
something in them was afraid that they might feel sexual. A shop-
keeper must not surrender to the customer, he is there to take his
money.'

Of course, such sweeping statements are certainly not universally
applicable, but they may give us food for thought as to the possible
element of truth in them, and the size of that element. In surrendering

our natural instinctual reactions to the life that spells health, and surrendering to the taboos because we are concerned to ensure our safety, our economic advantage, rather than to obey our instincts, is medically and psychotherapeutically a valuable concept in revealing the initial sources of all illness, nervous, psychoneurotic, psychological and even physical.

This patient added an interesting rider to his remarks. He said: 'I am the last person to want to think and talk about such things, about what should be as natural as eating and sleeping. It is the fact that every woman I meet is such a shocker in her sexual abnormality that the consequent frustration has caused *even me* to start thinking and philosophizing.

It is perhaps such remarks as these which caused even me, his analyst, to reflect that there is perhaps something in my theory that not only anxiety but also the emergence of the ego are the fruits of frustrated instinct. It would seem from this material and these reflexes that society is encountering a very great difficulty in achieving an ideal adjustment between the demands of the id (instincts) and the prohibitions and taboos of the superego (originally the parent figures).

Nothing is achieved except perhaps temporary and illusionary satisfaction in shutting one's eyes to the issue. I feel that an important contribution in the direction of a better solution would be to recognize that these taboos and restrictions, however necessary and essential they may be for the protection of the individual and the community, are in fact as they exist today, instituted by superego equivalents and not by the latest, highest and most recently emerging mental faculty, namely, the ego.

Of course, instincts are the oldest patterns, passed on during the whole history of the biosphere, if not before. Second in appearance comes the superego. We begin to see manifestations of the existence of a superego as soon as man begins to institute restrictions and taboos —extending for instance to the death penalty for a menstruating woman who entered a cornfield, and all the nonsense, not excluding human sacrifice, that went on in the days of primitive man. It may be that we forget that it was the superstitions, cosmologies and religions invented at that time which are the parents (with strong likenesses) to the superstitions and beliefs of this civilization, and thus we fail to see that the restrictions, laws and constructions of our human institutions of today are the work of these primitive irrational mechanisms embodied largely in our superegos and have not necessarily very much relationship to our emerging reality principle, scientific methods, or ego.

Therefore, like primitive man, we are the victims both of an internal conflict between irrational forces (id and superego), and of an external conflict between our personal desires and social restrictions which may be unwarranted and irrational. We are so indoctrinated and have so much of the primitive superego past with its characteristic of opposition to instinct inside us, that it does not seem to occur to us that in the field of social life, particularly when it comes to restriction of instinct, scientific methods are called for, as they are in every other field of human endeavour and activity.

In other words, the whole problem of id-requirements and the requirements of organized society should be assessed scientifically and not assumed to be solved. It should become as simple as the question of drinking water. We drink water when the instinct prompts us to, when we wish to drink water. There is no enormous social or religious fuss about it. Instead we combine, build hygienic reservoirs and have what we want when we want it from the simple mechanism of a tap in our homes.

I am not suggesting this has an exact analogy to the problem of sexuality, but what I am suggesting is that the probable reason why the scientific view has not even begun to operate in regard to sexuality, whereas it has gone quite a way with regard to oral ends, including water, is because of our indoctrination with some old-fashioned and should-be-out-of-date psychotic ideas. The latter does not solve the problem, it only prevents the beginnings of a scientific investigation that would lead us to the solution.

In short, marriage, while offering a solution of the conflicts that social life or even social sexual life does not solve, may mean merely that our conflicts are carried into a new situation, where the closeness of the relationship makes them more evident and vivid to us and to each other. Nevertheless all these things are part of the experience of living, and perhaps of recognizing that our lives and habits individually and socially, our customs and institutions, are not common sense products of the ego, but are brought about by much stronger forces, namely the dynamic emotions which biologically are responsible for life . . . and for death, and perhaps for an admixture of the two in varying proportions in every human situation individually, socially or institutionalized. They all reflect the chaotic state of the unconscious psychotic mind.

CHAPTER VII

GROWING UP

The study of man's psychotic behaviour in relation to growing up involves a consideration of the psychology of both parties to the process, the infant and the adult. It is not possible to start at a logical beginning, because even prior to the baby's birth there are all sorts of factors at work. The matter of conception itself involves psychological factors, for instance, as to whether the couple did or did not want to have a child. It is a curious reflection on our allegedly ego-ruled world that this most important event of life should in fact usually be left to something in the nature of chance, if not accident.

It is conceivable that the happiness or unhappiness of the pregnant mother may have some relationship as to whether the pregnancy was wanted or unwanted. I am convinced that the mother's emotional state, including morbid emotions such as anxiety, has some prenatal effect upon the unborn infant's subsequent psychology, and even endocrinology. But all this is a field in which chance would seem to be the prime mover, and even in this enlightened age we appear to be almost as helpless in this field as we are in our gyrations round the sun. Perhaps this is another instance to convince us that we are the chance products of natural forces, rather than that we live according to our own choice in an environment designed by us for our own wellbeing and happiness.

However, if we choose the arbitrary beginning of birth from which to make a start, we may find plenty of psychological peculiarities intruding even into this natural event. The history of the process is of course laden with conspicuous psychotic superstitions and misconceptions of what is good, proper and healthy for the welfare of mother and child. I believe in some parts of India it is still a superstition based ritual that the mother must lie upon septic goat-skins closely associated with an abundance of cow-dung in the form of cakes or patties. This may remind us that it was not more than a century or so ago, up to the time of Lister, that surgeons in this country were in the habit of dressing wounds with septic ingredients, including sometimes even earth. No doubt ignorance of asepsis was the promoter of such practices, but their main instigation appears to have been something in the nature of superstition—or psychosis.

In this enlightened age, sepsis is rigorously avoided but it may be shown that the enlightenment regarding physical matters is not equalled by enlightenment regarding mental or psychological influences. Perhaps more advanced nations have now passed the phase of undue anxiety-driven interference with the natural process of childbirth. It was merely a temporary indication of rushing in, through ignorance or superstition, where angels fear to tread. In this respect it might be regarded psychologically as a negation from the carless and perhaps almost equally dangerous habits of primitive people.

No doubt our current management of these matters indicates a relatively greater sanity, though it is impossible to believe that it leaves nothing to be desired, for no practice psychologically based on superstition does not introduce some imperfections, particularly as regards the attitude of mind and consequent behaviour of the expectant mother. For instance, does she really want to be separated from the mental and emotional support of her beloved husband and family during such a crisis in her life, or is this separation in subservience to the mental comfort of her medical and nursing attendants? If the latter, it may be asked why should our behaviour be determined by such a relatively irrelevant consideration? Is this another instance of our allegiance to authority enslaving us and causing us to accept unnecessary mental tensions and discomforts? Cannot the baby be born just as well and safely without a miserable interruption in the mother's way of life and would not both mother and child be benefited more in consequence?

Little matters like this are not entirely inconsiderable. For instance, might it not be that a certain amount of the prevalent failure to produce breast-milk would be obviated in more natural and happier circumstances? Furthermore, there is no other species of mammal that has its newly-born offspring immediately whisked away from it by the other female mammals of its species, whose unconscious psychology may well include a conglomeration of emotional attitudes towards the helpless infant which are not necessarily maternal. There may be every variety of emotional reaction from indifference to positive hatred, and although these would be, at least in a well-ordered home or maternity hospital, refused overt expression, we know from our psychological experience that it is almost impossible for a living person to avoid at least some covert expression of their repressed emotionally-charged complexes.

There is also the possibility, though this may be regarded as speculative, that the baby, like the infant, reacts to the real emotional attitude towards it, however repressed and unconscious this may be, in a more direct manner than does the relatively repressed adult. In other words, the baby probably knows, or rather feels, that unloving hands are touching it, and anxiety reaction within it may be none the less real and injurious, probably more real and injurious because unconscious. There is little doubt that the right person to handle the baby as soon as she is fit to take any notice of it (and that may usually be only a matter of minutes), is the mother who gave birth to it. It is probable that it will feel more at home with her. She will have the same smell that it has become accustomed to while in her uterus, and it is conceivable that it will feel at home and safe with that person, and that person alone, like a dog would with its master, or a puppy with its mother. These other people who whisk it away and take possession . . . are they really acting in the baby's interest (in a sense we should ask the baby), or are they obeying some envious and possessive phantasies of their own, to the detriment of the unhappiness and therefore of the health of both baby and mother?

Perhaps the best answer that can be given to these enquiries is that anyhow the baby sleeps practically all the time, and therefore is unaware of who is tending it. Personally I am not entirely satisfied with this answer, nor do I think would be the child analysts, for after all the baby is not asleep *all* the time, and it is quite within the realms of possibility that even in sleep the organism senses in some intangible way whether it is in a secure, natural, anxiety-free situation or not. It may even be that the baby's sleep will be sounder, less disturbed, more anxiety-free, were it in the atmosphere of its mother, perhaps pervaded with the odour of her milk, to which it alone is sensitive.

Anyhow that is how nature would have decreed it, and do we know enough, are we wise enough, arbitrarily to interfere in the way we do? At least we do not seem to me to know enough and be wise enough to discount the unconscious forces and the unconscious motives in the minds of ourselves and other interferers. Thus we may, at the very dawn of life, be introducing some modicum of psychological injury at the most impressionable moments of the newly-born life.

The behaviouristic consequence of our over-confident ignorance and psychotic mechanisms reach a new accentuation when the newly-born reaches the moment of instinctual desire to suck and feed from its mother. There is little doubt that it is its mother, or rather her nipple and breast that it wants, and nothing else. Of course it will usually (but not always) accept substitutes rather than hunger and die. What is ignored is the undoubted fact that these deprivations leave their psychological mark to its dying day. The fact that it survives, or does not always perish, is an insufficient answer. I am reminded of the answer I received from the matron of a hospital where patients were habitually wheeled unconscious through an interminably long and incredibly cold corridor from the operating theatre to the ward. I was told: 'Well, they survive'. But in mobilizing their physiological reserves against any tendency to get pneumonia, they may conceivably have been reducing their much needed resistance to post-operative sepsis and similar eventualities. These babies mostly survive, but how many of them subsequently lie on our analytical settees, or worse?

What is nearer the mark is the importance of its immediate reactions in the form of successful feeding. I do not think it would be possible for such a large proportion of cultured women immediately to turn their babies over to bottle feeding if they had an adequate conception of the subsequent psychological effects of breast-deprivation. The study not only of child psychology but even of adult analysis shows us without a shadow of doubt that the earliest repercussions of reality upon an organism are important and permanent in direct proportion to the earliness of their impact. In other words, you may lock an adult up in prison for a year, and probably do him less harm than a week-long deprivation of a newly-born baby from its mother's breast. The adult may get over it, the baby may never get over it. This is the sort of thing that is revealed by analytical investigation, both of children and adults. Perhaps every species of mammal is, after all, better placed than ourselves. Animals do not have to endure the consequences of their progenitors' or their species' psychosis. If the mother has no milk for them, they simply die and it is all finished off. It may be that that would be better. Perhaps it is better to have a healthy species or a healthy race, than one infiltrated with distressing and misery-giving neurotic and psychotic elements.

Another point in this connection, and one with an importance of its own, is the question of when and how much and at what frequency the baby, especially if on the breast, should be fed. To my mind there is only one logical answer to this question and that is, ask the baby. We adults would not like it, in fact we might become aggressive or create a riot if we were left to hunger, however important the reality considerations might be alleged to be. Even in adult life we do not find it easy to endure frustration of our instincts. Why then should we expect the helpless baby to endure these and suffer no harm? I am sure that the harm it suffers is incalculable. If we must regard compromise with so-called reality considerations as essential, (after all, the mother may have to be considered as well as the baby), we should remember that the first reality consideration is to prevent the baby from accumulating uncomfortable or painful tensions. In so far as these are avoidable, they must at any cost be avoided. The most we should do in endeavouring to get the baby to adjust to reality is something very small indeed.

As the adult mind has already been so injured from birth onwards, we find it difficult to determine the appropriate balance between instinct demands and reality demands. In consequence of this difficulty of ours, we tend to be all one or all the other, thinking that we are doing no harm in conditioning the flexible mind and body of the helpless baby to suit our 'reality'. Perhaps these erroneous ideas reach their climax in the pernicious theory and practice of baby feeding by the clock. The only proper clock to go by, the only clock that we can rely upon as not injurious to the baby's psychology and physiology, is its stomach. None of us would care to be 'treated' according to somebody's theory, we would expect to be consulted regarding our wishes, and would regard treatment along such lines as the only non-injurious and indeed tolerable treatment. In the case of the baby, this matter is thousands of times more important. A wonderful little book which should be given to all expectant mothers is a collection of data of baby-feeding compiled by a woman psychoanalyst, Merell Middlemore, and entitled *The Nursing Couple*. Here she rightly regards the mother and child as a firmly and intimately related unit, a closely-knit partnership which no man or nurse should put apart. Maybe the mother will need help, but not interference, and this applies even more specifically to the child.

Dr Glover has said that an unanalysed adult can be counted upon to treat a neurotic or nervous person incorrectly. I would like to draw attention to the fact that every baby, infant and child is more than a neurotic person, he is most definitely psychotic, as is abundantly revealed by the data of every child analyst, and no unanalysed adult can therefore be expected to treat him appropriately. Our chief hope in these matters follows the same lines as those of our untutored brethren, mammals of every species. Their treatment is determined by their instincts. Perhaps ours is one of the rare cases where a little learning is a dangerous thing, one of the cases where total ignorance is to be preferred, as then at least instincts will have the field to themselves. Of course there will be the occasional disturbed or abnormal mother who will destroy or eat her young, but on the whole the instincts will prove themselves healthy and productive of healthy offspring, with the best chance of a relatively healthy maturity.

Anthropologists tells us that in some of the Pacific islands, mothers are in the habit of breast-feeding their babies and *infants*, even up to the age of six years, whenever their young show a desire to regress to nipple-sucking. They simply run to their mothers and are given suck. It is alleged that such tribes suffer far less from neuroses. In one instance during the last World War, when a Pacific island had been bombed alternatively by Japanese and Americans, there were many traumatic neuroses amongst both invaders, whereas at the same time the natives, who had suffered double the bombardment, had evidently taken it all quite calmly, without any neurotic disturbance. A body of psychologists attributed this phenomenon to the breast-feeding habits of the natives, for adult neuroses are founded on the pattern of the preceding infantile neuroses, however, inconspicuous the latter may have been.

To sum up, it may be said that the defects in our behaviour to the newly-born, as in all other departments of life, may be due to two antithetical causes, or rather to an admixture of the two.

1. Our thoughts and conduct are determined by our unconscious emotionally charged phantasies. These are determined by our instincts, but their charge is strong enough to seduce our ego, and in consequence of this our conduct is more or less inappropriate to the requirements of the real situation.

2. Having repressed our emotionally charged phantasies and the instinctual impulses from which they arise, we endeavour to deal with the situation entirely on an ego or superego plane, as it were by a sort of theoretical rule of thumb.

In consequence of this we tend to be either too much id or too much superego, too lenient or too strict. Our ego, which should be the orderer and determinant of our conduct, is perhaps too recently developed and too weak to be able to do enough about it. Most usually it is seduced by the superego, we side with the 'ideals' which we wrongly assume were represented by our parents.

Other mammals and some primitive races, with perhaps an undue proportion of uncritical acceptance of their emotions, are likely to do much better, and to make fewer mistakes, particularly in this department of life where instincts are usually representative of the libido or life-promoting instinct, and superego representative of death. In our case the result of these deep-seated unconscious forces in our psyches is a compromise between life and death, a compromise which allows life but introduces enough death to cause the result to be a mixture of neuroses and psychoses, perhaps corresponding to our own, which has been accentuated by a comparable process.

As a determinant of our thoughts and actions, the ego lags behind these other two powerfully charged forces (id and superego). If it is alleged that our executive activity is the department of the ego, and that therefore it must be the ego which is determining our behaviour, the answer is that the ego is still too weak to be the real determinant of almost everything that is us. What really happens is that it passes through a succession of phases during the progress of civilization, phases in which it alternates between undue seduction by the id and undue seduction by the superego, both of them causing its reality behaviour to be largely inappropriate. Since Victorian times at least, we in this country have shown more superego seduction of our ego than was previously the case. It is on account of this relative inadequacy of our ego to appreciate reality as well as to appreciate the needs of our internal or instinctual and superego 'realities', that justifies me in my allegation of a universal psychosis.

In the above material a good deal has been said about the unconscious psychotic motivations of the adult in her treatment of the baby and infant. At the same time it has been hinted that the baby and infant are fundamentally very psychotic persons, whatever thin overlay may come about in the course of development. Child analysts have made this plain to us without any shadow of doubt. Nevertheless the child is usually regarded as normal because it is pretty much the same as its siblings and contemporaries, and we have got used to accepting it as it is.

I am not alleging that the infantile psychosis is brought about by the inappropriate behaviour meted out to the baby and infant. Its psychosis is too severe to be conditioned by actual experience. The state of mind, together with its developmental potentialities are obviously something inherent. Nevertheless, inappropriate treatment can and does accentuate or ameliorate the state of affairs within certain limits. With regard to the psychosis of the young child, what would we think if we saw an adult behaving similarly, playing these interminable games, for instance with figures, dolls, little toys or what not. We would certainly think he had gone mad. Perhaps we do not adequately appreciate how much the child's emotional life is taken up, absorbed and expressed in these incessant games of childhood, with their accompanying phantasies, conscious and unconscious. They are the outlet for the child's complexes and emotional tensions, no less than the ordinary activities of living are some degree of outlet for the adult.

Melanie Klein tells us: 'Full use had to made of the symbolic language of play which I recognized to be an essential part of the child's mode of expression. The brick, the little figure, the car, not only represent things which interest the child in themselves, but in his play with them they always have a variety of symbolical meanings as well which are bound up with his phantasies, wishes, and experience.'[19]

It seems that Melanie Klein, unlike some child analysts, does not hesitate to give the infant, however, young, her interpretations of her findings, and thereby to achieve thereapeutic amelioration. Of one case for instance she says: 'Peter (aged three years and nine months)... had strongly objected to my interpretation that the toy he had thrown down from the "bed" and who was "dead and done for" represented his father. (The interpretation of death-wishes against a loved person usually arouses great resistance in children as well as in adults). In the third hour Peter again brought similar material, but now accepted my interpretation and said thoughtfully: "And if I were a Daddy and someone wanted to throw me down behind the bed and make me dead and done for, what would I think of it?" This shows that he had not only worked through, understood and accepted my interpretation, but that he had also recognized a good deal more. He understood that his own aggressive feelings towards his father contributed to his fear of him, and also that he had projected his own impulses on to his father. . . .

'. . . a great deal of relief is experienced in play and this is one of the factors which make it so essential for the child. For instance . . . when I interpreted his damaging a toy figure as representing attacks on his brother (he said) that he would not do this to his *real* brother, he would only do it to the *toy* brother. My interpretation of course made it clear to him that it was really his brother whom he wished to attack; but the instance shows that only by symbolic means was he able to express his destructive tendencies in the analysis.'[19]

According to Melanie Klein: 'This archaic mode of expression is also the language with which we are familiar in dreams, and it was by approaching the play of the child in a way similar to Freud's interpretation of dreams that I found I could get access to the child's unconscious. But we have to consider each child's use of symbols in connection with his particular emotions and anxieties. . . .'[19]

Similarly, Paula Heimann, another well-known child analyst, says: 'Unconscious phantasies are associated with the infant's experience of pleasure or pain, happiness or anxiety; they involve his relation with his objects. They are dynamic processes, because they are charged with the energy of the instinctual impulses, and they influence the development of ego mechanisms. For example, introjection develops from the infant's unconscious phantasy of incorporating the mother's breast, which accompanies the desire for the breast and the actual sensation of sucking and swallowing when in contact with it.

'Conversely, the mechanism of projection develops from the phantasy of expelling an object.

'In order to understand the infant's psychic development and many of his physical processes, we must appreciate his unconscious phantasies. . . .

'The instinctual urges and the phantasies which they imply reign supreme. Perception of the reality of the self and of objects is poor, and phantasy flourishes the more. . . . When he is caressed and gratified, he has the ideally good breast. . . . He omnipotently possesses it. . . . He incorporates the gratifying breast and is one with it. He goes to sleep with his loved object. If things go well, he will do the same thing in adult life.'[19]

However, the analysis of children is not the only route whereby analysis can discover the outstanding psychological importance of phantasies in babyhood and infancy. I have a woman patient of over fifty years of age, who has experienced a life-long feeling of intense insecurity, symptomatically expressed by every conceivable phobia, including the familiar ones of cancer and war. The source of this miserable anxiety state has, through her analysis, been traced back to babyhood, more specifically to being left to cry it out in her pram. Apparently this unnatural treatment, regularly repeated throughout babyhood, failed to remove and accentuated the ordinary feelings of insecurity produced physiologically by hunger.

This patient's early upbringing may draw our attention to the dangers of people not having a clue psychologically. Her mother was very young (about nineteen) and too readily accepted (naturally she studied her own convenience) the family doctor's idea that babies should be allowed to 'cry it out', so as to teach them to be good. The effects of such treatment certainly include an appearance of being good—really a morbid apathy—overlying an incredibly intense reservoir of repressed hate. It was the intensity of this repressed hate inside her that led to her fears and phobia. In consequence she has little faith in 'science', but is of the opinion that 'mothers who succeed best in bringing up their children are those who have a genuine maternal instinct (love), untainted by science or by books on psychology'.

In the light of analytical investigation, the mental world of babyhood, infancy and childhood may be seen to be a world of dreamy psychotics, presided over by an incompetent and rather clueless world of attendants, who are themselves not entirely free from their infantile psychosis in so far as their activities are themselves determined by unconscious fantastic residues of their own early life.

In a paper entitled 'Infantile Conception of Reality', Melitta Schmideberg reminds us that like embryology and ontology, the current state of affairs is largely an epitomized reproduction of what our human race has gone through in the course of its development from primitive to modern. 'The thinking of primitives in animistic terms is in keeping with the distorted impressions which the very small child has of the world about it. . . .

'The infantile distortion of reality, in animistic terms, depends on the child's conception of the world as peopled by all-powerful giants, and may be reconstructed from dreams, myths, fairy tales, and psychoneurotic and schizophrenic symptoms. . . .

'Both the child's and the adult's conception of reality are distorted by emotions and unconscious fantasies. . . . Thunder and lightning may be . . . explained as noises and fire produced by gods and giants. As Frazer pointed out about the savage, his magic ideas are akin to scientific thinking in being correct deductions from mistaken premises. The same holds true for the child. . . .

'The infantile ego reality systems are reflected in fairy tales, in art, in the magic of savages, in folklore, in expressions of language, the pleasure of conjuring, and in schizophrenia and obsessional phenomena. . . .

'The baby and the savage enjoy freedom from the limitations imposed by a more developed knowledge of reality. Their magic beliefs include seeing effects as causes, that like produces like, producing effects by imitating, that two things once in contact continue to act on one another.' Schmideberg gives examples of the customs of primitive people based on such beliefs.

'The phase of animism in the baby seems to be the earliest phase in which he tries to connect things and happenings based on simple associations. The phase corresponding to the magic of savages is one of intense intellectual activity occurring at around twelve months. To the small infant mute in his crib, the adults walking, talking, turning on a light, must appear as miraculous as anything in a fairy story. Omnipotence of deeds, thoughts, and words or sounds, is demonstrated by savages, by fairy tales, and by obsessionals and schizophrenics. Sounds may be regarded as concrete objects by children and schizophrenics. The young child cannot think in abstract terms. He takes things quite literally. He does not detach the name from the thing. He can barely differentiate between thinking, saying and doing, and between mental and physical sensations. . . . Folklore has hundreds of methods of getting rid of illness, like a concrete object to be thrown away.'[18]

This description of the mind of the child, given to us by a child analyst (daughter of Melanie Klein) seems to support the suggestion that ontogeny repeats phylogeny, and that in the course of our development from babyhood to adult life we are going through the psychological phases of our early ancestry. It may also cause us to reflect that fundamentally we have not advanced very far beyond these early people, whose beliefs and behaviour we are so ready to recognize as absolutely crazy or psychotic.

CHAPTER VIII

EDUCATION

In the light of the insight we have gained into the psychology of babies, infants and small children, we should, I hope, be rather careful and humble before we rush in to interfere. Although the child differs slightly from primitive man, and from the schizophrenic or permanently insane adult, he differs chiefly in virtue of the fact that he is still undergoing the process of growth and development. Perhaps if we met a savage or a madman we would be a little careful in making allowances for his state of mind, and be a little wary of the way in which we interfered with it. Perhaps our humility would be due to a fear of his size and strength, which advantages the child has not. Nevertheless the appropriate approach to the child, appropriate to his addiction to psychotic phantasies, is far more important in every respect than the approach to an equivalent adult.

Surely our first considerations should be to obtain the child's transference, to reduce his anxiety, to encourage him to feel that we are on his side and will protect him from all the bogies that infest his internal and external environment. In short, it seems to me that our approach should be comparable to that of the psychotherapist or analyst. Our first business is to gain his confidence and never to betray it. That is surely the only undamaging way in which we can so much as hope to begin any sort of 'education'. Here I am rather tempted to ask whether it might not be better for us, having got the child's confidence, to endeavour to get him to 'educate' us. At least I feel that we should begin this way, and continue this way until we feel sufficiently educated for it to become almost inevitable that we take a natural part in the proceedings. By that time the child may be ready to welcome our contributions, and it is only then that they will be relevant and helpful rather than disrupting and damaging.

No doubt a modicum of some such process or technique is actually at work in our educative approach, at least to the small child in nursery schools, but I feel that it is probably only a modicum, and is more instinctual or unconscious on our part, and perhaps instigated more by our sense of ignorance than by knowledge. In other words, it would seem that we are up to a point wise enough to sense our ignorance and keep quiet, rather than to rush in like the proverbial bull in the china shop. Perhaps this is the best way we can do it. It is certainly not the worst. If education means the intrusion of reality appreciation into the fantastic world of the child, it should be very gently and warily introduced. In fact I am inclined to say that perhaps it should not be 'introduced' at all. The child should be allowed in the course of growth to move gradually from his phantasies towards an equally gratifying acceptance of some modicum of reality. Perhaps we will be more humble in our educative efforts if we ask ourselves 'and what is this reality which we are offering the child? Is it actually reality or is it some delusion or misrepresentation of our own?' We had better learn about his world first. In the course of development he will probably find less difficulty in learning about ours.

Freud very rightly says: 'Actually, the substitution of the reality-principle for the pleasure-principle denotes no dethronement of the pleasure-principle, but only a safeguarding of it.'[20] For the time being it is our job to safeguard the child's pleasure-principle, for its health depends upon this process. In the fullness of time as he grows up he will have to safeguard it himself. In due course he will have to recognize this fact and do something about reality or at least about what we call reality. Freud says: 'A momentary pleasure, uncertain in its results, is given up, but only in order to gain in the new way an assured pleasure coming later.'[20]

As was indicated previously, the living organism does not want reality at all if it can possibly avoid it. The impact of reality is primarily felt as an intrusion or interruption of our pleasurable experiences and preoccupations. It may be objected here that many realities, such as the mother's breast in babyhood are objects which on the contrary aid or are necessary for our gratification. My thought is that probably such gratifying aspects of reality are not the essential nature of what we regard as reality, they are usually accepted as though they were a part of ourselves, or an attribute of our omnipotence. The ego or reality principle proper to my mind arrives when the pleasure-principle is not only frustrated but actually interfered with, and brought to a stop. This sort of reality would obviously be felt to be something bad, something which however objectionable we must learn to understand in order to overcome so that we can continue our gratifying experiences and phantasies.

Perhaps what we regard, or come to regard, as education proper belongs characteristically to this aspect of reality appreciation. Freud appears to think so when he says: '*Education* can without further hesitation be described as an incitement to the conquest of the pleasure-principle, and to its replacement by the reality-principle; it offers its aid, that is, to that process of development which concerns the ego; to this end it makes use of rewards of love from those in charge. . . .'[20]

According to this it would seem that the immature organism will only agree to some acceptance of the reality principle if it is at the same time compensated for the pain of this process by receiving 'rewards of love from those in charge', that is to say, only provided its security in love is increased so that it will be able to indulge in the pleasure principle more freely, with greater security and with less anxiety.

It may be that it is through introducing these facts too early in our attempts to educate, that we are apt to achieve some sort of stunting of the infant's capacity for original and independent thinking. We will succeed in regimenting him like we do the horse, a castrated animal. Not only psychologists but many original thinkers have felt this danger.

A male patient of mine, who had seen a film depicting circumcision rites in East Africa, including the rites of genital mutilation called circumcision, which were compulsory before admission to the status of manhood, turned to me and said: 'All that is nothing, it is merely physical mutilation. In this country we have substituted for it something much worse, namely *mental* castration. That is our equivalent of the savages' initiation rites. I went through a public school and it has nearly been the death of me. Perhaps some people survive in a mutilated state that escapes notice, but in my case it has left me scarred mentally for life. Nobody bothered to understand me and I went through the most awful agonies. Bells ringing every three-quarters of an hour and having to jump up and rush to another class-room—one's whole train of thought interrupted and turned upside down. What has it made me into? A grasshopper. I cannot sit at a desk and work, it has created such tensions and strains in me or increased the tensions and strains I already had to a degree when I cannot sit at a desk to earn my living.'

Perhaps the last part of this patient's remarks gives us the clue. He was already suffering from a considerable amount of repressed energy and intrapsychic strain before he went to school, but he perhaps rightly claims: 'The business of the school should have been to relieve me of the tensions I was already enduring. My head was full to bursting. And instead of relieving my tension, all they did was to try and push any amount of irrelevant stuff into my already over-stuffed head. Call that education? I call it mutilation.'

Another male patient of mine, who met with more bullying than head-stuffing, said to me: 'What these schools teach one is to submit to being beaten into a frazzle. All that does for most of the victims is to create in them a pattern which they relieve by beating others in their turn. They acquire a sort of compulsion to undo the wrong done them by passing it on to others—at least some of them do. Unfortunately I could not manage this, I remained beaten, that is why I am here.'

Another patient said: 'It is a sort of initiation which is a battle between the young and the old, the initiates and the elders. Either you become an elder and spend the rest of your life initiating or castrating the young, or you remain a eunuch like me. In any case the so-called education does not matter. The thing just forms a load in your mind which indoctrinates you into the ways of similar mentally castrated people. This I could not accept, and so I have remained a sort of useless load stuffing up and clouding my mind.'

A very intelligent woman patient said to me in reference to her son who was an outstanding scholar, and had just achieved a double first at Cambridge: 'Doctor, I am afraid. The boy is growing up just like his hopeless father (a professor). He is abnormal. This intellectualism, which I suspect that even you think may be meritorious, is nothing more or less than a perversion, an abominable perversion. The boy has no use for friends, he never looks at a girl, on vacation he lies in bed until eleven or twelve o'clock reading a book. No, not his studies, it is detective thrillers he reads. He is so completely introverted and perverted that I tremble for his future. He will never be happy. This is a perversion which we are all encouraged to achieve in schools and universities. We are all striving to achieve it or being encouraged to do so, and the unfortunate ones are those who succeed like my son— and my husband. They are doomed and all associated with them are doomed. It is through this in my husband that I am here for analysis. These people (husband and son), they displace their libido on to something which is not alive. It may bring fame, but fame at the expense of a normal way of living is wrong. I would rather my son was a healthy labourer, who could marry and have children. He will never be any good to himself or anyone else, that is why I have reason to be frightened.'

It may well be that I am here drawing attention to exceptional cases, neurotics and scholars. But what we learn from the exceptional cases often has more application than is generally realized to the normal individual and to the process as a whole. The question may be asked, if our system of education can produce illnesses or accentuate illnesses already present, what is the matter with the technique, the technique that rides roughshod over the person inappropriately subjected to it, and to some extent brainwashes or indoctrinates even its most appropriate proselytes. The answer must be it is the same determinant common to all human thoughts and activity, namely that we are so compelled to express or discharge the impulses and tensions within us, however sublimated, that we do not or are unable to assess reality, in this case the reality of the developing mind, well enough to know whether we are helping or hindering the progress of *its* reality appreciation. Probably we help a bit and hinder a lot. But the point is that these results are only advantageous to the blind

compulsion to be ourselves, and to discharge what we have accumulated and are paid to discharge in the form of education. It would
seem that anybody, at least anybody without a great deal of insight
into his own unconscious motivations cannot really choose his behaviour appropriately to the real situation with which he is, or should
be, dealing. He may nurse the illusion of choice, but if he were
analyzed he would probably find that he could not behave in any
other way, but was simply obeying his acquired reactive patterns as
an animal obeys its instincts, whether or not they fit the reality requirements. In this sense one cannot say that the ego is free from
neurotic and psychotic compulsions. Perhaps we are satisfied if it
'gets by', and if those whom it apparently injures also appear to get
by. We conveniently forget the less successful effects which are
encountered in the analytical room and the hospital bed.

The pleasure principle in the developing child and young person
does not always have added to it a developing reality principle, or
so-called adult ego, but is instead commonly rudely and injuriously
interrupted, assaulted as it were, with the result that the realities
introduced may not seem real and the health which was there before
and might have improved, becomes impaired. My lady patient might
well have asked are we producing able men or perverts and neurotics?
Perhaps the best we can produce is something approximating to ourselves. The culture and mythology of our age is the reality we are
accustomed to, whether we live in the Stone Age or now, and we are
introducing and indoctrinating the initiates (having somewhat
damaged them) into our milieu. It is the best we can do in view of our
unconscious mechanism.

The point I wish to make is this: in ancient and primitive times and
amongst primitive peoples of today, the boy and very often the girl,
developing into an adult, usually just before sexual maturity is
reached, manhood or womanhood, is as it were seized by the elders
and mature people of the tribe, and subjected to a symbolical castration, according to the tribe's particular initiation rites. The purpose
and direction of this interference is made only too apparent by the
fact that its climax is focussed upon the initiate's genital organs. As
has been described in this book, some tribes, copying their neighbours,
extended this ceremony to the adolescent females, suffering fifty per
cent of deaths amongst their victims, apparently just sufficient to lead
to an abandonment of the process. The expressions of jealousy and
sadism had gone too far. It would appear to the modern observer that
in any and every respect these ceremonies always go too far, leaving
as they do physical injury and incalculable mental injury.

The psychology of the situation may be summed up as follows: the
young person is about to enter into a normal heterosexual life. Those
who have already arrived at the privileged position somewhat resent

these new intruders, perhaps they are unconsciously jealous of the
advantages of the relatively young arrival. Certainly they appear to
turn their at least unconscious sadism, short of murder, against him.
Thereby they say, as it were: 'If you are going to enter mature
sexuality, it will only be after we have given you a terrible lesson for
aspiring to it. Then perhaps you will realize that it is we who have
spared you from complete castration, and that your sexuality can be
indulged in only by virtue of our benevolent permission. So you will
realize that forever more you have an allegiance primarily to us.'

This interpretation is verified by the fact that if the initiate recovers
from his circumcision, or rather genital mutilation, heterosexual
licence is immediately granted to him and in some tribes, I believe,
he runs off with a young woman, often similarly mutilated, even
before it is physically practicable for intercourse to be indulged in.
The psychological lead up to such an orgy is openly accepted by all
members of the tribe, provided the youth at least has undergone the
initiation. Sometimes it assumes a more or less public exhibition,
accompanied by open jubilation and dancing, perhaps the equivalent
of rock'n'roll in our society. There is much open jubilation and
excitement. The fathers having as it were symbolically castrated the
young man, made him understand that they and they alone are the
bosses, now do not care so much what he does. After all, they have
had the satisfaction of venting their jealousy and sadism.

All initiation ceremonies are clearly interpretable along such lines.
Even in some modern pseudo cults, reminiscent of the past, as for
instance in freemasonry, the would-be candidate who aspires to
acceptance by the brothers is first subjected to a symbolical initiation.

It may all seem to be a game in these days, children playing out the
unconscious residues of their early history, dramatizing their complexes. But the point I wish to make is that in our most civilized way
of life, we are unwittingly doing the same thing and it is not necessarily
a game, it is our very way of life. We do not subject our adolescents to
the open 'shocking' ceremonies of primitive people, our symbolism
has become more remote from the meaningful core (the genital
organ), and therefore its significance has become more obscure,
though none the less detectable by the trained eye.

Today its main form is no longer called initiation, it is called
education. The psychology and the psychopathology are nevertheless
identical. The individual from infancy onwards is wanting to find and
is looking for something exciting and gratifying. We may say in a
sense that he wants to 'educate' himself, he wants to learn what the
gratifying object is and how to find it. I believe that a lot of his
phantasy life which is made so much of in analysis, and particularly
in child analysis is only there as a result of frustration. He is making
the best he can of a bad job, dreaming himself into the pleasures which

have been denied him, and which he is unable to attain—like the baby hallucinates the breast and sucking it, as can be seen from his lip movements, when he is unable to get what he wants. The only 'education' which the growing individual spontaneously wants is one which will show him what it is that gratifies and how to find it.

A very much alive and bright woman patient of mine told me of how in her childhood she felt that parents and all adults were concealing something extremely important from her. She knew that there was something she did not understand and she knew that they were determined to keep her from understanding it. According to her this created a mental gulf between her and her parents, but she did not give up. When she got the opportunity she used to search their belongings for clues. She remembers how as a small girl she furtively examined most carefully every item in every drawer of her mother's chest of drawers. She did this again and again. Finally she came across some rubber instrument which she felt revealed some part of the secret, if only she could understand what it was for and what it was all about. She says she puzzled for days about this rubber thing, and the thoughts of it used to come back to her years later.

It is well known that not only these frustrated children, all children, are preoccupied with their games or symbols, the unconscious meanings of which are not gone into but merely experienced emotionally, they nevertheless have time to feel intrigued by some vague thought of what keeps mother and father ticking, why they go into a room together to sleep, listening and observing and puzzling. Their 'education' is deliberately thwarted and therefore they go back to their symbolical playing out of their phantasies in the form of games.

Referring to development in the child, Alix Strachey says: 'Much of his earliest and powerful epistemological drives are directed to matters of sex, since it has such intense impulsional and emotional importance for him. If these drives are thwarted at the very beginning it is highly probable that the whole development of his instincts of curiosity may be seriously arrested and the once bright and enquiring child may turn into a dull and uninterested one.'[21]

Nevertheless the early instinct-determined compulsion to understand what gratifies and to learn all about it, presumably so that we will be able to overcome our interminable frustration, never dies, though it may be strongly repressed, mutilated and wither a bit. After all, while there is life, the life instinct must be there, however hidden, and however much its objects are displaced, substituted and symbolized. Whatever department of learning we may subsequently embrace, the seeking and finding that goes on in it are all symbolical of our primitive seekings for the gratifying object. Though this is true of every department of learning, in some it is more obvious than in others. For instance to the uninitiated the study of the university curriculum in *medicine* unconsciously means sex. The unconscious mind is engaged in searching every item of every drawer in the old chest of drawers, just as my patient was as a little girl. But now the chest of drawers has become the body itself, and its functions a permitted, publically encouraged and even rewarded form of investigation. This is therefore an excellent sublimation of adjustment between the conflicting claims of libidinal desire to achieve gratification, and parents and society who forbid it with castration threats, a solution of the conflict. The only trouble here is that the aspirant to this sublimated form of gratification may find that it entails more castration than gratification; the sadism of the superego is not to be denied.

Perhaps my theory regarding the unconscious motivations in the choice of medicine as a study and career may be more acceptable to the non-analyst if he thinks of that department of medicine which concerns itself with childbirth and diseases of women, but I would insist that displacements of the original sexual interest, with its puzzlements and frustrations, need have no limits, even for instance in the specialization called ophthalmology, a concentration of one's attention upon the functions and diseases of the eye, may be similarly motivated unconsciously. Perhaps the individual who chooses ophthalmology has more resistances, a less direct approach. An interest in mother and her functions can extend not only to her chest of drawers, but even to her jewel-box.

A method of approach which may be less naive would be that of knowing what goes on in her head, or mind, the things she is concealing from us, for surely there must lie all the answers to the riddle, therefore we become psychologists or analysts. So it would seem that education can offer us, if not a direct achievement of omnipotence, at least some modicum of pseudo-gratification in the form which one of my patients calls a 'fob-off'.

It may be that one of the determinants in our embracing of all these manifold displacements of 'fob-offs', rather than persisting in the direct pursuit of our original search for the gratifying object (which began with the breast), is that sooner of later fear, attributable to the attitude of the parents, interferes with the direct approach. In consequence of this, conflict arises in the mind and the repressing elements of this conflict result in our sometimes all too readily seizing upon a symbol or substitution. Hence we have all the manifold gadgets and ramifications of civilization in place of the original biological interest. A great deal of repression of the original interest goes on, so that we finally reach the stage of becoming incapable of knowing directly what are the principal preoccupations of our minds, since they are relegated to the unconscious.

Now these considerations may bring us to the current recognition that some degree of sex education is called for, at least at puberty or adolescence. I know the mind too well to be taken in by this apparently frank enthusiasm for sex education. I have more than a suspicion that the tendency is to keep all the conflicts connected with sex still safely repressed in the unconscious, and to delude ourselves that we are facing up to everything by substituting in place of them some conscious-level medicine-or-anatomy-or-physiology-like knowledge which, like all sublimated knowledge, owes its chief subservience to the repressive and fear-inducing superego.

We remain castrates of the father-image whichever way we turn. Our initiation ceremonies, whether primitive or 'educational', have seen to that. I do not wish to decry the value of our sublimated attempts, but merely wish to put them in their proper perspective to show how far the mind of man, including modern man, is removed from an ability to appreciate the truth, how full of substitutive delusions it is, and how justified I am in my allegations of a universal psychosis.

The call for sex education, however plausible, should not be identified with a new-found liberation from morbidity. We are rightly told that all knowledge should be imparted quite naturally, whether it has any bearing on sex or not. What we are unable to appreciate is that we have no knowledge (and therefore cannot impart it) of our basic mental content, such as the phantasies which reside in our unconscious and which cause anxiety (that is why they are repressed into the unconscious), and that it is this anxiety which causes the repression of knowledge, even repression of what was most obvious in our early infancy.

Innumerable instances can be quoted from analytical experience of almost incredible ignorance or blindness to what were once the most natural and perhaps the most interesting facts. For instance I remember the case of a patient who, at the age of fifteen, spent an entire holiday in a strenuous endeavour to avoid looking at two moles on his mother's neck, as the thought had occurred to him that this was where he had been suckled. As his mother sat immediately opposite to him at every meal, his struggle was all-absorbing. He had already successfully repressed the knowledge as to where his mother's breasts really were.

What should we tell this and similar children in our sex education? Should we tell them where the breasts really are and what they are, or would it not be better to get from them, to learn from them, what this thing can be which is so terrifying that it cannot under any circumstances be confessed or known. Perhaps we know nothing until they have taught us. The difficulty is particularly important as they themselves remember no need of the breast. In other words, it is the phantasy that matters, not the facts. We can teach them a lot of more or less irrelevant facts, but we do not know their unconscious phantasies from which all their defences arise. It is *we* who need education, not they. In the light of these emotional reactions we can immediately assume that the 'breast' has nothing to do with what the anatomy and physiology books can tell us, but that it must be some terrifying monster, probably something which devours us if we look at it.

In other words, sex education is not something which we can teach the young, it depends rather upon our learning from the young what may be the phantasies which caused them not to dare to know—about sex and about much else which may be associated with it. The anxiety belonging to these phantasies takes them beyond the normal limits of repression of sex knowledge to those of apparent feeble-mindedness. None of us are free from some degree of this psychosis.

If we thoroughly examine the attitude of the mind towards any subject, we find that not only its reactions and behaviour, but even its judgements are more or less far removed from reason and logic. They can be shown to be biased, if not entirely determined, by factors which have little or nothing to do with reason and intelligence. This peculiarity of mind and behaviour is not fully explained by psychology's simple division of mental processes into reality principle versus pleasure principle. For instance, there may be conflict between one pleasure drive and another.

In no spheres of action, thought, and behaviour is the reality principle so completely over-ruled by the factors of un-reason (emotional forces, biases, conflicts, etc.) as it is in the sphere of sexuality. This is all due to our having come up against fear of our projected sexual aggressive and sadistic impulses. No wonder we accept the displacements and 'fob-offs' offered by our educators. It is doubtful if it is even possible for any human being to deal with the subject of sex, in deed or even in thought, in accordance with reality values and reasonable judgement. No matter how complete may be one's knowledge of anatomy and physiology, one is none the less a victim of phantasies. Thus pictures and music do not lose their appeal. The need for romance and adventure is still uncurbed. In a word, reason, knowledge and intelligence, or what is left of them after emotional conflict has impaired their efficiency, seem to occupy a different compartment of the mind. This has no effect upon some less accessible compartment of the mind, which latter determines our emotions and behaviour, at least, our emotional behaviour.

I have had a case of a woman who, at the age of sixteen, suffered from a phobia which was the plague of her life. She was afraid to pass a man in the street, even if he were on the other side of the road. It was revealed that this fear was connected with a phantasy that if she passed a man she would become pregnant. And this phantasy was effective in causing her phobia in spite of her knowledge of the facts of sexual intercourse and reproduction.

Admittedly this was at the immature age of sixteen. But an intelligent and capable patient of twenty-six, firmly believed that she was four months pregnant and that it was in consequence of an alleged rape. Analysis elicited detailed information which showed beyond any shadow of doubt that she had unconsciously endeavoured to be raped —her manoeuvres had been quite elaborate, but owing to the man's premature ejaculation had failed. The sequel was also of psychological interest. In her fright she had attempted a large variety of remedies to abort the 'pregnancy'. Eventually after three weeks' efforts she produced some haemorrhage, but it did not lead to abortion for it ceased within a week. In another three weeks or so, she had produced a second haemorrhage, after almost ceaseless efforts, and the duration had been similar—and again once or twice. Now four months had elapsed without the abortion, and she was desperate. After listening to the details of her story, most of which I have not here recorded, it was quite easy to inform her with confidence that, far from being pregnant, she was still a virgin.

It is almost incredible, unless one is in contact with the facts, that an intelligent adult can, under the sway of her unconscious wishes, so ignore all the facts well known to her ego in favour of a phantasy produced by her sex anxiety conflict.

This case reminds me that an educated woman, the mother of a child of five, came to me with her husband, and told me quite seriously that ever since the birth of her child, she had become pregnant every month, and that at the critical moment when she was prepared for suicide, as regularly as clockwork the abortion would come on. The most amazing feature of this case was that her husband sat there the whole time giving his assent to her theories.

Unconscious phantasies can provoke theories which go much further than determining our judgements. They can even determine our anatomical and physiological functions. Many cases are on record where, under the stresses of phantasy, a woman's menses have stopped not only for one or two months, which is common enough, but for a full nine months, during which period her abdomen has enlarged, and other changes consistent with pregnancy have taken place, only to disappear at the end of nine months with the giving birth to nothing more serious than wind or air. All this can take place in a virgin. Further, I have had a woman, past the age of fifty, celebrated for her intelligence, who for eighteen months confounded a series of doctors by periodic bouts of agonizing pain in her abdomen, which proved on psychological investigation to be nothing more or less than a psychogenic reproduction of her previous childbirth experiences. I have recorded this case in Chapter Ten of *Clinical Psychology*.

If the unconscious forces of the mind can so affect the body, how much more may we expect them to affect our mental functions of thought and reason?

We may consider the question, why does ignorance of the so-called facts of sex exist at all? Why does there exist this conspiracy of silence? Why does the parent who knows something of the facts wish to conceal this knowledge from his child, or conversely we may ask why do some adults wish to burden the child with knowledge he is not seeking? Why are so many facts and truths subject to censorship?

Already, before we reach the problem of education or the problem of ignorance, we have this great, big, general *symptom* to understand, and perhaps to 'cure'. Every symptom has *causes*, if not reasons. It is perhaps noteworthy that even when attempts are made to be open about the facts of sex, all facts relating to the father's part in it are rigorously excluded.

What we are all particularly blind to is the emotional situation underlying the conscious intellectual preoccupation. In order to maintain the intellectual thread of the intellectual work, we are at the same time repressing, keeping out of our consciousness, what otherwise might amount to emotional disturbances threatening to disturb this intellectual preoccupation. The point I am coming to is this: when pupil and teacher meet to discuss sex something is going on between them that neither of them is discussing, which perhaps each of them is equally strongly repressing. So, perhaps, while the situation is overtly that of an education, it is still, essentially, the old, old situation of concealment.

The following example, taken from the clinical transference situation, illustrates what I mean: a woman of forty, who was in the habit of talking quite freely, though on a superficial plane, when she arrived in the consulting room, always showed some reluctance to lying on the settee, and when finally she assumed this attitude she always became perfectly silent. Of course, it was obvious to the analyst that this silence was far more eloquent than anything she had said or could say. What did it mean? It meant that the entire situation was dominated by the fact of her posture. This was the posture that in her brought all hands to the pumps. This posture meant her ship was sinking. This was the posture in which sexual intercourse took place. I may mention that her ego-control never had been overwhelmed by sexual feeling. Though she had borne two children, she had invariably enjoyed complete sexual frigidity.

This illustration is brought forward to show that the really important situation in analysis, as in life, and perhaps in sex education, is the unspoken, often unthought-of, situation. While we are intellectually or consciously employed or preoccupied with matters legitimate to consciousness, these may be merely serving as a covering to cloak or hide from us the real goings-on, under the surface, which latter may be, and commonly are, unconscious phantasies of sexual exhilaration, accompanied by their appropriate physiological and chemical changes. The activity of education may be no exception to this general rule. *Education* should surely include a revelation, rather than a concealment of this unspoken situation.

Sex education, like education in general, is a plausible ambition, though what these clinical excerpts may bring to our notice is that we are failing to recognize that there is a dark region of the mind that has a screen around it, which appears to be impenetrable to the light of facts, or to conscious knowledge. Indeed education, whether it be general or sex education, has the unwitting ambition of increasing the strength and impenetrability of this screen. It represents the elders who perform the initiating or castrating ceremonies, the superego. That life continues is due to the fact that even the utmost and most protracted efforts on the part of the castrators and superegos does not really succeed in making the screen quite impenetrable. The id breaks through in act if not in thought, and thereby the race continues, intellectualism remains as a substitutive 'fob-off', more or less confined to another department of the mind and separated from the basic life by the screen between them.

We keep the subjective element in sex more or less repressed while we busy ourselves with the purely objective or intellectual assessment. Perhaps this is the essential difference between education and life. I merely wish to correct the erroneous idea that in dealing with the objective aspects, we are dealing with the whole subject, and the idea that the conscious intellectual process can have any effect upon the unconscious phantasies which have been determined by early sexual conflict, and which in turn are the determinants of subsequent sexual behaviour. My contention is that our ego is not wholly on one side or the other, but is to a variable degree split between its allegiance to or seduction by each side in turn. How marked this split can be is illustrated by the following example from analysis.

A certain reformer was in the habit, with the permission of the headmasters of a number of schools, of lecturing to the pupils on what he called 'sex education'. I subsequently analysed two of his pupils, and it appeared that 'sex education' consisted almost exclusively of a public exhortation to the boys not to masturbate. However, it seems that this was balanced by a friendly relationship established with a few selected pupils, which enabled him in privacy to masturbate them himself. We may not have much difficulty in assessing the unconscious factors behind these fervent exhortations. Personally I should think that like Rousseau and his sex reforms, this man may consciously have meant quite well. He, like the pupils, was the victim of his unconscious conflict. His ego was evidently split and alternated between allegiance to or seduction by superego on the one hand and by the id on the other. Education for him apparently represented the castration phase of his sex life, and his homosexual practices were, of course, the sex phase.

We may be inclined to jump to the conclusion that if not a rogue or a criminal, this man was certainly mad. But the point I wish to make in this assessment of sex education, and of education in general, is that there exists a split in all of us, though it may not obtain such overt or undesirable expressions. The impression of wholeness or sanity to which we vigorously adhere is no more than a wishful delusion. The forces that drive us both in our beliefs and in our activities emanate from the unconscious, from complexes or repressed phantasies which have their roots in the frankly psychotic period of our infancy, and in the interminable struggle which has gone on intrapsychically ever since. My endeavour is to show that this struggle is not confined to intrapsychic processes, but attains its expression in all our attitudes and activities including those which are institutionalized.

In short, the world of man, even of civilized man, is a reflection of his intrapsychic state. Indeed it may reveal to us more of the nature of his repressed and denied unconscious mind, and the incompatibility and conflict within it, than can anything of which he is directly conscious. That is how it comes about that the world of man is as irrational as the infantile unconscious.

Probably the dramatic attempts on the part of older people to castrate the younger generation, whether by the symbolical mutilations of primitive initiation rites or whether by the more protracted and covert methods of training, and education, would not succeed so well as they do, were it not that the child, even the infant, has already developed, through the introjection of parents and mentors, a similarly castrating mechanism called the superego within his own psyche. In observing these cultural phenomena, we are witnessing no more than a more or less overt dramatization and acting out of what is already present and growing within the hidden recesses of the mind.

CHAPTER IX

SPORT, GAMES AND SOCIAL EXPRESSIONS
OF AGGRESSION

Children are even less capable than adults of verbalizing their thoughts and feelings. They are conspicuously less capable and more inhibited in this respect. After all, animals can hardly verbalize at all, their 'language' being limited to a few emotionally charged sounds. At this level of life the tendency is to express emotions, feelings, thoughts and phantasies by action and action alone.

It is a long time since child analysts first discovered that this was no handicap to analysing even the mute child. The clue was to watch it at play. The toys it chooses and what it does with them are all interpretable as symbols with which it expresses and acts out the phantasies which it is unable to put into words. The child analyst can learn a lot simply by watching the child's activities. For instance Melanie Klein tells us of a case who, symbolizing a child of her own by her doll, used to play 'the role of a severe and punishing mother who treated the child very cruelly'.[19] Klein tells us that this child's 'ambivalence towards her mother, her extreme need to be punished, her feelings of guilt and her night terrors led me to recognize that in this child, aged two years and nine months—and quite clearly going back to a much earlier age—a harsh and relentless superego operated'.[19]

But there are innumerable instances on record of the play of children revealing, as they always must reveal to those who can read the meaning in the symbols, the drama of the child's emotional life. The point is that these observations show us that the play of children is far from meaningless, it is like the active life of the adult, a vehicle for the expression of a very often rich and complicated emotional life, with elements far more dramatic than the 'blind' adult is likely to suspect.

All the child's games are symbolical of activities which represent every aspect of the child's emotional life. That is why it needs so many toys and gadgets as props for its dramatic production.

Children's play is of course not limited to such elaborate forms, they take pleasure in running and skipping and jumping and swinging and sliding, in roundabouts and almost every form of exhilarating locomotion.

The psychoanalytical theory is that eroticism is certainly not confined to genital regions, nor indeed to the orifices of the body, but

permeates every region and function of the body. The skeletal muscu-
lature is an important source of discharge of tension and of pleasurable
feelings, and a lot of children's games are based on what is called
muscular eroticism. In addition to this the child enjoys locomotor
eroticism, hence its pleasure in swingings and slidings, whether or not
these are accompanied by muscular movement.

Of course such things are only relatively more important to the
child. The adult is still capable of some degree of enjoyment from all
these pre-genital sources. He may, like the child, enjoy skating,
swimming, water-skiing, speed boat racing, gliding, flying and car-
driving, and a hundred and one other activities, some of which like
athletics in general are attributable to locomotor and muscular
eroticism, whether or not there is some added element such as competition, victory or defeat. Even muscular exercise, though to some
not very exhilarating, probably implies some propensity for more
enjoyable muscular activities.

The locomotor and muscular eroticism expressed and enjoyed in
the playing of games, sometimes reveals itself as merely symbolical of
the sexual act itself. Every analyst has become familiar with dreams
in which although the dreamer was overtly (in the manifest dream)
doing something as innocent as swimming, flying or rising in the air,
he had, through the exhilaration of the experience, actually had an
ejaculation, revealing clearly that the activity presented to consciousness, and remembered by the dreamer, was a cover for some
comparable pleasure that was taking place at a deeper level, and with
physiological accompaniment. Analysands have dreamt of every form
of sport and game, and with or without this physiological confirmation the overt or manifest activities of the dream have proved on
association of thought to be genital sexual equivalents, often with an
added admixture of aggression, such as when a football is kicked
through the goal.

When it comes to muscular activities, especially those which introduce an element of competition, we are dealing with a form of expression, an outlet for energy, which however much erotic or libidinal
feeling is involved, certainly tends to serve as a vehicle, perhaps the
most important vehicle, for the discharge of aggressive tensions.

Competitive games, including team games, bring this out very
clearly. Of course there is always boxing and wrestling which may
well be regarded as overt expressions (in play form) of our difficult-to-
discharge aggressive impulses. Few people seem to realize how many
of our team games originated with something more like a fight between erstwhile friendly rivals, and even today amongst the Latin or
excitable races, such innocent games as football arouse passions not
only in the players but perhaps more conspicuously in the spectators,
which often approach the verge of open fighting. Nevertheless games,

however rough, may be regarded as a very fortunate and useful mode of discharge of tensions which otherwise might become frankly destructive.

Early in the history of public schools this was recognized by the authorities, and used to such a degree that it has occasionally threatened to become the chief activity of the young male community. If they fought it out on the playing field, the theory was that they would become more manly (i.e. aggressive) and less prone to sloppy sentiment, day-dreaming, masturbation and mutual erotic activities. Games were something open and healthy, and they must learn to find their enjoyment and their training in these. No doubt some boys could utilize them for an expression of their unconscious aggressive and sexual phantasies better than could others. This is certainly true of adults, games no longer being compulsory, those who can discharge their tensions this way are more likely to continue to play, others will find some alternative mode of relieving their feelings and phantasies.

Every analyst has had games-playing patients, through whose activities and experiences he has gleaned that the playing of games, like children playing with their toys, can reveal symbolically a very real drama, comprising every shade of feeling from success to failure, from gratification to frustration, from life to death. I do not think any analyst has taken the trouble to work out fully all the emotional experiences which the symbolism of a game encourages the player to enjoy or suffer.

Adrian Stokes says:[22] 'Games must dramatize the unrhythmic chanciness of reality: a large element of luck is essential to their wide appeal: the player makes trial of his good fortune as well as of his skill; he is "chancing his hand", his potency and his power to compel.'

What the non-analyst will find difficult adequately to appreciate is that every gadget or instrument connected with every game has a symbolical meaning to the unconscious mind, and an activity which is symbolical of some action, often aggression or defence, in the unconscious drama. If it were not for this sort of thing, games would not exist at all. They have no other determinant or *raison d'etre.* Nevertheless the symbolism is variable in its meaning, and probably changes from one moment of the game to another. Perhaps the rugby football is something different while you are hurling it out of the scrum to what it is when the player outside the scrum grabs it, probably knowing full well that he will not get very far before retribution overtakes him. Nevertheless the excitement or hope of managing to overcome all opposition with the aid of his brothers, and reach the defended or 'forbidden' ground the other side of the important line, is sufficiently exciting to make him exert every ounce of his energy and risk all sorts of penalties.

No doubt games have become more organized and perhaps more

civilized as time has gone on. We are told of a game of football recorded in a history of Derbyshire published in 1829: 'A Frenchman
passing through Derby remarked that if Englishmen called this
playing, it would be impossible to say what they would call fighting.'[22]

Tennis began something like squash, within a built-up courtyard,
which has been interpreted by Stokes as symbolizing, perhaps like all
architecture, the mother's body. Subsequently chalk lines came to
replace brickwork, and of course other important alterations took
place.

A large number of games use a ball and holes as well as some
hitting instrument for their expression, golf of course conspicuously
so. Adrian Stokes says: 'From the point of view of the attack, it is
beyond question that a genital aggressiveness characterizes ball games
whose players possess feet, hands, stick, bat with which to manoeuvre
the ball . . . generally, the ball is itself the phallus.'[22] In golf the
player has the advantage of letting out his aggression in driving from
the tee, but control and patience is often much called upon. When
finally he reaches the green, symbolical of the female genital regions,
he has to conduct himself very carefully. His reward lies in skill and
care and accuracy; only thereby will he manage to get the ball into
the hole before his rival.

There is an important element of competition with other males in
the form of rivalry in most games, for instance in cricket. Stokes says:[22]
'To be any good one must freely want to smack the ball. As in war, the
aggressive component, already contingent perhaps in the very fact of
taking violent exercise, is more apparent than the libidinal . . . it is
obvious that considerable aggression is used in hitting, kicking, and
flinging the ball: indeed, here lies the principal opportunity for the
catharsis of aggression.'

Finally Stokes tells us: 'One could argue that games, a substitute
for warfare, have become one of modern warfare's opponents.'[22]

Perhaps enough has been said about games to indicate that like the
play of children, they serve the purpose, usually blindly, to discharge
otherwise pent-up impulses and emotions. What makes them of
special psychological interest is that their forms and elaborations, like
those of children's games, reveal psychological construction in the
form of unconscious phantasy, and that they have no other source,
determinant or cause for existence other than these unconscious
phantasies and the wishes, fears and emotional tensions associated
with them. Like children we are clearly playing out our deeper madness in these irrational ways, but here we know there is an element of
irrationality in that we call the process play, or a game. In this respect
we are perhaps less obviously psychotic than when we play out our
lives 'seriously', deluded that our activities are truly rational or
necessary, or must be done for objective or reality good reasons.

How dangerous this can become will be made evident presently in the chapter on war. But in the meantime to emphasize the fantastic irrationality of our behaviour, I would like to refer to at least one blood sport, as this form of play reveals more undeniably the aggressive and sadistic elements involved in these voluntarily pursued pleasures. Like other games, hunting, shooting and fishing appear in our analysands' dreams with great frequency and variety. Sometimes the dreamer is the hunted animal and the dream may become a nightmare. Sometimes he is the hunter sadistically triumphing over his quarry. Like hunting, shooting dreams are not so frequent nowadays as when the sport was more popular, but almost invariably firing a gun and bringing down a bird on the wing is a thrill which on association proves to be something of the nature of a very potent aggressive rape, whether or not it includes the unconscious phantasy of destroying the rival's (father's) rising phallus (the bird) in the process. The unconscious phantasy so finds its way into a symbolic form of expression in a more direct and satisfactory manner than it could achieve by some other cultural activities. It must be the strength of the emotional drives connected with this phantasy which are responsible for maintaining these sporting activities.

Fishing dreams are perhaps amongst the most common. Practically all our patients, whether fishermen or not, catch fishes in their dreams. Sometimes the fishing is interpreted as a finding of the lost phallus, and perhaps hooking and landing the fish is the successful finding and restoring of the object that was lost. Curiously enough a fish is practically always a genital symbol, usually phallic. No doubt other elements of the unconscious phantasy sometimes include Oedipus gratification at the expense of both father and mother. The result is that the successful catch causes the good feeling in the dreamer, comparable to having restored or/and gratified his potency desires. In the light of such dreams it is possible to recognize the deeper determinants in the activity of fishing and one of the most important causes of this perennial pastime.

The interpretation of these recreations in general outline does not of course do justice to the innumerable elaborations which show the complicated organization of the psyche, and lend more precise meaning to the existence of the activities. Also to my mind the accumulation of these minor details when their symbolical significance is understood helps to eliminate any doubts we may have had about the source in the unconscious and the nature of the unconscious phantasies from which they spring. For instance in the case of fox-hunting, such a host of practices and rituals have been elaborated that they may astonish us on their first impact upon us and give us the impression that here is something more than a sport, indeed something savouring very much of a religious rite. For instance in fox-hunting, the practice of blooding the newcomer at a kill is commonly called 'christening' him. He is not allowed to wash the blood off his face until the evening. From some people's reaction to this it may indeed be as Ingeborg Flugel says: 'An initiation ceremony'.[23] He has been made to share 'Both the honour and the guilt attaching to the deed'. One of the most curious features about this sort of sport is that it was estimated in the case of stag-hunting 'a special honour actually to kill the hunted animal when brought to bay, and only those of a certain social standing were allowed this privilege'. The most curious feature of these rituals is that it was dimly supposed to be 'a privilege which . . . was not unappreciated by the animal itself'.[23]

It seems to me that some elements of this same religious or pagan rite appertain to the ritualistic bull-fighting in Spain. If only we could all delude ourselves that the exhausted bull is appreciative of the privilege of being killed in this manner, we would perhaps mitigate any tendency to conflict or to the suspicion that we were being sadistic or inhuman. We are reminded that the honour of hunting and killing the hunted animal is in meaningful contrast with the severity of the punishments meted out at the time of the Norman kings to anyone who poached and killed one of their game. Ingeborg Flugel says: 'With regard to the ritual (of fox-hunting) we may refer once more to Erasmus' description of the "gentleman" who "shall throw down his hat" and "fall devoutly on his knees before despatching the game". Such extreme signs of respect as are here indicated surely give the clue to the whole attitude involved in these ceremonies. They overwhelmingly suggest a religious sacrifice—an institution, the most primitive and the clearest examples of which are to be found in the ritual of totemism.'[23]

She proceeds to show further details of a parallelism to totemism: the ambivalence, fear, hatred and even friendliness, differing according to the seasons, the honour and respect shown to the fox contrasting with the cruel manner of his death, 'a common feature of totemism and of the corresponding sacrifices of divine persons or animals in the higher religions'. The ambivalence is revealed further by the fox's remains being divided into good parts, highly valued (mask, brush and pads) and bad parts, which 'are thrown ignominiously to the hounds'. With further reference to the parallelism to totemism, she points out that it can be 'killed only in certain ways and in certain seasons, as a collective deed performed with the due ritual', and also that 'to shoot a fox in modern England is almost as wicked as for a member of a totemic community to kill his totem otherwise than in the appointed manner'.[23]

There are innumerable other little parallels with the pagan or religious attitude. There is the same symbolical feasting and abstinence, followed after the kill by something approximating to the totemic orgy of eating and drinking. Ingeborg Flugel tells us: 'The smearing of blood upon the face may even be a shortened and symbolic expression of the more primitive practice of drinking the blood; for in certain initiation ceremonies of Australian tribes the initiates are covered with the blood of fellow-tribesmen, which at the same time they drink.'[23] Frazer considers that like eating the totem or sacrificial animal, the smearing with blood is also 'beyond a doubt' an identification with it. In this ceremony it would seem that we have regressed further than the age of merely human and animal sacrifice, right back to the age when such sacrifices had totemic elements.

It may be seen that the motivations or determinants of our recreational behaviour are powerful emotional forces, powerful although complicated by counter-forces, all blindly acting upon one another in the unconscious, and emerging in the form of symptomatic behaviour with all its aggressive libidinal control and ritualistic (superego) elaborations. Recreation, play or games has a special characteristic of not being obligatory or compulsory for us through any reality determinants such as physiological needs to maintain our life. Therefore it can only be explicable by the sort of irrational emotional determinants above referred to. May it not be that much of our behaviour which we are inclined to accept as rational, is similarly determined, and on account of our guilt, shame or other reactions to it, rationalized in the sense that we plead that it was reasonable, justified, so that we had no other course but to behave as we did behave.

CHAPTER X

FEAR

In one patient after another, the analyst observes the operation of what may be regarded as the basic law, or the basic psychological law, of life.

It can be put in terms of instinct gratification. If an individual's or organism's instincts are being gratified, he is naturally happy. He finds the world a good place, a place that loves him and he in return is naturally full of love.

Complications and difficulties arise only when instincts are frustrated. So long as an instinct remains frustrated, the world is a bad place, a place that hates us, and which we hate unless and until we can conquer it or remove our frustration and continue with instinct gratification (i.e. with life).

Now the first reaction to a frustrating world may vary very greatly from one animal to another, and from one level of life to another. The baby cries or screams, that is all it can do. Some animals immediately mobilize their energy in the form of aggression to remove the frustration, and so on.

Civilized man, or the more intelligent individual or animal may approach the frustrating situation in a scientific spirit. He is using his ego. He investigates the nature of the frustration, be it inorganic or in the form of a person, and mobilizes the reality situation in a manner designed to enable him to cease to be frustrated; in short to get his own way, such as gratification of his instinct desire or drive.

Nevertheless, however civilized the individual or group of individuals, if, in spite of the scientific method, technique or psychological technique, they remain frustrated and fail to achieve what we could call basically instinct gratification, sooner or later aggression is mobilized and they will fight to get what they want, or what their instinct must have. It may be such that they revert to the primitive 'technique'.

Thus it would seem that 'war' is inevitable, or at least not always avoidable. If one creature wants something which the other wants, or which the other is determined he shall not have, or shall have only over his dead body, then there will be a fight, one will survive and the other will be a dead body. This seems to be a basic law of nature, fighting it out to the death, or life.

The exception to this rule would seem to be where another instinct, such as that of fear, proves stronger than the instinct which is being frustrated or denied. It has been said by some of my more aggressive patients that civilization is only possible through there being a vast majority of frightened people, too frightened to insist upon having their own way in life. It is not that they do not want to gratify their instincts, but something has arisen stronger than the instinct, namely fear, which has caused them to obey it rather than to fight for instinct gratification. Nevertheless it would seem that if it is fear rather than instinct gratification which brings the creature's energy, aggressive or otherwise, to a halt, then this is illness, in life, possibly something on the way to death. The creature has, in a sense, already given up life for fear he should lose it by trying to claim it.

I have been trying to keep these contrasting forms of behaviour or natural (psychological) laws on a primitive or instinct level. It will be seen how extremely difficult it is to do this consistently, as our minds have already become so complicated. The battle or war already goes on intra-psychically. We have introjected our parents and mentors in the form of superegos, and the battle between the desire for instinct gratification (or life) and the abandonment of this battle in the face of fear has, in itself, developed into a very complicated psychological situation. Not the least of these complications is the apparent symptom of substitution in which a primitive desire is abandoned in favour of a more civilized or more superego desire, such as that of gaining social kudos, originally parental approval. Then of course there is the further complication of the projection of the superego into ideologies and religions, and all the complications which this must lead to in cloaking the primitive or original situation.

To strip the original situation of all its cloaks and disguises may be to reduce the basic laws of psychological life almost to a formula, and the formula would be instinct striving towards gratification, meeting frustration, frustration being met first or last by a scientific method designed to remove it and failing this (or preceding this), by a mobilization of aggression to meet it, aggression being held in check by fear and the net result being a conflict between the instincts of aggression and fear, a conflict in which, if the aggression wins, life is fought out in an external life and death struggle, whereas if fear wins, life is fought out in an internal life and death struggle. The operation of these conflicting forces appears vividly during the analysis of all our patients.

In considering social habits and human behaviour in general, they may be classified from a point of view of source, in accordance with one or other of the ingredients from one of the three structural levels of the mind, id, superego and ego. It seems possible that there is another basic instinct or component of the id which is not to be ignored as a source of thought and action. The only debateable point may be whether this emotion or instinct should be regarded as a fundamental component of the id, or as a reaction to various levels of the psyche such as the ego to internal (id) or external sources of danger. I am referring to the emotion or instinct of fear. (This subject is dealt with more extensively in my book *Fear, Punishment, Anxiety and the Wolfenden Report*).

Paula Heimann concludes regarding the origin of anxiety with the following statement: 'Danger arising primarily within the organism provides the stimulus for the human being's innate capacity of fearing. This pattern may be regarded as the intra-psychic disposition for recognizing external dangers *and using against them defences learnt originally in the response to internal danger*.' (my italics).[14]

My own view is that these 'defences learnt originally in the response to internal danger' were even earlier, in the course of evolution, learnt by the more primitive organism as a reaction to *external* danger or frustration. The evolutionary pattern is that the organism, long before the arrival of psychic structure and perhaps long before the development of what we now call instincts, reacted to environmental frustration to its physicochemical re-adjustments, by some process (physicochemical or otherwise) which could be regarded as a precursor of aggression. At the same time an organism, frustrated in its metabolic physicochemical readjustment, may be conceived of as experiencing discomfort or tension, a precursor of anxiety. This would be an appropriate reaction as such a condition, if not remedied (if the frustration were not overcome), would be a movement towards death instead of the normal movement towards life. It is through millions of years of such experiences in the course of evolution that such intra-psychic ingredients which we are here discussing came about. In other words the external danger *preceded* and *initiated* the sensations of 'internal danger', which the psychoanalysts talk about.

My conception is an evolutionary as well as a developmental one, namely that reactive patterns, instincts, and all the ingredients of the psyche were gradually built up as a result of experience, including especially adaptation to environmental stimuli. When in the course of evolution inheritable internal reactive patterns have been acquired and passed on, whether in the form of instincts or indeed any intra-psychic content, including unconscious phantasy, then admittedly these enter into all new experiences or repetition of old experiences.

Thus it may become true to say, as do the psychoanalysts, that the position is reached when the psyche has internal sources of anxiety and uses defences which it has 'learnt originally in the response to internal danger', to assist it in recognizing and dealing with external dangers. The point I would make is that the reactive pattern of internal danger and defences against it has originally been acquired and built up and inherited in consequence of even earlier external dangers or frustrations, in the course of millions of years of experience. In short, the internal condition of the psyche is itself a register of aeons-long experience of response to environment, and adaptation.

What makes the responses or behaviour of present-day man in any community inappropriate to reality and in this sense psychotic, is the fact that he has built up a psyche of past experiences which, so far as community life is concerned, are obsolete and from a reality point of view inappropriate. Physiologically it may well be that he is tolerably well-adjusted to his environment. The build-up of environmental physicochemical reaction appears to enable him to survive today, but the build-up of psychological reaction formations, instincts, beliefs and customs is more appropriate for relieving internal psychological or physiological stresses and distresses rather than for any appreciation of reality, and belief and behaviour appropriate to it. In other words, his psyche is evolved essentially as an aid to or tool of his physiological needs, his need to reduce internal discomfort, including anxiety, and thereby to ensure or facilitate his physicochemical equilibrium. There is no reason to believe that he has an apparatus suitable or competent for a wider field of reality perception, judgement, or appropriate reality behaviour.

Thus we may expect to find what we do find, namely that his beliefs and customs are a consequence of psychological (fundamentally physiological) needs, without very much environmental or reality appreciation, and largely at variance with even that limited knowledge of reality with which science presents us. His behaviour in general, intra-psychically and socially, can be shown to be a response to internal needs of a homeostatic nature, and to include a distortion of reality in order to maintain such beliefs, and to rationalize his unreality behaviour.

This is never more conspicuous than in the field of social phenomena. These phenomena in particular seem to me symptomatic of psychotic processes in the individual psyche. Naturally this is most conspicuous to us when we study the social customs of primitive peoples, particularly savages, their (to us) obviously crazy rites, for instance human sacrifice, and insane superstitions and beliefs. It may prove more difficult, though not impossible, to convince civilized man that his beliefs and customs, including institutions are, if not totally insane, at least riddled with a superabundance of insane elements. Perhaps it is inevitable that this should be so, for it can be shown that they have evolved, and are designed essentially, for the purpose of projecting and relieving urges, tensions and conflicts which he had found impossible to tolerate without the aid of projection, socialization and institutionalization.

As with neuroses and psychoses, the intolerable feeling of anxiety is usually the immediate source of these symptomatic phenomena. Elliott Jaques writes: 'My own recent experience has impressed upon me how much institutions are used by their individual members to reinforce individual mechanisms of defence against anxiety, and in particular against recurrence of the early paranoid and depressive anxieties first described by Melanie Klein.'[19]

This author goes on to speak of such institutions, including also the 'gratification of libidinal impulses in constructive social activities'. I must point out however that the latter source or mechanism, like the former, is an expression of a psychological need rather than a reality evaluation or adaptation. Stress is laid particularly on human institutions having come into being as a 'defence against psychotic anxiety'. In short, those impulses and phantasies that would otherwise give rise to psychotic anxiety, become externalized or pooled in the form of the social institution, and thus I have authentic psychoanalytical support in regarding social institutions as a more or less symptomatic expression of human psychoses, and thus it is maintained that we would 'expect to find in group relationships manifestations of unreality, splitting, hostility, suspicion, and other forms of maladaptive behaviour'. It is further said that those individuals 'who have not developed the ability to use the mechanism of association in social groups to avoid psychotic anxiety' would manifest ordinarily recognizable psychotic symptoms, including those of anxiety, destruction, hostility and schizoid or schizophrenic manifestations.

The mechanism is typical of that of the production of neurotic and psychotic symptoms, namely that anxiety feelings, which are too strong to be consciously controlled, erupt together with the defences mobilized against them, into some form of symptomatic expression, in this instance a social form of manifest behaviour. Thus we see that as with neurotic and psychotic symptoms, anxiety and the conflicts and defences associated with it, are the dynamic source of symptom and social-symptom formation. Elliott Jaques says that intractability to change of social attitudes and behaviour can be 'seen as the "resistances" of groups of people unconsciously clinging to the institutions that they have, because changes in social relationships threaten to disturb existing social defences against psychotic anxiety'. It is alleged that 'individuals make unconscious use of institutions by associating in these institutions and unconsciously co-operating to reinforce internal defences against anxiety and guilt'. Thus he concludes: 'The character of institutions is determined and coloured not only by their explicit or consciously agreed and accepted functions, but also by their manifold unrecognized functions at the phantasy level.'

Analytical experience teaches us that this is true of practically all

social as well as socially institutionalized behaviour, certainly not
excluding political tenets, beliefs, discussions and controversy, but
there are some institutions and forms of social behaviour in which
these unconscious mechanisms are even more conspicuous than in
others, for instance, war. I am strongly of the opinion, and I think
nearly every analyst would agree, that the essential causative factor
in war springs entirely from the unconscious mind, particularly when
it has joined with other similar things in the unconscious minds of the
individuals comprising the community. If only it can be agreed by the
members of a community that some object such as another community
or nation is bad, the relief of the internal stresses of the minds of one
and all is not to be gained by any other environmental adjustment.

The need to relieve ourselves of our 'bad objects' and sadistic
impulses is infinitely greater than we commonly appreciate. If an
enemy can be found he can have the lot, and how gladly we project
them and discharge them into this new-found conjectural bad-object.
What is more, the process enables us, on the side of the gods as it were,
that is to say with the full approval of our superego and seduced ego,
to give vent to all the bad impulses, aggressive and sadistic, which we
have failed to project, and thus as it were temporarily at least we are
relieved of our unendurable uncomfortable internal conflict, and have
merely an external or reality one in place of it. The point is that this
reality conflict embodies the ingredients and the exact equivalent of
the previously endured internal conflict. It can now be seen and
reacted to on a reality plane. How mad it is from a point of view of our
adjustment to reality, and for that matter from the point of view of the
enemy's adjustment to reality is now plain for all who have eyes to see.
It takes a psychologist to point out that it is his symptomatic behaviour
revealing in a general sense nothing more or less than psychosis
within the mind which may previously have been invisible or at least
less visible. We escape neurotic and psychotic internal distress by
reality distress, which admittedly in this instance may turn out to be
just as bad. Remember, our internal condition is, to start with at
least, less bad, because we now have a fear of known and identifiable
enemies instead of a fear of unknown and invisible enemies, whose
psychic existence we may have been only too ready to deny but nevertheless very conscious of the fear or the intolerable state of morbid
anxiety or latent psychosis.

CHAPTER XI

WAR

War, on account of its potentially disastrous effects may be regarded as the most serious symptom of man's psychosis.

Speaking of the psychological appeal of war, J. C. Flugel tells us that it can be summarized under four main headings, Adventure, Social Unity, Freedom from Individual Worries and Restrictions, and the provision of outlets for aggression. As regards Adventure, he says: 'Civilization, we are often told, demands a dull routine to which we do not all take kindly and the eagerness with which we read "thrillers" and adventure stories shows that many of us retain throughout life some of that zest for adventure, for a life that is less settled and secure . . . we may . . . be called upon to perform some . . . heroic deed, like the exploits of the great figures of history, of romantic fiction, or the screen. This is connected with the increased possibility of risk and danger.' Apparently some of us are only too ready to discard the safety-first motto and to embrace the excitement of the 'spice of danger'.

Another factor which he claims has 'only become apparent as a result of psycho-analysis, consists in the satisfaction of what he calls 'the nemesistic urge and of the need for punishment so often associated with it'. Here he says the appeal of war is associated with sacrifice and asceticism. These urges have to do with a need for punishment or pain. Flugel adds: 'In war, moreover, there is always the hopeful possibility that the larger share of the punishment may be enjoyed vicariously through the sufferings of the enemy.'[24]

Speaking of the 'social unity' appeal, he says: 'War brings together all the members of a nation, inasmuch as it gives them a greatly increased number of thoughts, interests, emotions and purposes in common.' Competition between individuals, groups and classes gives place to a 'sense of co-operation'. There is a 'great common worthwhile purpose in which all can participate . . . war . . . has proved the most effective means of overcoming the economic problem of unemployment and of actually providing jobs for all'. He speaks of a condition of 'humility and happy pride'. Apparently all this makes war seem 'noble and uplifting and makes so many peace-time activities seem in comparison trivial and insignificant'. It gives us a wider freedom and 'for the time being holds out a prospect of id gratification without incurring guilt'.[24]

Last and certainly not least Flugel speaks of war as 'an outlet for moralized aggression. . . . Individual aggressiveness, whether it be in the nature of an "appetite" or a natural "reaction" to the inevitable frustrations of life, is itself constantly frustrated, and in its cruder manifestations is normally condemned, alike by the law, by the conventions of polite society, and by the superego. In war, however, aggression is provided with a channel that is ego-syntonic and socially approved, indeed socially demanded, and the individual is therefore willing and even eager to make use of it.' He provides us with the aphorism 'as a means of doing evil and of feeling good while doing it, war is without a parallel'.

Freud has similar views about the appeal of war when he says: 'Thus, when a nation is summoned to engage in war, a whole gamut of human motives may respond to this appeal; high and low motives, some openly avowed, others slurred over. The lust for aggression and destruction is certainly included; the innumerable cruelties of history and man's daily life confirm its prevalence and strength. The stimulation of these destructive impulses by appeals to idealism and the erotic instinct naturally facilitates their release.'[25]

Edward Glover in his book *War, Sadism and Pacifism* tries similarly to trace the psychopathology of this social (or anti-social) phenomenon. He says: 'It is obvious that war impulses can be identified with the impulses of destruction . . . war provides perhaps the most dramatic piece of evidence that destructive impulses can be completely divorced from biological aims and pursue individual ends.'[26]

Tracing these outward manifestations to their intrapsychic source, Glover says, I think very relevantly: '*The instinctual enemy is internal and unknown.* . . . Projection implies a psychic displacement; *an attempt to convert an inner (psychic) stimulus into an outer (reality) stimulus, an inner enemy into an outer enemy.* It is one of the oldest of mental mechanisms, it serves a useful purpose in emergencies, but its retention as an adult mechanism is one of the greatest dangers to existing civilization. *And it operates with especial vigour in most group relations* . . . we know from the animistic systems of the savage, that he has peopled the external world with evil spirits, *a projection of the primitive impulses he has such difficulty in mastering:* and he believes himself to be in constant danger of attack from these dangerous and malevolent beings. The little child, of course, does practically the same. . . . *We can vaguely apprehend in this externalization of conflict a phase of biological adaptation.*'[26]

Alix Strachey goes into the regressive mechanism inseparable from the process of group psychology.[21] It would seem that what was originally a healthy process, namely the process whereby an individual attaches himself to objects or persons (the first instance being that of the infant attaching himself to his parents), can subsequently become a potentially unhealthy process. In short, having developed his own individual superego by means of this 'healthy' process, and become accustomed to relieving his tensions by symptomatic behaviour expressive of the balance of forces contained in his individual conflicts, the influence of a group can and does have an ego-dystonic effect. It would seem that he is only too ready to hand over his superego, as it were, to the group, thereby evidently getting rid of a great deal of its restrictive influences.

He regresses to the more primitive mentality of the group and by virtue of a relative absence of superego and relative id support and encouragement, gains courage to exchange his individual relatively restricted behaviour for the freedom permitted in unison by the group. His mental condition has regressed to a more primitive stage of development, in common with that of other members of the group, and behaviour which would be intolerable for the individual is now encouraged or enjoined. It may be said that he has exchanged his personal 'symptoms' for those of a more primitive animal, or combination of animals called 'the group'.

By dint of this regression they may seem to us even more obviously insane. As Strachey says, the regressive process is not limited to behaviour but naturally affects belief and thought and perhaps every element of mental functioning, including unfortunately a considerable weakening of ego control and reason.

She goes on to say: 'On top of this, it must be remembered that members of regressive groups have actually more destrudo in their mental composition than have individuals in their private capacity, from the very fact of having regressed to an earlier developmental stage.

'Furthermore, the ties of mental dependence and of identification which the member forms as well with persons within his group detract from the strength of similar ties which he has formed with persons outside it. This, if it does not increase his *hostility* to the latter, does increase his *indifference*. And it decreases the efforts he makes to inhibit his hostility.

'All this, it is obvious, makes groups that are powerful a serious potential danger to the outside world, and history is full of its struggles, sometimes successful sometimes not, to keep them in their place.'[21]

I have quoted this extract, as it seems to me to be the most important contribution that Alix Strachey has made in the whole of her long book expounding *The Unconscious Motives of War*.

History tells us of the long succession of leaders who could so inflame the emotions of a mob, small or large, influencing them in the first place to identify him with their ideals or moral values, then playing upon their emotions, inducing them to hand over their superegos, as it were, to his custody and then having no difficulty in bringing about the most insane of all insane collective behaviour, namely that of war.

The mechanism which we have been discussing at some length, though essential as a factor in war between groups or nations, is of course not in itself a primary determinant. There is the most important and most neglected of all scientific considerations effecting humanity, namely the natural biological phenomenon of increasing birthrate. Flugel says: 'It is commonly implied that any nation with a high birth rate, and therefore a real or potential rapid increase of population, has a right (if it has the necessary power) to demand fresh territories for its overflow. Except in the rare cases where unexploited land is actually available, such a notion must inevitably lead to war.'[24]

History, including recent history, shows us very vividly this natural phenomenon at work.

We have seen that so far as individual psychology is concerned there are a million factors which, if they do not actually drive the individual to promote a national war, certainly drive him to embrace such a movement with alacrity as though it were a solution of all his problems. One feels that however great or small the reality factors determining war may be, the existence of these psychological forces in the minds of people (and indeed of all living creatures), are held in leash only by the relatively weak hand of reason. But may we perhaps be heartened by the thought that this relatively weak hand, which has, time and again, throughout the history of the world failed to control these forces, has in very recent times been enormously reinforced by an 'instinct' which can be even more powerful—namely *fear*. The study of animals as well as of man shows us that if anything can control the impulses and instincts of a creature or group of creatures, it is, above all else, fear. Fear or pain, of injury, or annihilation, or rather fear of the certainty of annihilation. The effectiveness of this as an international force in the present day would only depend on individuals, and nations, great and small, having or acquiring sufficient knowledge and reason to leave them with no doubt whatever regarding the consequence to themselves of unleashing aggression.

Unfortunately, a further consideration comes in here, perhaps several considerations. One is that there are, and always have been, individuals and perhaps groups or nations who court not only a risk of death but even a certainty of it. Another and perhaps equally important consideration is that emotional pressure, if sufficiently powerful, has been known to break through any and every repressive barrier.

Turning to the dynamic contents of the individual's unconscious mind, which is the source from which all energy drives originate, we should first consider the beginning of these drives in infancy and childhood. Ernest Jones has told us that practically every stimulus

which the new-born baby encounters from its environment feels to it
unpleasant if not actually painful. Thus it would naturally tend at
first to be provoked into feelings of hate, anger or aggression, and to
regard its environment as bad. Be this as it may, there is no doubt that
children feel a great deal more hate than the adult appreciates.
Naturally they do not express their hatred by aggression, because they
know that at the best it will only expose their weakness and make
them appear ridiculous. Therefore children bottle up their impotent
hate or rage . . . until in later life war offers them a chance of getting
their own back. They have a great deal to get back, for adults have
doubtless given them a raw deal throughout their lives, including
even in their later childhood the disciplines of school and cultural
indoctrination.

It is not every horse that can be trained to endure a harness, and it
is not every individual who can beneficially be trained to accept the
restrictions of culture. Perhaps it would be truer to say that none can
be trained fundamentally, only apparently, and perhaps that is why
we have wars. Even if we do succeed in controlling ourselves when
there is little or nothing to upset the balance of forces inside or outside, it is usually only a question of the degree of stimulus when the
balance will be upset and a disproportionate amount of aggression
released. There are a very large number of people who are over-
sensitized to even a modicum of hostility on the part of anybody
around them, and who will in consequence react with a disproportionate degree of aggression or rage.

A patient said to me 'If somebody, anybody, shows some ill-
temper, my reaction will be ill-temper with a vengeance.'

The truth about this patient is even worse than this. If anybody so
much as corrects him or tries to tell him anything, or is in any way
self-assertive, he will react as though he had been violently attacked
and had to fight back for his life. At the same time he naturally
projects all the responsibility and guilt on to the other person. A
striking case like this brings to one's notice how general such reactive
patterns are in practically all persons, although they are certainly not
always so evident as in this man. He says: 'I never know when I am
going to be snapped at, therefore I am on the alert all the time, ready
to knock the other person's block off. . . .'

It was pointed out to this patient that he was unwittingly *creating*
an environment that attacks him and thus 'confirms' his unconscious
phantasy or illusion of conflict or war. He replied: 'So certain am I
that *you* want to attack me that it is a relief for me to get at you, to
attack you and to get the thing over. What a relief it would be for me
to tell that contemptible black-guard (so-and-so) what I think of
him . . . and indeed to tell all the rest of them what I think of them.'

The point about this clinical excerpt is to show that whereas this man is actually tending to create a hostile (or war-like) atmosphere, he is firmly convinced that he is not the aggressor but the victim, fighting back for his self-respect or very life. The tendencies to a similar reactive pattern are far more widespread than we realize, and are probably only precariously held in check by reason and public opinion. Of course they are no longer held in check when public opinion encourages them. It brings to our notice that because there was hostility there between the child and parent, and subsequently intrapsychically between the id and superego (introjected parents) once upon a time (in infancy), we were endowed with a permanent state of tension, unconsciously watching or hoping for an opportunity for relief in battle.

This is brought out even more clearly in the case of another male patient of mine in the following words: 'The perennial trouble of my whole life is that I can never find a *causus belli,* but deep within me there is always a gun panting to go off. My life is spent in trying to prevent it from going off, but as a result I have this intolerable tension locked up inside me, enough to drive me mad.'

A moment's reflection may cause us to think how eagerly such a man would seize upon any *causus belli* that presented itself. Indeed, one might have reason to fear that he would be driven to imagine one, or to seize upon an illusion in the absence of a reality, but the point is that once objectively or subjectively a justification or excuse presented itself, what an enormous relief he would experience in being able to let the 'panting gun' have its way, and all the 'intolerable tensions' bottled up inside him explode outwardly. Perhaps any amount of external destruction would seem warranted for the sake of the internal relief at long last experienced.

The analyst may see an analogy (or even a basic pattern) between this phenomenon and many physical processes inherent in the nature of life. For instance, the impulse of man or any mammal to discharge the contents of a loaded rectum cannot be withstood indefinitely without an intolerable internal condition arising, comparable to that which this man describes in connection with his aggressive impulses. Perhaps one has, in the capacity of a doctor, to meet a case of intestinal obstruction to appreciate fully that the inherent peristaltic movement of the bowels will not be gainsaid indefinitely. A rising compulsion automatically takes place and if movement in the normal direction is definitely obstructed, the bowel does not relax its efforts but even reverses its peristalsis and endeavours to eject its contents in the opposite direction. The automatic forces of life are as powerful as this.

If we consider the two instincts sex and aggression, it may be said that within the social structure some provision is made for sexuality, whether sublimated or not, whereas little or no provision is made for the discharge of aggressive or destructive impulses, except perhaps by means of very tenuous and highly-sublimated sublimations. This probably means that the greater part of these forces, as in the case of this patient, has to be permanently countered by pain-giving repressing forces. If there is always 'a gun panting to go off', and no *causus belli* to be found to relieve the tension, surely the mind of man with its ingenuity will not only be looking for *causus belli* but ever and anon will find one, or persuade himself that he has found one. Anyway, his mental dice would be loaded and this 'discovery' is essentially for the purpose of releasing the gun, as he cannot bear the tension of holding the explosion back any longer.

I think most psychologists would agree that this is the psychological basis of war. In the light of these considerations, there would not seem to be much hope of peace everlasting, unless it has the epitaph R.I.P. upon it. Tanks will go on filling up, and on account of metabolical or physiological functions, explosions will continue to take place, both in the service of life and of death. Psychoanalysis tells us 'the infant . . . simultaneously experiences and seeks to satisfy libidinal and destructive impulses . . . from the beginning of life (he) is under the influence of the two primary instincts of life and death. Their derivatives in the form of self-preservative and libidinal impulses on the one hand and of destructive and cruel cravings on the other are active from the beginning of life.'[19]

Every person who is analyzed reveals sooner or later that he or she has, for the sake of parental love, domestic and social felicity, for the sake of civilization, in short for the sake of peace, *repressed* a great deal, if not all, of his or her aggressive and destructive impulses. Psychoanalysis would group these under the general heading of death instinct. It appears that the death or destructive instinct is responsible not only for death and destruction, but for every psychosis, neurosis, physical, social and every other ill. According to Melanie Klein it is the primary source of anxiety, and through that of everything that makes for illness.

An unconscious factor in the promotion of war which is certain to escape notice by all except analysts is the ambisexuality of all persons, and the consequent 'need' of males, generally speaking, to repress and deny the existence of their feminine component, in the same way as females generally repress and deny or disguise their masculine component. Even the boy is not exempt from having to make war against his unconscious opposite attitudes. That is why he is often so 'over-masculinized', boastful, pseudo-aggressive, deprecatory of feminine attributes, and so on. Very often he is busily, or even violently denying his attraction to male persons, for at all costs he must reveal no femininity even if he has to burst himself making a display of being a superman.

Apparently it is not enough that his feminine component should be repressed from consciousness and denied, he must do better than that and actively demonstrate that he has so much maleness that it would be ridiculous to suspect him of even a modicum of femininity. Of course the whole thing is an unconscious process largely determined, as psychoanalysis has shown, by a defence against unconscious phantasies not only of femininity but also of castration.

Thus we get the reactive formations and over-compensation. As Alix Strachey says: 'The boy makes himself extra manly, or makes himself out to be more manly than he is, and he puts away all girlish things with high and noisy contempt. In this way we see that the phallic boy's excessive masculinity is nearly always not only a protest against the possibility of castration and internal injury, but against his own desire for them or what entails them.'[21] She adds: 'Here we have a Nazi type in the making.'

This remark may remind us that the whole build-up of Nazi Germany, and perhaps particularly of its leader, was largely determined by these unconscious but none the less forceful motives. One can see also how the consumption of this extra manliness might well express itself in such phenomena as coat-trailing, picking a quarrel at the cannon's mouth, sabre rattling, and finally finding oneself precipitated into war. This would be just one instance where an internal conflict has attained an external dramatization.

Even more important than the foregoing is the general prevalence of paranoia amongst apparently normal or near-normal people. It is worth drawing attention to, if only for the fact that it is the source of so much misery, friction and 'war' in both private life and public. It commonly escapes diagnosis. Suttie rightly says that paranoia is distinguished (commonly) by 'great force of personality'.[32] This, together with the support of logical and intellectual faculties sometimes presents such a strong personality, instead of the sane atmosphere around the individual tending to make him more sane, he often has a tendency to make them embrace and believe in his delusions. In other words, he cannot be a follower and is liable to become a dangerous leader. More strong-minded people than are generally recognized have at least a minor element of paranoid characteristic about them. His tendency is often to attribute all his own bad characteristics to other people, or some other person, and make him a scapegoat while he identifies himself with the self-righteous avenger. One can see how dangerous such a mental mechanism is in the promotion of war, for then there is a nation-wide conspiracy to project all bad things on to the scapegoat of an enemy, which naturally makes nothing too bad for him, and lends much strength to one's own elbow.

Before we become too contemptuous let us remember that almost all so-called normal persons have divided not only themselves but the entire universe into concentrations of good properties on the one hand and bad on the other, in some beliefs designated as god and devil respectively. As Strachey reminds us 'The mechanism of projection is very primitive and occurs in early infancy.'

There are few situations better than that of war to facilitate the unloading of the tensions and bad objects in the unconscious of the individuals who comprise a nation. As Elliott Jacques says: 'The members of each community put their bad objects and sadistic impulses into the commonly shared and accepted external enemy. They rid themselves of their hostile, destructive impulses by projecting them into their armies for deflection against the enemy. Paranoid anxiety in the total community, Army and civilian alike, may be alleviated, or at least transmuted into fear of known and identifiable enemies, since the bad impulses and objects projected into the enemy return, not in the form of introjected phantastic persecutors, but of actual physical attack, which can be experienced in reality. Under the appropriate conditions, objective fear may be more readily coped with than phantasy persecution. The bad sadistic enemy is fought against, not in the solitary isolation of the unconscious inner world, but in co-operation with comrades-in-arms in real life.'[19]

After listening to large quantities of analytical material from every degree of paranoid and 'normal' person, my reflection is that this is a universal disease. (Practically every person, however 'normal', who comes for analysis, sooner or later gets on to protracted vituperative abuses of his parents, as being responsible for all his miseries and troubles). We might call it a manner of seeing the truth according to our own feelings and emotions. One may question whether anybody is capable of truly objective judgement.

The point is that this applies not only to individuals but perhaps more obviously to entire nations. International differences in idealogies and political opinions are notorious. The most important reflection is this: does a nation ever go to war for an avowedly 'bad' object? I think not. Invariably a nation that goes to war does so for justice, goodness and truth, or some equally high principle, just as we punish and even hang people for justice, perhaps in the same way that they (if they are anything like my paranoid patients) murdered some bad person or other, out of their own sense of indignation or justice. Interestingly enough, its opponent, in the case of nations, is equally strongly motivated by similarly high and incontrovertible principles, thus one or other or both of them must be to some degree mistaken, deluded or paranoid.

One is tempted to ask whether the only incontrovertible principle is what is good for oneself. Perhaps the highest principle is the preservation, aggrandizement or enrichment of oneself, whether or not it includes the opposite effects on the opposing party.

While the mind is so constructed, is it likely that quarrels and wars will cease?

In other words, we have not been mistaken in regarding the phenomenon of war as symptomatic of psychosis. All that we have missed is that the psychopathology responsible for this flagrant manifestation of mental illness is not confined to international, civil or any other war, but is present in a greater or lesser degree in all individuals, groups and nations all the time. In other words war is but one, albeit a particularly incontrovertible and disastrous one, of the innumerable manifestations of what might be called the normal psychosis of all people, individually and collectively.

What we have been discussing in this chapter is chiefly mechanisms, albeit very primitive and early mechanisms, leading to certain forms of manifestation of internal tensions, specifically the manifestation of war. But we should not lose sight of the fact that mechanisms are not identical with sources. The primary source from which these mechanisms receive their dynamic force is nearer to the instinctual level, the id reservoir of dynamic energy. Our morbid processes begin with the need imposed by society and civilization to hold in or repress our instinctual impulses or drives. It is the ensuing conflict between opposing forces that results in indirect rather than direct forms of behaviour, forced upon us as it were in order to relieve degrees of tension which are otherwise found to be intolerable.

The details of this process and its psychopathology are most clearly revealed during some of our analytical sessions. The following excerpt will serve as an illustration. A very virile male patient told me that he had had the following dream: 'I dreamt that my girl-friend (of many years standing) had joined some people who were hostile to me. I had in my hand a leather handle torn off a bag, and I said to her, "I've a damn good mind to give you a beating with this".' He went on to say that before the dream he had had sexual relations with her, and after it had experienced a feeling which had been growing during the past few months. Instead of experiencing a satisfaction, he experienced increasingly a feeling of deflation, or to use his own words: 'Making love to her has come to feel more and more as though I am flirting with castration.' The handle torn off the bag of course symbolizes castration. 'I am sure it is because I am trying to repress the feeling that she is becoming more and more hostile to me. Therefore making love to her feels like surrendering to an enemy (castration). I have been trying to repress this from consciousness, but the dream brings it out in suggesting that she has joined people who are hostile to me.'

He goes on to say: 'All this threatened to come to a head the other day in a restaurant. We had a bit of a row. I said to her: "I don't like you any more". Then I realized that giving vent to my feelings like this would lead to one of those terrible rows that would ruin the evening, and make us miserable for days. Therefore I deliberately checked the expression of my hostile feelings, I was quite conscious of the process. I suddenly clamped down on it, and held it all inside me. I could see that she checked her hostility also, so that we could have a nice evening. After all, we had gone there to dance. But what I wanted to tell you was this: directly I suppressed my impulse to go for her, *I felt sick.*'

At this point the patient leapt from the settee and started shouting: 'I need more freedom. It's holding up the whole of my life, keeping myself in this sort of straight-jacket, it is as if I have had enough of all this, enough of being here, and enough of this girl, and enough of the whole bloody thing. *It's maddening.* The same old feeling was coming up again last night when I had the dream. I wanted to beat her. I know that you stand for my controlling myself, that is why I got off the couch, I was getting no more relief. What you call control, holding myself in, merely means that I am feeling slightly sick and must relieve it by walking about all over London.'

After he had calmed down a bit, the patient continued: 'It is aggression I suppose that one cannot get out. But this aggression of mine is my health. It is the health that I am keeping in. I am living in a world that is too ill for me. If I could have more freedom, freedom in sex and freedom to be aggressive, I could be well. The row that I had, or nearly had, with this girl started because I felt that she was on the side of the illness. That is why making love to her is no good. Yes, I know that we have been compelled to hold in our instinct pressures, especially aggression, civilization must be preserved even if it leads to a pain in the stomach. We all keep up this ridiculous pretence, pretending we are all nice people. Everybody is looking at the thing from the back of the neck to avoid seeing the truth. Nice people! *I know* that they are restless, I know that they are *not* really contented. The emphasis is all on taboos which create the morbidity, instead of on the instinct freedom. If they get any instinct freedom, sex or a fight, they get relief, but directly it is over they sit in a chair being nice and denying the whole thing. They are living on two levels, liars and hypocrites. I can feel that something wants to be healthy, that is the life instinct, *but* something is denying it, that is the death instinct. It is aggression held in and destroying health, and making me like all the others, an ill person. In attempting to make mankind sane and reasonable, all you and those like you are doing is to make an ill world, and probably it will lead to a more complete destruction that way. I can see how it works. Repressing one's aggression in order to preserve civilization leads to everybody seizing upon the social permission to let it out in war. I would rather have a war than be torn up inside with a pain in my stomach.'

Having leapt into philosophy, the patient continues: 'It seems to

me that having seen how bad wars are, people have seen that they
have got to invent something even worse than their own aggression
. . . and scientists have found it in the atom bomb. That is something
so bad that nobody will start this thing, or people who start it will be
the first to be wiped out.'

The material from this session may cause us to reflect that the process of living in itself mobilizes and utilizes our aggresive instincts, if
only to overcome the frustrations of living. This man is different only
in degree, in so far as his aggression appears to be so dynamic that he
could restrain it only at the expense of internal visceral disturbances.
He is revealing particularly vividly the familiar psychological conflict
between instinctual or id pressure on the one hand and indoctrinated
repressive forces on the other. In his case the energy involved in the
conflict, if unrelieved outwardly, disturbs his internal physiology. The
object of recording this analytical excerpt is to suggest that it is
different from normality only in so far as it shows up in vivid relief
what is less conspicuous but none the less present in normal psychological and physiological functioning. Like quarrels, rows and fights,
war is one of the symptomatic expressions of this conflict.

To show that this case is by no means unique, I will quote from the
session of another male patient. He said: 'Before they made me ill like
this, life felt so wonderful. I felt that Mother would want me. I even
felt that she would approve of my murdering my father and the other
children, so that she would recognize how wonderful I was and want
that wonderful me, especially when all the others were out of the way.
The world would be strewn with their corpses, and then she too
turned on me. When I was well (as a baby) I knew that *my* needs were
paramount. They were equivalent to life. To forego them was
equivalent to death. The tragedy that made me ill was that the facts
would not conform with the feelings. I suppose you would say that I
am still alive today . . . but it is a living death. I have lost the fight.
The feelings inside me might be expressed by saying that I was
fighting not for *my* life, but for *Life,* for God's life.' (Perhaps he was
identifying himself with God).

What few people and even many psychotherapists do not adequately realize, is the enormous quantity of repressed hate and destructive
impulses, not to mention libidinal impulses, which everybody has
inside him or her, and which few patients succeed in fully discharging.
Commonly the patient will say to the analyst: 'But if I freely express
what I feel and think, you could not stand it, but you would turn me
out.' More commonly they do not say this, because they do not even
realize it. They will only get well or better in proportion to the amount
of freedom they achieve in their analytical sessions.

Sooner or later, and usually later rather than sooner, most patients
arrive at a stage of analysis which is called the negative transference.

The great task of the analyst is to remove the last resistances to a free expression of this negative transference, which consists of the accumulated hate and destructive impulses of his or her whole life. Therapists who talk about short methods, hypnoanalysis, and some quick or magical way to the patient's unconscious, have not fully appreciated the full blast which the patient is holding in so as not to destroy himself, or more relevantly on account of his phantasy that he himself will be destroyed in the process. It takes a long time for the patient to gain enough courage for his resistances, unconscious as well as conscious ones, to be lessened sufficiently for the real nuclear forces of his unconscious to be permitted an adequate discharge.

Speaking from the point of view of the analyst, I may say it is only when one receives the full blast of hate, fury, murderous and destructive feelings and impulses that one can appreciate the psychological material out of which nervous and mental ill-health, and physical disease and death are made. It is the same stuff out of which murder and war are made. We have seen how if bottled up it can cause abdominal pain, and how if let out it can stimulate hatred, battle or war in its recipient. Of course the analyst should not be surprised when he gets the full blast of this sort of thing, but it commonly happens that he gets it from patients from whom he erroneously least expected it to come. Probably it is there in everybody, more strongly locked up in some than in others. To think that one can do psychotherapy and avoid this sort of thing is to live in a 'therapeutic' world of nursery tales in the presence of potential atomic bomb explosions.

When my patient tells me 'deep within me there is always a gun panting to go off', it is easy enough for the analyst to sit calmly, interested, making his clinical notes, but when, as sooner or later happens, in all analyses if they are to be successful, this gun is turned upon the analyst with all the patient's intellectual resources rationalizing 'causes' why he should hate the analyst and reduce him to dust, it is certainly not easy to take clinical notes while the patient is shouting.

The patient will himself believe that his reactions are to the current situation, and his relationship to the analyst, and it is sometimes almost impossible to make him realize that he is living his repressed early past in the present situation. Of course, as a baby he was inarticulate, and as an infant and small child he would not have dared to let anything like this reveal itself, his phantasy being that any hint of murderous impulses in him detected by parent figures would result in immediate and annihilating retribution. He has now gained courage to blow off his gun, using the analyst as the Aunt Sally for all the past miscreants throughout his life. The process is often not only impossible to exaggerate regarding its intensity, but also incredibly protracted and apparently inexhaustible. An inexperienced analyst may even wonder whether it were not best to have left the patient within the prison walls of his own superego, than to have invited or encouraged all this madness to blow to pieces the environment and the analyst with it.

Now the point I want to make is that the basic drives are lifelong and age-old, and consequently that their restriction by the environment, including of course parents, civilization and superego, is at least lifelong. As we have seen from some of our case material, the alternative often appears to be omnipotence of the id (or the child within the psyche), that is to say, libidinal and aggressive gratification without any inhibitions, including rape, murder and all the rest of it, versus a feeling, something which in its extreme can amount to a feeling of annihilation including castration, suffocation and an obliteration of all the drives of life.

In most individuals a certain amount of compromise must be achieved between these two extremes. The symptomatic behaviour of life is an expression of a compromise, very often sometimes including a greater proportion of the one (id) and sometimes a greater proportion of the other (superego). It would seem that we go through life in this peculiar and apparently unsatisfactory fashion.

Maybe we are like people sitting on the concealed crater of a volcano, very often not even knowing that it is there, but something in us knowing enough to cause us to feel some degree of discomfort and perhaps to experience various forms of behaviour all of which are unwittingly designed to reduce our internal tension. If they have ego consent we are justified in calling them symptomatic behaviour. If they do not have ego consent, but operate irrespective of the ego, or against it, they are simply symptoms, neurotic, psychotic or physical. It may be that the analogy of the volcano is not too inept, for there is no doubt that they are forces which sooner or later will encompass our demise, and return us to the original inorganic state.

CHAPTER XII

POLITICS AND PUNISHMENT

An analysis of the unconscious psychopathology of the phenomenon of war would show us that the unconscious elements involved include an attempt to get back to a lost paradise which involved perfect comfort and gratification, inseparable from omnipotence. In symbolical form it might be described as an attempt to get back to mother's breast, since the loss of which we have had nothing but unhappiness and torture. To overcome the frustrations in the way of reaching this Elysium, we are apparently prepared, or even compelled, to murder everything that stands in the way, including particularly fathers and brothers. It is as though we cannot bear the torments of frustration any longer, and must at any risk to our lives fight to attain complete id-omnipotence, removing all frustrations in order to do so. In short, we are merely acting out our Oedipus complex so long restrained, repressed or held in check. It is an institutionalized and nationalized form of what in the first or earliest family groups presented itself as the son killing the father who barred his way to the female, or even the pre-human form of the young bull destroying the ageing leader of the herd, or the younger stag destroying the older in the breeding season. These biological forces may be seen to have found their way into the most organized and institutionalized forms of human and national behaviour. To be more correct, I should say not that they have found their way into this, but are indeed the very forces and mechanisms responsible for its development.

The imposition of civilization, like the imposition of the superego, may be seen to represent an attempt, emotionally powered, to counteract these more primitive biological mechanisms. It would seem that with the progress of evolution, a modicum of countering force is gradually being brought into the picture to check and to modify the old patterns of behaviour. The result is the painful process of endeavouring to accept a greater and greater amount of instinct frustration, in favour of subservience to parent figures, superegos, civilization, and larger and larger group organizations. I regard this as the most recent of all biological processes, a process whereby an individual, a multicellular animal, is being forced to sacrifice a certain amount of his individuality in order to accommodate himself to a larger multi-individual 'organism'. It seems to me that going back very far in biological evolution, we may conceive of single cells having to sacrifice a considerable part of their liberty of movement, function and action, in order to attain the advantages of division of labour, protection and security. To my mind that is a biological process evidently inherent in the nature of life, or indeed in the whole principle of evolution; and this incorporation of individuals into groups and nations is a less evident process of the same principle at work. My contention is that this is a blind principle, and that reason is merely the latest and most insignificant contributor to it.

A lot of analytical material from a variety of patients makes it hardly possible for the analyst to avoid seeing that in the House of Commons the standard activity of argument and counter-argument, of cut and thrust, of boos and cheers, reveals that the whole process is emotionally determined and has little or nothing to do with science or truth. Innumerable analogies between social and political institutions on the one hand and intra-psychic structure on the other could be drawn, and I feel the exercise would not be an idle one, or irrelevant to an understanding of the evolutional development of the increasingly large social or national group from, shall we say, the individual animal or family group. For instance, one can see that there is an analogy between the Lower House, and the emotional conflicts connected with the id on the one hand, and the Upper House, and the superego on the other hand, not confined to the special vetoing function of the latter.

If anything were needed to prove that the political process is emotionally determined, and has little or nothing to do with science or truth, the history of legislation provides it in abundance, and upon almost every subject that one cares to mention. Take for instance the votes for women campaign of a generation or two ago. Unless we have accepted my view of emotional rather than logical determinants, this makes incredible reading today. The resistances that were mobilized against this obviously equable measure, the illogicality of the limitless arguments debated and even written up in books, and perhaps one might add the equally illogical behaviour of the advocates, reveals beyond any shadow of doubt that the pros as well as the cons, the cons as well as the pros, were determined purely by emotional forces causing the resulting battle to be solely emotional, often with palpably absurd rationalizations brought in, showing that reason was regarded simply as the tool in the service of emotions.

After years of obstruction, including sadistic activities and medical tortures of women almost amounting to martyrdom, it took the First World War to bring about a modicum of concession to reasonableness. Some say it was by dint of the women in the armed forces that the vote was won (more probably it was the belated effects of the

sado-masochistic struggle), but it is worth remembering that even
then this concession to reason was absurdly grudging. The vote was
given only to women of thirty years of age or over, thus excluding the
war-workers who were alleged to have won it. The emotional bias
against equal franchise was still alive.

I have quoted this as merely one instance to illustrate that political
struggles are emotionally determined, and not scientifically or
rationally. Probably every political struggle, not excluding civil war,
if subjected to scientific examination, would reveal corresponding
mechanisms. There is such a strong psychological tendency to create
good objects or good causes with which we identify ourselves, and to
regard the opposition as bad objects or bad causes, so that we can
then, exercise our reactive pattern, championing the good and fighting and trying to destroy the bad. The minority group is particularly
prone to feel the weight of hostility from the majority group, though
this is not always the case.

The psychopathology of many of these mechanisms can be over-
simplified by suggesting that 'bad' depends upon which structural
element in the intra-psychic conflict the ego decides to support. If we
regard the classical intra-psychic conflict as that between id and
superego, and the ego decides to support the id, it will then regard
superegos and all that it can identify with superegos as the enemy or
bad object, and want to fight them by dialectic and other means, as
though it were removing a bad object from the face of the earth. On
the other hand, if the ego takes the side of the superego it is apt to
regard objects which it identifies with the id as bad objects, unruly,
undisciplined, dirty, contemptible, of a distinctly lower order, and
often positively dangerous. Thus it will build up ramparts against
them.

This is an over-simplification because in the minds of most people
there is a certain amount of ambivalence, nothing is quite black or
white, but certain modifications and vacillations are apt to occur.
Something of the sort may be seen in cases where a person, towards
whom some ambivalence existed during his life (and this probably
applies to every person), has at least deceased. Our behaviour then
is as though our hatred of him, however much repressed, had killed
him. We bury this hatred with his body in our funeral rites, and
endeavour to preserve only the good object part of him. There are
unconscious superstitions (if I may use such a phrase) that the soul
which animated the person is not extinguished, but that it may still
do bad things to those who entertained hostile thoughts (however
unconscious) towards him. Although we do not openly avow such
beliefs as does primitive man, our behaviour shows that to some
extent they have not disappeared. Referring to the soul of the dead
person, Alix Strachey says: 'It is a ghost that passes through . . . solid

walls . . . to punish the living who have destroyed its body. . . . Or it actually enters their body, unknown to them, and does terrible things to them inside. Small wonder that so much of the funeral rites are designed to placate the dead one and to prevent him from doing a mischief to the living. Nowadays we throw a handful of dust upon the coffin to keep the corpse from arising and coming back, and in other places stones are still piled upon a grave for this purpose.'[21]

I would add that not content with this, we are in the habit of placing a heavy gravestone to ensure that there shall be no malignant resurrection, or better still in the modern fashion we prefer to cremate all the remains and be done with it. Alix Strachey alleges that: 'We wear black not only to express grief for our lost ones but to disguise ourselves so that they shall not recognize us if they should come back to do us harm. In some parts of Bohemia the mourners are still more thorough and put masks over their faces.'[21]

What may be lost sight of is that all this is fully in keeping with the regular practices of our social behaviour. Politeness amounts to a denial, perhaps very necessary, of the repressed opposite tendencies. We are saying all the time, 'No, we are not aggressive, we do not want to get the better of you, we do not want to take advantage of you for selfish ends. On the contrary, it is your welfare, not ours, which we wish to promote.' So strong is the repressed negative (transference) within us that we dare not meet a friend or acquaintance and stand or sit silently with him. Generally speaking we must make haste to reassure each other that we are not entertaining hostile impulses. The implication is that silence, or nothingness, would very soon be filled with phantasies of hostility. Better that the conversation should be absolutely neutral than absent, but in general we prefer to express some denials of hostility, such as 'I hope you are well', and so on.

Every item of our social behaviour has interesting symbolical meanings. Taking off the hat, as the analysis of the dreams of our analysands show us, is symbolical of castrating oneself, removing all our id, libidinal and aggressive, to deny any unwelcome tendencies and to promote the other person's positive relationship to ourselves. Bowing and curtseying are similarly symbolical, indicating that we surrender absolutely to the will of the other party. In a large proportion of people, except in those who have suffered, or imagine they have suffered by being debarred from positions of privilege, there is usually a tendency for the ego to identify itself with the superego, if only to exhibit to parent images and society how superior one has become to the infant or delinquent of one's nursery days. Many persons have a tendency to align themselves with the more powerful, or imagined to be more powerful, parent equivalents, and from this superior position to denigrate all who have fallen even a little short of the height which they imagine they have achieved.

This is the psychopathological basis of snobbery, a more superego-imbued variety of class war. Its psychopathology includes the nursing of an illusion we are no longer ids, but have now become superegos, something far superior, as the parents and society always taught us it was. Sometimes this psychosis can reach such a degree of intensity, that the individual appears almost to believe that he or she is without a body, a sort of disembodied soul floating above mere biological organisms! There is probably more of this in all of us than we are prepared to recognize. It is part and parcel of the conflict against intrusions of our early repudiated id tendencies. We can see it quite strongly in schoolchildren, maybe only because they have less ingenuity in concealing it.

The question may be asked as to why it is so important that we should be identified with superegos and repudiate ids, and for that matter why some other persons should wish to be identified with ids, and show hostility to superegos. No doubt it all goes back to the battle between infant and parents, between id and superego, and which side in that battle we have decided to adopt, or pretend to adopt, as our own.

The matter is not always so clear cut as I have indicated, but it has many ramifications into all aspects of our social life. For instance, there are few people who want to be identified with a delinquent or criminal class. Indeed, practically all of us want to be so sure that we will never be suspected of being as iddish as all that, that we cannot be too severe in our repudiation, vengeance and destruction of any person whom we suspect of entertaining such anti-social id tendencies.

One of the insuperable barriers to an objective or reality attitude towards the behaviour of ourselves and other people is that in spite of our superego indoctrination, there is an inexorable tendency to believe that what we feel is good, what gives us pleasure, must have an absolute value of goodness. A curious feature of this emotionally biased judgement is that the reverse may also prevail, and the switch from one to the other seems to be entirely arbitrary or adventitious.

I am afraid my illustration of this point is going to be rather subtle. For instance, the grown-up or adolescent family of a widow or widower are almost bound to regard their surviving parent's wish to espouse a new mate as an inexplicable and most undesirable evil. Their widowed mother, who had hitherto been regarded as a sort of madonna, is apt to become overnight an inexplicably horrible 'prostitute', or at least incredibly evil and even obscene. Naturally the offspring's choice of a partner in marriage is of an entirely different category.

Nevertheless, this may not always seem so to the widowed parent. In one's psychotherapeutic work, one has known many mothers, usually of the hysterical type, who have completely broken down at their son's choice of a woman who presumably in order to protect herself from undue emotional intrusion, seems to have debarred them from adequate access to their son's heart, or even to his house. Melanie Klein tells us that in the case of children, the sight or sound of intercourse between their parents is apt to be felt as the most disturbing and fiendish intrusion of hell itself. The feeling is of something incredibly evil going on, and the concurrent transformation of at least one (usually the father) of these previously good people into a sadistic devil.

It is probably from such emotional reactions, and their concurrent fantastic or psychotic phantasies, that there springs much of our adult incapacity to assess any and every sexual matter objectively. I think the psychosis of infancy goes further than this, and makes it difficult or impossible for us to assess any matter whatsoever that entails even a minor degree of conflict between id and superego (and what matter does not), objectively. Our judgements will be more than biased, even determined, by unconscious forces of which we have not the slightest suspicion. Judge not that ye be not judged is a dictum which we seem incapable of making into anything but an empty formula. We are compelled to judge, compelled by unconscious emotional forces, despite the fact that our judgement is almost certain to be subjective, but none the less violent. It may be said that even with crime, in the form of anti-social activity, we are psychologically incapable of stopping the violence, and leaving it at that, but on account of our unconscious sources of aggression the best we can do about it is to reverse its direction and to perpetrate the same, or usually even greater violence in the form of punishment. Psychologically this has much in common with the mechanisms of war. The best we can do about it is to fight on the side of 'right', and who on earth would fight on any other side . . . and yet we have wars. Evidently 'right', like bad sexuality and good sexuality, can be at least two-sided.

In the days of totem and taboo, people were executed for sexual activity that was not legally sanctioned, and although we do not overtly go as far as this today, there is plenty of evidence of identical reactive patterns. What may be regarded as particularly curious is that persons who are themselves indulging in illicit sexual activity are not free from the illogicality of condemnatory judgements upon others. Indeed, almost the most promiscuous woman I have known made a murderous attack upon her relatively asexual and blameless husband when he so much as mentioned his meeting with a French lady during his absence at war.

In other words, it would seem that what feels good to oneself must be good, broadly speaking, including one's illicit affairs, whereas what does not feel good to oneself, such as losing one's spouse or even parent or child, is immediately felt to be bad, or very bad, and

judged accordingly. It is not too much to pronounce the generalization that as every virile heterosexual man, like the Olympic elk, wants
every female, so any other male's sexual activities with any female
must be bad, unless one can identify oneself with him, and similarly
this goes for the heterosexual woman also.

From this basis it is easy to see that through the process of cultural
displacement, every good object, or advantage which we acquired
personally, must be an occasion for rejoicing, whereas advantages
and good fortunes befalling others, unless we identify ourselves with
them, must be unfortunate if not positively damnable. With all the
complicated psychological adjustments to this basic reaction, the best
we can achieve is a niggardly or reluctant yielding to another person
of their rights, provided of course that our rights are assured and
secure. Any person who takes advantage of this leniency on our part,
and gets what we consider to be a little more than his rights, may seem
to us dishonest, unlikeable, if not positively criminal. This is at least
part of the basis upon which we set ourselves up as judges.

When we come to the institutionalization of this process in the form
of law, and more specifically of criminal law, we would hardly expect
to find its psychopathology to be fundamentally different, nor indeed
its form of expression altered except in regard to its vividness and
violence. An attempt has been made in this book to implement my
contention that the phenomena of social life, as they exist today,
would not be properly understood without some evolutionary or
chronological survey. They are after all the most recent products or
manifestations of an evolutionary process which has taken hundreds
of millions of years to reach its present stage. By the same token legal
punishments of today would lack their true perspective without at
least some reference to their historical development. I would go
further than this and say that we should include in such a survey pre-
historical and even pre-human reactive patterns out of which our
present attitudes have evolved.

For instance, in the law of the jungle 'justice' and might are
obviously identical. Swift 'justice' would descend upon the starving
hyena who laid claim to a modicum of the lion's prey—unless of course
he was a successful 'criminal' and got away unseen! There is however
not only a similarity but an important difference between the
reaction patterns of human beings and their ancestors. The important
difference is not, as we might be tempted to assume, that contributed
by reason or 'justice', but on the contrary that contributed by unreason, projections of phantasy such as superstition, and emotionally
determined beliefs of which the animal is innocent. As Money-Kyrle[2]
has said, a giant ape, however intelligent, would not show the
characteristics of man unless he were endowed with a system of
delusions regarding the nature of life and death, and the belief in

spirits and magic. Then and then only would we find him burying his kind with provisions of food, and like ceremonies. Then, and then only would we say this was a primitive man.

Thus it comes about that from the earliest times of which we have any record, crimes were not judged by utilitarian standards but by the supposed offence given to some tribal deity. The present-day legal attitude towards acts of sexual perversion that do not infringe the liberty of the person (e.g. homosexuality between adults with mutual consent) and towards bestiality are only two instances of innumerable successors of the above attitude. The standard is not utilitarian, and the impression is that a psychological equivalent of the tribal deity is implied if not avowed. The idea amongst the primitive tribe is that if it did not punish the culprit, the outraged god would punish the whole tribe with a terrible vengeance (e.g. the story of Jonah). Thus it was believed that incest would anger the gods and bring down their curse on the crops.[27]

Our present-day legal attitude towards incest is, one feels, determined entirely by strongly charged emotional forces to the exclusion of reason. This seems palpably evident when we read of such a case as I saw recently in the newspaper, where a half-brother and sister had grown up in different parts of the world, and did not even know that there was any blood relationship between them when they met, fell in love and actually got married and lived happily together. Years later, through some misadventure, a middle-aged neighbour happened upon the truth of their identity. The law, and for that matter society at large, could not tolerate the situation.

It cannot be denied that there was overt sadistic enjoyment in the infliction of punishment during the childhood of civilization. In the exercise of this violent superego activity, those very urges that were being punished, namely, the aggressive and the libidinal (in short, the sadistic), were evidently much exercised and enjoyed. The urge to punish is thus seen to derive its dynamic force from those very instincts that it proposed to destroy. It is therefore merely another mode of expressing and enjoying those instincts. The particular mechanism employed is almost identical with that of neurosis where the instinct is gratified and the superego opposition is expressed in one and the same symptomatic act. The only essential difference is that in the case of punishment it is the criminal and not one's own instinct or id that is identified with the phantasied bad object. By virtue of this projection the punisher may now identify himself with the superego and freely enjoy the release of his instinct-derived impulses at the expense of the scapegoat; the 'neurosis' is now extra-psychic—in the outer world—instead of being intra-psychic.

If punishments in general emphasize the aggressive component of the sadistic impulse (masquerading as superego), a study of the centuries of the witch epidemic (1484-1793) provide us with ample material emphasizing the libidinal component.

It is difficult to believe that any amount of private infliction of torture and murder would ever reach commensurate figures as the Spanish Inquisition. The only comparable depletion of a population by human action would be due to war, another superego organization of the aggressive and libidinal urges on a national scale.

It might be assumed that the modifications of punishment which have since taken place, particularly the much later development of imprisonment as a punishment, must be an indication of the ego having taken the matter in hand. It might be thought that punishment was a sadistic enjoyment, but now is a product of reality considerations and of reason, in short that its psychology has changed. Such alteration is not necessarily the case. In the light of evolution it would appear almost miraculous if such a revolutionary change had in fact taken place. The same *principle*, that of punishment, has been, and is still being, maintained, and it seems likely that quite other elements than those of science or reality are responsible for the apparent changes in practice.

We have institutionalized with a vengeance this highly satisfactory mechanism, highly satisfactory at least to the persecutor, relieving him as it does of all his guilt feelings by enabling him to project them upon the scapegoat and at the same time giving him superego and community sanction for relieving himself of his aggressive and sadistic urges by castigating and even torturing the scapegoat. However many 'criminals' there may be in a community (Kinsey has told us that ninety-five per cent of the male population of America, if the truth were known, would be jailed for sexual 'crimes' alone!), nearly every one of them enjoys the castigation of any one or more of their number who has broken the eleventh commandment, that is to say, been apprehended and found guilty.

In my book *Fear, Punishment, Anxiety and the Wolfenden Report*, I have indicated that the psychology of crime and the psychology of punishment were fundamentally identical, the point being that there is usually an emotional compulsion behind both, rather than a scientific ego-assessment of reality requirements. There is a comparable psychology behind the incentives for civil war and indeed behind any quarrel or fight between individuals and groups of individuals. The mental mechanisms involved are common to all these phenomena and include a projection of internal 'bad-objects' on to the opponents and a facilitation by the superego and ego of the consequent release of destructive impulses against the opponent or scapegoat.

The superego and usually the ego will always support and reinforce the release of destructive impulses, provided these are directed against bad objects and not good objects. The point is that the whole process is emotionally determined and serves a psychological end to reduce internal tension, and in this sense may be regarded as an agent of the mechanism for relieving us of the intolerable accumulation of anxiety tensions. Socialized rationalizations usually make it very easy for the ego to be seduced into co-operating in this emotionally satisfactory release of energy.

We may ask if it may not be on account of further repression that we have hidden our injuries to accused persons behind prison walls. May this be the modern equivalent of that earlier repression of the sadism of punishment which found its expression in the Eastern habit of burying alive? Barnes says: 'The cruelties of present-day imprisonment are for the most part screened from the specific knowledge of the public. . . . The key to the defects, abuses and cruelties of the present prison system is to be found in the fact that, whatever the pretext, the actual purpose of imprisonment is not reformation but punishment. Of course, the older attitude of conventional penology was that punishment itself necessarily produces reformation, but we now know that in most cases exactly the opposite result is brought about.'[27] Barnes was more enlightened than many Members of Parliament today who are agitating for the return of the birch.

We may reflect that it was not so very long ago that the manifestly insane were manacled and chained and subjected to *punitive* detention. May it not be that this is still, though less manifestly, the case? On the basis of laboriously compiled statistics comparing the countries of Europe and elsewhere in the ratio of members of asylums to the number of prison inmates, Penrose concludes that: 'as a general rule, if the prison services are extensive, the asylum population is relatively small and the reverse also tends to be true.'[27]

Barnes says: 'If one were to plan an institution designed to promote sexual degeneracy one would arrive at the modern prison.'[27] We may reflect that this sexual degeneracy is just an attempt on the part of the psyche to find an outlet for mental tension which would otherwise further damage it, perhaps to the extent of a permanent psychosis.

To assess the degree of injury suffered by legal punishment of whatever degree or variety it would be necessary to conduct a clinical study of individual cases—perhaps a further extension of the sort of work done by Dr Palthorpe in her book, *What We Put in Prison*. Such a study would bring us to the conclusion that punishment implies injury, physical or mental, to its victim. It also provides, at the same time, a certain satisfaction or helpful outlet for those employing this mode of relief.

Bernard Shaw said: 'Imprisonment, as it exists today, is a worse crime than any of those committed by its victims; for no single criminal can be as powerful for evil, or as unrestrained in its exercise, as an organized nation. . . . To punish is to injure, to reform is to heal; you cannot mend a person by damaging him.'[27]

In conclusion, the psychology of punishment may be tentatively divided into three stages. The first stage may be called the pre-punishment stage and regarded as the free expression of the instincts of aggressiveness and sexuality, either singly or combined as sadism, together with the retaliatory reaction of their victim.

The second stage arises as a result of repression of the first. In consequence of this repression the instincts are anti-cathected, and obtain their outlet as superego activities—naturally directed against their original form. This last is projected on to a scapegoat and the sadistic activity is then freely and openly enjoyed at his expense.

The third stage is a result of a further degree of repression. The disease has progressed further so that now the open expression of sadism, even in the form of punishment, can no longer be tolerated. It becomes repressed into the unconscious, and its victim becomes similarly hidden behind the prison walls. Inside the prison—the objective equivalent of the unconscious—the same process goes on unseen by consciousness and inaccessible to ego-interference.

Many theories have been advanced in the past to explain the phenomenon of legal punishment. I have examined some of these in my book *Fear, Punishment, Anxiety and the Wolfenden Report* and will not recapitulate them all here. As might be expected, they prove to be obvious rationalizations.

The attempt to justify retribution as reasonable is manifestly absurd. That the retributive element exists in the psychology of punishment there is no denying. It is an emotional force. I would criticize merely the attempt to rationalize it, to justify it, and to disguise it as a function of the reason. The mental mechanism involved has nothing to do with reason. It will be shown that it consists in a projection of our own forbidden and repressed tendency on to the delinquent, where we can express our opposition to it without hurt to ourselves. Would it not be more appropriate to punish our own criminal id, to punish ourselves, instead of seeking this way out at the expense of a scapegoat?

Do we not thereby actually express upon him our own hate impulses—to teach him that hate impulses must on no account be expressed and to ensure that we ourselves will not express them.

The influence of deterrence is over-rated. Statistics show that a large proportion of both male and female prisoners have been previously convicted. We have it on record that of 167 thieves prepared for hanging, 164 had witnessed public executions for theft.

The theory of reformation must be based upon the hope that the aggressive or sadistic act has, after all, not been damaging; that it has, on the contrary, really benefited and improved the victim. Reality evidence apparently has little effect upon a belief which promises so much emotional advantage necessary to the placation of the superego or ego. Therefore, there is the tendency to cling to this satisfaction in spite of all the evidence to the contrary.

Punishment, the outward equivalent of total repression, precludes sublimation or reform. If not a physical injury or castration, it appears to be a mental equivalent of this.

An interesting confirmation of the ego-less origin of the psychology of legal punishment is that it fails to take into consideration the nature of the human material with which it deals. The ignoring of such a relevant reality factor is characteristic of the unconscious. 'Justice', like the unconscious, is depicted as being blind to reality.

It is recognized by analysts that the position an individual gets himself into, his role in life, the things he does and often the things that happen to him, are on the whole mostly engineered by himself, consciously or unconsciously. It does not necessarily follow that the person who gets himself punished is invariably a masochist seeking this particular role and this particular mode of gratification. It is normal to seek advantages for oneself and to avoid disadvantages. Delinquents are, for the most part, seeking personal advantage.

They will be motivated by their emotional needs and by their reality needs. There will be unconscious factors and ego factors responsible for their activity and for their getting themselves into the position of the punished.

The person whose unconscious urge for advantage is strong and whose ego is alive to reality will be unlikely to get himself into a position which is the exact opposite to that towards which his whole psyche is striving. The person who gets punished will, therefore, either be one whose emotional needs are abnormal (masochistic) or one whose ego is defective—or both—one who has not succeeded in coping with reality in accordance with his emotional requirements.

Nevertheless, I feel that the tendency would be to over-estimate the importance of the ego as a responsible factor in punishment. There is much evidence that it is, particularly in the case of those who get punished, merely a tool in the hands of powerful unconscious desires and compulsions. As the goal achieved is that of being punished we expect to find that these persons, ego-defect or not, are, for the most part, masochistic.

Apart from the fact that some persons (on account of unconscious guilt, etc.) actively *want* punishment and *must* see that they get it, there exists a large class of persons who are normally desirous of death. Only occasionally does this desire find expression in the form of suicide. It is noteworthy that one in every ninety deaths in Great Britain is due to suicide—a larger proportion than is popularly supposed. There is also the far larger class who do not actually commit suicide, but who put themselves in the way of death, and eventually achieve it by 'accident'. Then there is the still larger class whose behaviour shows a compromise between this death-desire and tendencies to self-preservation. Such persons get themselves into ill-health, tuberculosis, alcholism, drug addiction, bankruptcy, misery or imprisonment.

Now members of this large class of persons are not likely to be deterred by the prospect of misfortune, legally inflicted punishment or hanging. On the contrary, they are more likely to be unconsciously attracted by these possibilities or likelihoods. In these cases punishment, far from being a deterrent, is likely to be an incentive to their crime.

But in whatever way the prisoner unconsciously engineers his punishment or unconsciously asks society to punish him, this does not justify a would-be sane society in yielding to his request. In our therapeutic or reformatory treatment of patients we do not demonstrate love to those who ask for it, or hate to those who demand it. A psychotherapist who acted in this fashion would indeed himself have entered the emotional dog-fight and we should rightly judge him to be as much in need of psychotherapeutic treatment as the patient he was treating.

That such is actually the psychological position of a society that punishes is borne out by its failure to cure, reform, or even to understand its criminals.

The aggressive or destructive instinct is principally responsible for the phenomenon of punishment as it is at the root, also, of much criminal behaviour.

We know this about the aggressive or destructive instinct, that whether it has a primary nucleus or not (whether or not there is such a thing as the death-instinct) there can be no doubt that aggression is at least enormously stimulated, exacerbated, or perhaps even called into being by any and every instinct-frustration.

The subtlety of legal punishment lies in the fact that while it is law which, by enforcing suppression of instinct relief, thereby stimulates and increases the aggressive instinct, it is also law which, by enjoining punishment, permits an outlet for this aggression in its augmented violence.

Does the infliction of punishment bring any relief or gratification to the sexual or pleasure-seeking instinct?

There can be no doubt about the answer. The public who only a few centuries ago tied naked people to carts and beat them, found libidinal pleasure in the process. Spectators who paid 2s for seats round Tyburn Tree were evidently prompted by their pleasure-seeking instincts. Our modern jurists in ordering punishment, conspicuously such punishment as the 'birch', and those who inflict it or witness it, are probably not immune to, at least, a *conflict* in which the libidinal instinct, as well as the aggressive, plays a considerable part. My clinical experience has opened my eyes to the fact that conflict even to the degree of conscious agony does not preclude the possibility of considerable unconscious libidinal relief actually accompanying it. For instance, I have a female patient suffering from total psychosexual frigidity who spends her analytical session literally writhing in an agony of frustration and yet becomes angry and violent if it is so much as suggested to her that she should forego a session. Analysis reveals that under the conscious agony of resistance there exists simultaneously a gratifying though repressed phantasy containing all the joys of sexual indulgence. At a very deep level she is experiencing her early incestuous intercourse, while at the same time at a slightly less deep level is the resistance due to the phantasy of the terrifying eyes of her mother. The agony of this situation fills consciousness, whilst the id-gratification of the act remains repressed, but none the less gratifying. Moreover, this is the only way in which she can reduce her instinct-tension; and so we can better understand the violence of her insistence upon it. Hence the pain which the punisher feels or claims to feel ('it hurts me as much as it hurts you') does not preclude the presence of deep libidinal satisfaction.

Newspapers that specialize in catering for the emotional needs of the public do not hesitate to give priority to the most lurid crime. Crime and *punishment* are usually the richest emotional diet unless the international news promises something of a similarly stimulating nature.

Punishment is so fully explained on the basis of id and superego activity that it seemed to me difficult to see what the ego or reason had to do with it. Yet the ego must come into the picture if only on account of the fact that it has given sanction to the unconscious urges. Then it occurred to me that if we ask anybody who is not primarily a psychologist for an explanation of the phenomenon of punishment, he will reply, or endeavour to reply, in terms of its ego-psychology.

As one might expect the result is a collection of *rationalizations*. Had he lived a hundred odd years ago he would have found no difficulty in rationalizing, in explaining and justifying, in terms of ego-psychology and reason, the obviously sadistic barbarities of that age. Pure reason does not in practice command the situation. Like the delinquent, our reason is driven by unconscious forces—mostly conflicting forces.

It is clear that the majority of human beings, however intelligent, are victims of a mass suggestion, with the result that they unconsciously identify themselves with the State, and establish the institutions and customs of the State as the criterion of what is right and good. As psychologists we fail if we fall into this trap, and I think few of us escape scot-free. The force of it is too great.

Let us recognize the two essential truths that emerge from an analytical examination of the problem of crime and punishment. One is that the delinquent in his action against us is driven by un-conscious forces. And the second is that we in our action against him are no less driven by similar unconscious forces.

Admittedly there is an ego difference between the punisher and the punished. If the punished is similarly driven by his unconscious emotional needs, he is getting his relief or gratification, at least in greater conformity with his ego requirements. There is also frequently, though not invariably, a deeper non-ego difference. The punished is frequently unconsciously in need of punishment while the punisher is unconsciously in need of inflicting it. There is a difference therefore in the balance of the emotional conflict. There is a difference between masochism and sadism, though a difference which is more apparent than real, as is evidenced by their reversibility. The ego has to do merely with the execution of the act which gives release to the tension.

I can think of a no more inappropriate symbol for a scientific attitude towards crime than that of a blindfolded or blind lady, holding a pair of scales! Surely science ought to have both eyes wide open, but what I am pointing out in this chapter is that the eyes should look inwards first, in order to discount as far as possible the overwhelming emotional reactive biases which are and always have been from the time of the jungle the real determinants of our attitudes and behaviour.

CHAPTER XIII

CULTURE AND THE PSYCHOLOGY OF
AUTHORITARIAN INSTITUTIONS

It is many years since Freud came to the conclusion that: 'every culture must be built up on coercion and instinctual renunciation'. He went on to say: 'One notes with surprise and concern that a majority of men obey the cultural prohibitions in question only under the pressure of external force, in fact only where the latter can assert itself and for as long as it is an object of fear.' Thus it would seem that legal enforcement (which might well include at least a threat of punishment) may lie at the very foundation of culture and its maintenance. He goes on to say: 'it does not even appear certain that without coercion the majority of human individuals would be ready to submit to the labour necessary for acquiring new means of supporting life.'[28]

These and further considerations lead him to ask the question whether, in view of all the instinctual sacrifices they have had to suffer, and still suffer: 'Culture is indeed worth defending at all?'

There is no doubt that the psychology of the cultured or civilized person depends largely upon his reactions to parent figures during infancy and childhood. It is by introjecting the attitudes he finds around him that he develops a superego, without whose approval he would not be happy, and perhaps most unhappy, if his discarded instincts were freely gratified. This is easy to see if we remember that the most primitive instinctual wishes include those of murder, cannibalism and incest. It is difficult to imagine the civilized person happily indulging in these! Hence we may say that it is the introjection of civilized persons around, and the culture they stand for that gives rise to at least that minority which ensure that culture shall be maintained.

Child psychologists will tell us that we can see the process and the struggles or conflicts between the process and the primitive id, at work from a very early age. There is a tendency amongst them to divide children into at least three categories, according to the predominating force in their civilizing conflict. For instance they speak of 'the conforming child'. This is the child who has a positive or love relationship to its parents or the authorities around it, and appears fairly willingly or easily to submit or even readily to absorb their indoctrinations; the good child, the one who will do what the authorities want it to do without objection, perhaps who will be very ready and happy to conform.

At the other extreme we have the rebellious child, the naughty child, the one who is forever resisting the authoritative figures. Of course there is every degree of this sort of thing. It may be that this child would be the happier if it could get away with it, get its own way all the time, but in actual practice it is usually less happy because it is meeting rebuke, rebuff, frustration and disapproval. Its failure to adjust to the powers-that-be may present a serious problem. Such a child may in the end submit, and accept the inevitable, or it may be made ill in being forced to submit. It is naturally from this group that delinquents emerge. Child analysts have told us such a child imagines that people are hostile to it. It sometimes expects that even if it does not fight authority, those in authority will fight it. It is often full of fears and anxieties, sometimes of a fantastic nature. Probably it is a child which possesses a great deal of hostile and destructive impulses. These it largely projects on to the adults around and according to Melanie Klein even imagines, at least in its unconscious that they are cannibals that will devour it.

In other words, the child has projected its own repressed aggression and sadism on to these adults, and may grow up into a delinquent or criminal. Unfortunately the adult commonly has too little insight to be of much help in the situation. His tendency is to react like the punisher which is exactly how the child expects him to react. The child therapist knows very well that as a first principle that on no account must he react like the monster the child has projected on to him, in spite of the fact that this is precisely how the State does react towards its children.

We may look upon this group of reactions, the rebellious group, as revealing the struggle between conformity and the opposite. There is hope so long as the struggle is still visible. Perhaps the worst condition is a third category which the child therapist regards as the withdrawn child. It seems that this type of child has given up the fight as a bad job, and, refusing to conform, has simply withdrawn into a world of his omnipotent phantasies. Whereas group two may be the breeding ground for unsatisfactory adults or delinquents, group three is the breeding ground for neurotics and psychotics, although this is not necessarily the case unless the position becomes extreme. Within certain so-called normal limits, these processes may indeed have certain personal and even social advantages.

The first group is perhaps the most educable type of child, if we regard education in the light of Freud's suggestion that it is an attempt to replace the pleasure principle by the reality principle, the reality principle being defined as 'no dethronement of the pleasure-principle, but only a safeguarding of it. A momentary pleasure, uncertain in its results, is given up, but only in order to gain in the new way an assured pleasure coming later.'[20] An important emphasis lies in the fact that the child can give up this immediate pleasure-principle only by making use of 'rewards of love from those in charge'.

With regard to withdrawal, or perhaps a normal element of it, Freud says it can lead to a reunion of both pleasure-principle and reality principle in a peculiar way, for instance in the form of art. 'The artist is originally a man who turns from reality because he cannot come to terms with the demand for the renunciation of instinctual satisfaction as it is first made', and indulges in phantasy. 'But he finds a way of return from this world of phantasy back to reality; with his special gifts he moulds his phantasies into a new kind of reality, and men concede them a justification as valuable reflections of actual life.' He achieves all this 'without pursuing the circuitous path of creating real alterations in the outer world'.[20]

These and other considerations may lead us to see that culture, cultural groups, and cultural institutions are built up largely out of this struggle between indoctrination by authority figures on the one hand, and rebellions on the part of the id on the other hand. It would seem that generally speaking, sufficient superego (introjected authority figures) is built up to maintain civilization or a cultural group, together with its authoritarian institutions. No doubt a certain amount of pleasure principle is lost to the individual in this way, but the gain, like the gain of the conforming child, may to a large extent outweigh the id sacrifice, particularly as in the fullness of time some of the most primitive id wishes, such as those of cannibalism, appear to be completely vanquished or relegated to the unwanted recesses of the mind.

I would like to point out that the processes involved have little or nothing to do with reason, but might be more correctly regarded as some sort of biological evolution, though admittedly belonging to a branch of biology which has not yet been recognized as such, and in which activities or movements are largely determined by unconscious psychological processes.

Culture and cultural institutions are obviously dependent upon the formation of a group of individuals, commonly an enormously large group of individuals. If it is conceded that in evolutionary history the first group was the family group, it will be readily admitted that this at least had a biological foundation in so far as it was formed and held together by heterosexual instincts, and subsequently by maternal, paternal and filial instincts, including those of the need for protection and companionship.

The authority figure, beginning in early life with the parents, and the psychological reactions beginning in infancy to these parents, have the most important effect throughout life in the cohesion of society and the cultural group. Strachey says: 'We see then that the intra-group attachments thus set up in each member of the group are of three kinds; ties of mental dependence, ties of identification and libidinal ties.'

As Strachey reminds us: 'Freud cites as the two most outstanding examples of organized groups of this kind the army and the (Roman Catholic) Church. Both have a supreme head invested with auto-cratic power: in the first case, the Commander-in-Chief, and in the second, Christ Himself, with the Pope as His earthly representative, and in both there is a rigid hierarchy of officers or priests, as the case may be, to consolidate the top leader's power and to bring it home to the rank and file. Both, too, consist only of men.'[21]

It is easy to see that there are innumerable bodies within a nation, social culture and civilization, which correspond in psychological structure to those mentioned. There are, for instance, all the fighting services, public schools, Boy Scouts and Girl Guides, sporting clubs, ordinary clubs, local bodies, or as Mrs Strachey further reminds us, even such little bodies as a group of botanists who join together periodically to read papers to one another. Following this line of thought, there is no end to the groups we could bring forward. There are of course trade unions, small, large and united. There are parti-cular social classes, some founded on play, others on work. There is the large group of business men and black-coat workers, the civil service, the different professions with their sub-divisions, and an inexhaustible list.

These groups of course are not necessarily limited to one sex. Even some schools have much of the same psychology, in spite of being co-educational. In all these cases there is some degree of identification with other members of the group. All the doctors will stick together if need be, and all the legal profession, and so on.

As a result of the regressive force of the group, Strachey tells us that 'each member is inclined to think a little more highly of himself . . . and his society and to feel a little more strongly on their behalf than he would otherwise do and than the facts warrant'.[21]

It may be said that even amongst psychologists and psycho-therapists who should *know* better, the group mentality tends to destroy an individual freedom in assessing the pros and cons of their particular system, or probably of analysis and psychotherapy in general. It may seem that some groups, some more than others, whilst expressing the irrationality of the process in many spheres of life, are nevertheless themselves inclined to erect the equivalent of a 'leader', a 'king' or even a 'god', whose word sooner or later tends to become infallible. And yet Strachey, a psychoanalyst, reminds us: 'In comparatively recent times, for instance, the Pope has, as head of the Roman Catholic Church, officially taken on the attributes of Infallibility—an attribute which, one would have thought, could only belong to God.'[21]

Thus we may see the enormous power of these emotional forces which subordinate the individual, including his very mind, powers of thought and judgement to that of the group mind, and all this even in those who claim to have the greatest insight into the process and mental mechanisms at work. According to Strachey, 'An organized social unit . . . obliges them (its members) to inhibit many of their instinctual impulses and to sublimate others, and it provides them with a superego. *Nevertheless, it does cause their minds to regress to a point at which they are unable to take a realistic view of their own group or of objects outside it, especially in relation to their group, or to make independent ethical judgements about them.*' (my italics).

And again: 'The regressive attitude which such groups engender in its members is apt, moreover, to impair their capacity to grasp difficult ideas or ideas that are at all abstract.'[21]

In the light of an insight into these mechanisms and their power to debase the faculty of intelligent judgement and thought, it is more understandable why an occasional individual (indeed very few) have a resistance to merging or submerging themselves in a group, military, religious, political, professional or intellectual. On the other hand it must be recognized that the vast majority of mankind, based perhaps upon the reactive patterns of infancy and babyhood, seem absolutely to *require* the protective and security-inducing feeling of the equivalent of family guidance and protection, and lose no time in burying themselves inextricably in one or more of the groups we have been considering, despite their regressive effects, or perhaps because of them. All want again the security of childhood at any sacrifice of reason and intellectual integrity. No doubt the process is largely anxiety-driven, and the first consideration of all mental operations is the reduction of anxiety before we can function physiologically—however much at the expense of healthy or sane *mental* functioning.

Allegiance to authoritative father-figures is discernable throughout the history of man. It is of course one of the characteristics of religion, but it is surprising to see how practically no department of social or group life is without it. It has intruded even into the realms of science where one would expect it to be most carefully disbarred. For example, right up to the time of Galileo (1564-1642), the progress of science had, for all those centuries, been practically arrested by the erection of Aristotle as an authority outweighing the evidence of all experimental work. Apparently even so-called scientists were banded together to accept the authoritative dicta (however erroneous) of Aristotle, rather than to believe their own eyes and ears and mathematical calculations. Both before this and after for many more centuries, as we well know, the indoctrination of religious authority was felt to be so much more dependable than the evidence of scientific experimentors, that practically no progress in real knowledge was made until a century ago. Thus we see that this tendency of the human mind to cling to father in the face of everything, has been felt by man to be so important for his feelings of security and his mitigation of anxiety that scientific and intellectual progress has stood still for this psychological or physiological purpose. Obviously knowledge and sanity did not matter to us, it was simply the security of father's protection that was required.

Thus it can be seen that reason, reality and scientific knowledge, although inadequate to compete with these fundamental emotional requirements and, other emotions such as those exhibited by the rebellious child on behalf of the id, do occasionally show some tendency at least to intrude and to enter into conflict with the established order. No doubt the position of authoritative dominance was usually maintained not only on account of fear of the parents and the introjected parents' superego, but also in every psyche to a varying degree there was a tendency to fear the repressed instincts of one's own unconscious id. Perhaps the rebellious child, like the rebellious intellectual, may at times have felt that he needed the suppressive and protective forces of the superego rather less strongly than the good child or the God-fearing man. Be that as it may, there were occasions when an individual, either alone or in concert with others, would produce some tentative challenge to the accepted order. Such instances are shown by the pioneers of science, Copernicus, Galileo, and a host of others. It is thus noteworthy that from these I would say emotionally provoked rebellions that some little advantage was won for progress of the human mind in place of its habitual surrender to the regressive forces of the group.

The anxiety bottled up in the psychotic recesses of the mind is of such magnitude and intensity that there is small wonder that practically all individuals cling together in groups, large or small, very often with a parent figure in leadership. Psychologically we are very like the infants we recently were, tolerably reassured from anxiety only when in the bosom of the 'family'. This phenomenon is so conspicuous that it has led to the late Dr Ian Suttie[32] contending very ably that the principal drive in life was a compulsive desire for companionship which naturally originated in the need of the infant for security above all else, the security of its mother's presence and companionship, without which anxiety supervened and also hate; and life became impossible.

Suttie's emphasis on this point helps to bring out the theory of this chapter, namely that subservience to authority and the institutionalization of such subservience is an emotionally activated compulsion of all persons, as it is the only measure they can find to counter intolerable anxiety and for which they readily sacrifice individual and rational thinking.

There is probably no department of civilized life, including its institutions, where this parent equivalent, our reassurance, is not of primary importance. For instance, in the field of politics we have an innumerable succession of parent-figure equivalents, from our Member of Parliament to Cabinet Ministers, and especially Prime Minister. Apparently this is not enough, and we must continue the emphasis on our need by the institution of Royal Families. If our problem appears to be one of law, we must have our trusted solicitor, if one of health we must have our family doctor, and above him of course all the various array of consultants with their magical medical equipment, and indeed the entire medical fraternity. The same applies to our anxiety about the after-life according to the particular religious denomination or sect to which we belong.

Examples could probably be extended in every direction but they are all reduceable to one and the same denominator, namely the need of leader, elder or parent equivalent in whom to put our trust and through whom to allay our anxiety. This is of course in addition to our needed identification with a usually very large group of sibling equivalents. Usually the parent alone is not enough for the child, he or she requires the other children also, in order to be happy or free from anxiety.

Our reality relationships were forced upon us, however niggardly, originally, as today, by instinctual desires and needs, of which no doubt the need for food came first, being followed inevitably by a need for protection against inclement weather. It may well be this latter which has led to those groups of humans who live in less kind climates developing a more complicated civilization than those who can go naked and unsheltered with impunity. As with the case of food, the former were forced into building themselves adequate protection against wintry weather, or enduring many discomforts and perhaps perishing.

In short, if there is anything that makes us turn to 'reality' and cope with it, it is again our instinct needs comparable to our emotional needs. The exercise of any such faculty as reason, common sense or reality sense is at the best a very late attribute reluctantly forced upon us in subservience to the instinctual and emotional needs here stressed. These latter always have been and still are the predominant driving forces of our lives, and the determinants of our behaviour. We will bind together as brothers and sisters in order to feel less frightened of the terrifying universe. We will elect, or run to already elected parent figures, further to mitigate our anxiety, and to save us from the anxiety of thinking for ourselves. Not only our behaviour in all its ramifications, but our very thoughts and beliefs are determined by the same irrational panic which makes the same infant scream if mother is not available.

Both at the dawn of life and the dawn of group life, and at the present day if we only knew it, our world is peopled with projections from our psychotic unconscious. It is full of all the bad and destructive and uncontrollable impulses of millions of years of our struggle for survival. It is full of the same bogies that the infant and primitive man feels around him unless he can run to the sheltering arms of his parents, leader or tribe. Thus whatever he knows or, having emerged from infancy and eaten of the Tree of Knowledge, grows to know, about the real nature of the parent who once protected him so adequately, he must at all costs still have an omnipotent and adequately protective parent, real or imaginary. It would be terrible without this benevolent and omnipotent figure, he would be as it were alone in the universe (with all his own projected evil), knowing only that the mysterious and awful thing called death must overtake him sooner or later. How much less terrifying and how necessary for the alleviation of anxiety is it for him to recreate his accustomed milieu of infancy with its security of parental love and omnipotent protection. He is fortunate in that he does not have to build up this phantasy or illusion all by himself. It has already been built up for him by authoritative figures, through a long traditional ancestry.

In other words, his proclivity for still rushing into the protective love of omnipotent parents is well catered for by these very parents lending the authority of the tradition of many generations to assist him in his pre-conditioned path of discarding reason and any sense of reality in favour of this emotionally gratifying regressive force, which again makes him a secure member of the group and an obedient servant of his leader on exactly the same pattern which was so firmly conditioned during the earliest years of the formation of his mind, and which from that time onwards has served to allay the bogies of anxiety. All that is required of him to live in this accustomed security is to believe and to be good.

CHAPTER XIV

BELIEF IN GOD

In the last chapter we have seen how the reactive patterns inevitably laid down as a result of our immediate environment at the dawn of life tend to determine our behaviour ever after. It is as though, having learnt the comfort and security of mother's arms, and subsequently of the family environment, we can know of no other tolerable situation in which to live. We must, as the first condition for feeling comfortable and secure, cling to or recreate around us at least symbolical equivalents of this primary environment. It is as necessary to us as the air we breathe; religion is the end product of this need.

This need does not apply exclusively to the human being. It seems that at least all mammals—and probably many other animals also, such as birds—having experienced a maternal and a sibling relationship immediately after birth, react similarly and find this a primary need throughout their lives. While I am dictating this, the family poodle, having been locked in the kitchen while the rest of the household departed, is howling away, obviously in a state of intolerable mental agony. The cure proves the diagnosis. We have only to let her come into the room where we are, or lie outside the door where she is aware of our presence, and all is peace and quiet.

This phenomenon is very conspicuous in the case of sheep and probably of all gregarious animals. Every farmer knows that if you separate a sheep from the flock it will tear about the countryside in a state of panic, evidently looking for the flock, but in such a state of blind emotional distress that it may even meet with death. No doubt this accounts for them all sticking together and following one another —like sheep. We are very familiar with the fact that the human infant feels similarly, and if there is no human companionship is liable to feel frightened and to cry.

We may now ask what is the dog believing, what is the sheep believing, what is the infant believing? By their conduct it is pretty evident that they are all in a state of anxiety or panic, they are believing in approaching doom. They cannot hope to live alone without the familiar environment of parents and siblings. I would say that their behaviour reveals that they are the victims of phantasy, the victims of erroneous belief. Perhaps they all need some belief, however erroneous, to counteract their unconsciously determined erroneous belief in immediately approaching doom, but in their case nothing has been prepared for them.

To what stage of development or evolution will they have to advance before they are competent to invent an appropriate anxiety-relieving belief, or to absorb one that has been invented for them? It may be said that in a sense they already have some such erroneous belief, at least in their unconscious. For instance, it is evident that when the baby's assumption of its own omnipotence begins to fail as a result of its contacts with external reality, it immediately begins to endow the mother and other figures in its vicinity with this delusional conception. Its necessary feeling of security is based upon a feeling that it is loved, and a belief in the omnipotence of the benevolent figure. Thus we already have two essential ingredients of practically every religion.

There is much evidence to prove this psychological theory, including of course the evidence which I have just described of the panic which ensues when the benevolent omnipotent figure is absent, and has not yet been replaced by any belief in its mythological equivalent. It may be that the difference between other mammals, such as the ape, however intelligent, and man, however primitive, is that the former have not reached a stage of inventing an imaginary or mythological substitute or compensation to take the place of the reality of separation from parent or family. If separated from the group they feel and behave as though all is lost; the foundations of their emotional environment, and feelings of security in the shape of the actual presence of parents, siblings, or substitutes for them, have been swept away from under them, probably for ever. But the human being, however primitive, has an imaginative or delusional substitute for this gap in his accustomed environment. It is as though his mind said: 'Mother, father, brothers and sisters have always been present, and although I cannot see or sense them at the moment, as they have always been present they must still be present in some invisible form. Anyhow, I shall cling to that belief as it is the only one which relieves my anxiety and enables me to go on living.'

Indeed it can be shown that the reason he must cling to this belief in an unreality, is because he is already full of frightened phantasies which he has largely projected on to the surrounding environment. So long as mother is there, and loves him, she will protect him from all these bogies (from his own unconscious mind), with which he has peopled the surrounding world. Take her away and his bad phantasies (really his own repressed destructive impulses) in the shape of evil spirits or bogies all around him, will soon encompass his destruction. If mother is not there or, *if in the course of intellectual development*, she can no longer be regarded as omnipotent, he must have something or someone who is omnipotent, to stand between him and the destructive forces around, created by the projection of his own repressed destructive impulses.

The history of religion, in so far as it may be regarded as beginning with animism, may dimly show us the successive stages of this delusional system. First of all, the world around is peopled with evil spirits, demons, etc., which cause primitive man to go about very often in fear and trembling. Subsequently he invents *mana*, which I am inclined to think, in addition to its ingredient of omnipotence, also commonly contains more benevolence than malevolence towards him. The mysterious qualities of the mother-image are there, ready to take various shapes and forms. At a very early or primitive stage of culture, he tends to endow real persons with these attributes. Thus, having outgrown his belief in the omnipotence of his mother and father, he may be content to endow the chief or the king with these attributes, and feel that he is protected by this powerful or supernatural being.

I would point out that this early endowment of socially powerful individuals with *mana* is never entirely abandoned. Even in our present civilized state, we still get some consolation from a variety of such *mana*-endowed individuals, in the political field prime ministers and royalty, and in the more individual field such parent substitutes as doctor, solicitor and priest. Their number and variety is innumerable. In this respect particularly we are blind to the realization that we are largely living in a world of superstition. This widely disseminated superstition is however of considerable importance in lessening our anxiety by the previously mentioned mechanism of benevolent omnipotence (or at least partial omnipotence), that protects us and keeps evil forces from encompassing our destruction.

However, sooner or later in the course of our developing intelligence and increasing appreciation of reality, we become relatively less able to feel that these persons, consisting of the same flesh and blood as ourselves, have a sufficient quantity of *mana* or degree of omnipotence to ensure our everlasting security. We need something more than the host of better-educated and superior individuals. Or it may be that we have discovered that we cannot always rely upon their benevolence. Therefore we have to find an equivalent of the parent who was so all-satisfying at the beginning of life, an equivalent that will be benevolent and omnipotent. If he is not all these things, and also in the shape and form of the original parent, he will be relatively useless to us as a safeguard against all the bogies which assail us, and bring about our death.

The unfortunate thing about this universe, and about the specific nature of our particular need, is that such a figure is extremely difficult to find. We may say, therefore, that from our point of view there is something wrong with the universe, or perhaps more likely something wrong with us and our conditioned emotional reactive patterns in relation to the universe. Something must be done about it. We cannot exist in a milieu different from that in which we were bred; anxiety would overwhelm and destroy us, as it would the lost lamb. It is our developing sanity which is responsible for this impossible state of affairs. Many animals can just stay with the herd and be relatively satisfied and free from anxiety. Very primitive man can conceivably endow some super-father-figure with all the necessary *mana*, and feel that all is tolerably well. But with our increasing sanity we have lost the power to obtain adequate consolation from these palpably inadequate projections of our omnipotent phantasy. At the same time the resulting anxiety (due to our repressed and projected bad phantasies) may become too severe to endure.

In the history of religion, mankind found that by the sacrifice of some modicum of his developing sanity, he could gain a great deal of reassurance by re-instituting the lost omnipotent parent. Perhaps he started by imagining that the parent and the parent's parent, and the whole host of super-parents were not really dead and vanished. They lived on in some peculier way, watching over him and his siblings (the other members of the tribe) and ordering their lives. It was a short step from this to the construction of totem poles, which demonstrated in a concrete form that these ancestral figures of the past were still available. This may not be so very different psychologically from keeping photographs of our deceased parents and ancestors around us. Some modicum of a comparable consolation may be derived unconsciously if not consciously. Of course parents are not necessarily a hundred per cent benevolent. Anger and hatred have actually been experienced by every child, and no doubt this accounts for some of the hideous expressions on the totem poles, but the balance must be in favour of benevolence, otherwise how would one have survived?

Further in these primitive religions, an even closer intimacy and influence from the parent image is not beyond reach. We may possess him, use him as a sacrifice, kill him and eat him. To us this may seem a strange thing to do with the parent whom we wish to preserve so that he can preserve us, but after all it may be suggested that how can he preserve us better than by being incorporated into our bodies and made part of us? It may be thereby he cannot get away, and we shall never lose him.

Such a psychological process is no doubt an important determinant in the behaviour of primitive peoples. Frazer's researches have shown beyond a shadow of doubt that the chief religious ritual of primitive beliefs was that of human sacrifice originally, and especially regicide or parricide, at one time accompanied by cannibalistic incorporation. Before we repudiate this madness and dissociate ourselves entirely from it, we should remember that we still harp upon this ceremony in our own religion, and even symbolically act it out, including the cannibalistic incorporation. It is all part of the evidence to show how important, how essential is the parent figure or its omnipotent substitute for countering the anxiety created by our terrifying unconscious phantasies.

The above material shows how overwhelmingly strongly we are conditioned to imagine the existence of a successor to the benevolent and omnipotent parent. One feels that he is already there in our psyche, even before he is born in consciousness. Now obviously it would only require the acceptance of some magical or supernatural force in the universe for this perhaps indispensable wish or need to take shape, usually in anthropomorphic shape like that of the parent, in our conscious phantasy. It has been said: 'Religion begins with a soul or spirit, and ends with a god'.[34]

The psychological process that leads to the belief in a single god is known to have passed through many stages of development before it reached this level, from totemism to many of the elaborate mythologies culminating in those of Greece and Rome, to the dawn of pre-Christian religions. It would seem that once the sense of reality, or in other words sanity, is surrendered in favour of this overwhelming need for consolation, there is no limit to the intrusion of this form of consolation into our materialistic or reality world. It is as though the mind has just surrendered and let go, and indulged in an ever-increasing abundance of dream-like phantasies in preference to emotionally unrewarding reality thinking.

Naturally the emotional phantasies that are built and acted out have many facets, some of them largely determined by id or instinct lusts, and others by superego prohibitions and gratifications. But it would seem that when primitive man has had his fill of regicide, murder, cannibalism, incest and particularly capital punishment, he, even at that stage of development, finds time to indulge in speculations regarding the nature of the world or universe in which he finds himself. Reality is not known and apparently need not be known. He can and does invent as much as he likes according to his heart's desire.

In reviewing these matters, however inadequately, we may well have come to the conclusion that he was not only psychotic but certainly a danger to himself and others. The point I am suggesting is that having accepted beliefs determined by nothing more or less than his emotional desires, such as belief in the supernatural, particularly supernatural beings in the image of his parents, there was nothing to prevent him from extending this delightful process to everything in the universe and not in the universe. Unfortunately beliefs are not harmless, they result not only in ritual, but also in what we would call social behaviour of the most crazy kind.

Nevertheless, like war, they are nothing more or less than a dramatization or acted-out expression of that which was already within primitive man's psyche. Perhaps, like our modern civilization expressing its symptomatic behaviour (including war) and its symptoms, especially in the case of admittedly neurotic and psychotic persons, primitive man is showing a familiar psychological tendency to unburden the internal tensions and complexes within the mind by making an environment suitable for them, in which they can be acted out for better or for worse.

When we pass on to the more complicated mythologies, such as those of Greece and Rome, we may reflect that mental evolution or development does not necessarily move from illusion and delusion towards reality-testing and science, but rather in the direction of further elaborations of emotional phantasies which have no other determinants than dream-life with its wishfulfilments and compulsive nightmares. Perhaps our monotheism robs us of a great deal of freedom in these respects, a freedom which even the Greeks and Romans were not yet ready to give up. They peopled the world with an enormously interesting and imaginative hierarchy of supposed gods, and sometimes it would appear that not even the top one was really omnipotent. Above Apollo was Zeus, and above Zeus was Fate. What is more, these gods indulged in all sorts of human-like and what we would undoubtedly call extremely criminal activities. They were forever castrating father-figures, having incest with mothers, sisters and daughters, and not content with murder *ad lib*, they frequently indulged in eating their victims, who were usually blood relatives! Such absurd beliefs, which have to be studied to be appreciated, were not limited to Greeks and Romans but are to be found in every part of the world during the development of man and his religions. We get such childish things as the belief that the universe rests on an elephant, and the elephant on a tortoise, and hundreds of similar fairy tales, accepted as religion.

I feel that a lot of these complicated sagas, which we now agree to relegate to the museum of myths, are a more accurate description of the phantasies based upon our early family experiences. After all, there were many people with whom we had dealings as babies and infants, and why should we subsume them all under the image of an all-powerful mother or father. I fancy that in order to make some concession of ego-reality or superego, or to defend itself against criticism, monotheism has insisted upon its adherents depriving themselves of a good deal of enjoyable emotional freedom. Perhaps it is being something like a parent who has forbidden its child to believe in Santa Claus, because the neighbours would laugh. However, the monotheists appear to tolerate this deprivation, provided the main parent image is not taken away.

But even in monotheism we can observe a tendency with other members of the family to work their way back, as it were, into their original relationship. For instance, in many monotheistic religions there is a son (ourself), or the equivalent of a son, who finds a place by his father's throne, and it is only natural, as we see in the Roman Catholic religion, that the poor downtrodden woman, or mother, should be at least acknowledged if not restored to something approaching her original position in the family. After all, the emotions which were felt in infancy towards the real mother naturally require a successor upon whom to direct themselves.

Freud says: 'The derivation of the religious attitude can be followed back in clear outline as far as the child's feeling of helplessness (for lack of a father).' My impression is that like Freud, the church, being a man-made institution, places the Father in an unjustifiably important position and the mother in an undeservedly unimportant position. Freud actually writes: 'Everything is the son-father relationship; God is the exalted father and *the longing for the father is the root of the need for religion*' (my italics).[28]

Having been a mother-adored infant myself, the idea of longing for the father absolutely revolts me. (Maybe that is why I am writing these chapters). Personally I never wanted him anywhere near me; it was mother I wanted, only mother; and if I had lived in the days of totemism, human sacrifice and cannibalism, I might well have appreciated the ecstasy of eating mother (and perhaps any woman as young as she was when I was an infant) but father I would simply have wanted to murder and leave it at that!

Every analyst has at times discerned that his neurotic and particularly his psychotic patients are commonly in closer touch with unconscious phantasy (the source of all our behaviour and beliefs) than are more stable or normal persons, therefore I submit this clinical excerpt as evidence of the connection between religious belief and the Oedipus complex. In a patient's own words: 'I still have phantasies of seducing your wife, although I have never met her, and this shows me that I am still living largely in the Oedipus situation. I think it has something to do with my wanting you to befriend me. I want you to be the Good Father, that is to say, the Father who will understand me, who will understand all and forgive all. It occurs to me that that is what every religion offers—a good Father who understands all and forgives all. Everyone is looking for this Good Father, and wishing to get his approval. I am sure the reason for this is to relieve the anxiety due to our feelings of guilt. And what have we been guilty of? I know the answer, because I am still at the Oedipus level. We are guilty of wanting to seduce mother, of phantasies of seducing mother. The counter to this terrifying idea is to find the Good Father, so that He will forgive us and help us. Above all, to attain the Good Father's approval, you must negate sex. And what does sex mean to anyone at the Oedipus level like I am? It means guilty designs on mother.

'The Catholic religion is the only one that is still on the increase, and I can tell you why that is. It is because it is the only one where you can still love and worship the Good Mother, the woman (the Virgin Mary). Thus you can get more out of the Catholic religion, you get Mother as well as Father. You get her without any increase in your guilt feelings. On the contrary, she intercedes for you and helps to attain Father's forgiveness and approval. The important thing for the child to be free from anxiety is for it to be loved by both parents. The trouble about guilt is that guilt is the one thing above all others that would cause the good parents to withdraw their love. That is why you must get rid of guilt, be redeemed of your sins and reinstated with the parents and have their esteem and love. No child can feel happy and secure without this, and apparently judging by the universal appeal of religion, no adult can either. Perhaps they are all in the Oedipus situation like I am, only they don't recognize it so clearly, And yet you say that *I* am a bit crazy and *they* are sane.'

However, personal psychology apart, I should have thought the baby or infant (especially the boy) turns to his mother from birth onwards, as it did at the suckling stage, and father hardly exists—until much later when the principal reactive patterns are well established. An infant separated from its mother even for a short time, during sickness in hospital for instance, commonly becomes psychologically ill. Waifs and strays who are taken into hospital not unusually become psychotic until they are given appropriate psychotherapeutic treatment by a substitute 'mother'. Clinical material shows us that we all must have *good* parents in order to feel well and free from anxiety. A patient tells me: 'If the parent is felt to be bad, the child feels *lost*—without security and support. It then becomes ill; the sick, whether children or adults, are children without parents.'

In his clinical work the analyst discovers that all patients (all people) are looking for a good, potent, parent figure. Therefore the satisfaction of this need must be *essential* for a feeling of well-being. Not infrequently a patient reveals to his analyst that life for him is impossible without the good parent image of the analyst. Should something transpire which gives the patient the idea that the analyst is not good after all, but bad ('bad' usually means not loving the patient), the patient is in an intolerable state of distress and can regain his health only by destroying the bad analyst and recreating a good one in his place, (though in reality they remain the same person). If parents are felt to be bad, it is as bad as having no parents, and the result is insecurity, anxiety, illness, or delinquency, and even death. It seems that we *must* feel that we have good parents. Even if the parent beats us, the impossibility of living without a good parent is so great that we automatically sooner or later make the beating good in order to keep the parent good. In this way we may become masochistic. By the same token we create a *good* God: to avoid anxiety and psychosis. In the light of our analytical work it would seem sometimes to be a necessary psychological mechanism even if it does mean substituting delusion for distress.

If the mother is the primary recipient of our earliest emotional reactive patterns, why then is it so many religions from totemism onwards, exalt the Father? I can only suspect that fear must have been an over-riding determinant. This might well apply to union with the male siblings, or band of brothers, also perhaps encouraged by a fear of the incest prohibition with its corollary of castration or capital punishment by the father or 'brothers'.

Be this as it may, it seems in most religions the father with whom the individual is concerned. God is usually a masculine figure of large proportions, as all fathers seemed to be to us when we were small. He retains the omniscience and omnipotence which the infant and child attributes to the real father. Undue dependence upon God might well be a sign of some immaturity, a continuation of the role of the child whose anxiety was so great that he had, as it were, to cling to this adult figure. I think it may be said that Christianity practically acknowledges the identity of God and Father when it describes God as the Heavenly Father.

The principal points I wish to make are:

1. That the reactive patterns of very early life are sufficiently powerful to condition us (a) to a reluctance to abandon our only anxiety-relieving early environment, and (b) to create one like it in so far as it has to be abandoned, otherwise we would be overwhelmed with the same anxiety as we would have felt as infants, as the animal feels when separated from the herd.

2. That there is no objective observation that warrants or justifies a belief in the reality of such a figure.

3. That on this latter account such a belief has no more justification than all the, to us, obviously crazy beliefs of the elaborate religions and mythologies of our forbears.

In so far as reason and science have been enthroned as the last Court of Appeal, theism has had quite a struggle to maintain its principal tenet. On this account the concept of an anthropomorphic god (such as an old man with a long white beard) has been waived in favour of a better approximation to scientific and reasonable concepts, and many intellectual manoeuvres have been made to enable it to do so. For instance, Spinoza defined God as a 'substance consisting of infinite attributes',[29] alleging that He is the whole of what is, and that nothing exists apart from Him. This is very like the tenet of Hinduism, and it is impossible to distinguish from the doctrine of pantheism. It is therefore suggested that Spinoza deprives the word 'God' of any specific meaning.

The allegation that because there is a universe there must have been a creator of it has been exploded by David Hume, and shown to be illogical. Even Immanuel Kant has argued that the concept of causation cannot be applied to totality of phenomena. Paley strongly supported the interesting conception that 'the invisible things of God are clearly seen through the things that are made', and from this inferred an almighty designer.

But Hume cogently asks: 'Do we know so much about matter that we can say dogmatically that it could not have originated the degrees of order and arrangement which we observe in the universe?'[29]

One may add that since the days of Hume, so much has been discovered regarding the inexorable laws of molecular physics and chemistry, that they support the argument that all the degrees of order and arrangement which we observe in the universe could have originated from these. According to Hume: 'The most probable hypothesis is that the power behind phenomena is as devoid of goodness as of malice—"a blind Nature, impregnated by a great vivifying principle, and pouring forth from her lap, without discernment or parental care, her maimed and abortive children".'[29]

Robertson goes on to remind us that ' "Epicurus's old questions are yet unanswered. Is he willing to prevent evil, but not able? Then he is impotent. Is he able, but not willing? Then is he malevolent. Is he both able and willing? Whence then is evil?" '[29] Dean Inge says: 'There is no evidence for the theory that God is a merely moral Being, and what we observe of His laws and operations here indicates strongly that He is not.'[30] Bishop Henson says: 'It cannot honestly be denied that grave difficulties attach to the creed of Theism', and Bishop Gore asks: 'How much can we . . . rationally believe about God?'[30]

Thus it will be seen that even the intelligent clergy who have devoted their lives to this subject do not find it at all easy to separate the popular conception of theism, especially that of an anthropomorphic god, but I realize that arguments on a conscious level are certainly not the purpose of this book, and I am reluctant to put aside even temporarily my thesis of unconscious motivation, and of unconscious phantasy with its reactive pattern, as the only important source of our behaviour and beliefs. I had mentioned a little earlier that monotheism, in so far as it is the successor of the polytheism, demonology, and mythology and animism of primitive races, must involve some sacrifice of the natural tendency to believe the truth of our phantasies and dreams, and to project these on to our environment, and so dramatize and relieve the tensions of our internal conflict. But I would add that we do not entirely renounce many of the elements of these unwarranted beliefs and mythologies. We have indulged in many elaborations of phantasy besides that of creating and believing in the existence of a Heavenly Father.

CHAPTER XV

RELIGION, AN EMOTIONALLY DETERMINED
BELIEF

Having firmly established in our minds the belief in an omnipotent being, or in omnipotent beings, in accordance with our infantile reactive patterns, and in the image of the original parent figure or father, it is only natural to consider that he brought into existence not only ourselves (the human race), but also our environment and all that in it dwells. Thus it is a short step from belief in God to belief in the creation by God of all that exists.

In ancient cosmogony sometimes the phantasy is that creation is undertaken by two gods, male and female, this corresponding better with its source in the concept of father and mother. Occasionally it is a female god that instigates the process, but more commonly a male god. Both these latter ideas have been classified or stigmatized as a process of parthenogenesis, or generation by a single individual without the co-operation of a mate. Perhaps they indicate a more complete omnipotence on the part of the creator, and therefore support that necessary phantasy. For instance, the Hindu religion corresponds to our own in this respect, the single (male) deity responsible for creation being called Brahma. However, it is noteworthy that in Hebrew mythology, God is not content with a solitary male person (Adam) as the progenitor of the human race, but soon creates from one of his ribs, (a phallic symbol), the woman (Eve). Jointly these two become responsible for peopling the world, and thus we are back to the more accustomed mechanism of reproduction. The garden of Eden is symbolical of the womb, and the imagined heavenly bliss of 'innocent' babyhood on mother's bosom.

It is noteworthy that even at this early stage, the concepts of temptation and sin are introduced, and what is particularly noteworthy is that they are associated with sexual knowledge, or sexuality. The above symbolism and that which follows is repeatedly revealed to analysts during the dreams and associations of thought of their patients. The serpent is obviously the evil phallic symbol which tempts the woman. The woman offers Adam the apple, a well-established symbol for the female genital. Having sinned they feel guilty, and proceed to hide the truth under a covering (of leaves), a covering which in its symbolical form at least has never since been discarded.

Perhaps it is worth noting that sin is here identified with natural behaviour, and not with the falsehood of dissemblance. Parents, such as the Almighty Father, never do like sexuality in their offspring, no matter of what age, and therefore this mythological concept is in keeping with unconscious reactive patterns of the human mind. As has been pointed out even by ecclesiastics, it is very much out of keeping with logic and reason that an omnipotent God should create people of a certain nature and then consign them to banishment and torment for acting according to the nature which He had put into them. Even ecclesiastics have recognized the illogicality of this. The Rev. A. W. Momerie says: 'The character of the orthodox Deity is as bad as it can be. He was furious with Adam and Eve for having disobeyed him. They had eaten something—*eaten something*—which he had told them not to eat. In consequence of this single and trifling act of insubordination, he became so incredibly vindictive that he condemned the wretched pair, with all their unborn—and therefore innocent—descendants, to a life of suffering and an eternity of torment.'[30]

Thus we see that whatever element of mythology we examine, its determinant appears to be unconscious emotional reactive patterns rather than anything logical or reasonable. It is further pointed out that a benevolent parent who allowed his child to burn himself by the fire in order to teach him not to disobey, would be condemned by us as a fiend, rather than regarded as a benevolent deity. Presumably at the time when these mythologies were invented, people were more overtly and uncritically sadistic than at our present stage of evolution.

It might seem presumptuous to attempt to review the over-studied details of the Christian religion; also it would be unnecessary, for we have the considered pronouncements of many intelligent clergy who have devoted their lives to this subject. Some of them have not hesitated to offer us their well-considered conclusions, and even their criticisms. These are commonly of the opinion that the Old Testament cosmogony as related in Genesis has no greater claim to our credulity than the innumerable and obviously fantastic mythologies that preceded it in the history of man.

For instance, the Rev. R. Sinker writes: 'No one would suppose that the knowledge of the details preserved in Genesis was *directly* imparted by the Holy Spirit, using Moses as a mere mechanical agent ... The Biblical and Chaldean accounts of the Creation and the Flood are, in spite of all their differences, so closely allied that they clearly have an organic connection, and cannot conceivably present mere incidental coincidences.'[30]

But the Rev. Professor S. R. Driver tells us: 'The irreconcilability of the early narratives of Genesis with the facts of science and history must be recognized and accepted.'[30]

Bishop Gore says: 'In my judgment . . . the early chapters of Genesis—the accounts of Creation, Eden, the Fall, the Flood—are not historical records, but inspired folklore; and the subsequent records of the beginnings of Israel are tradition, and not strict history.'[30]

Bishop Barnes, who was sufficiently outspoken to receive much adverse criticism, himself said in a sermon in 1927: 'The stories of the creation of Adam and Eve, of their primal innocence and of their fall, have become for us folklore. But by the men who built up Catholic theology they were accepted as solid fact. Man's special creation was one of the primary assumptions of the Catholic system. In it the Fall explained the origin of sin; and a horrible theory of the propagation of sin, reared on the basis of the Fall of Augustine, was accepted by official Catholic theologians. Darwin's triumph has destroyed the whole relevant theological scheme.'[30]

If there are no logical or authentic grounds for these beliefs, we may well ask from whence do they spring? The only possible answer is from our unconscious phantasy or dream life, with its accompaniment of wishful thinking, and a facile attempt to explain reality in a way that comes most easily to us, and suits us best—at least at the stage of development when it came into being.

With regard to the alleged 'Fall of Man', the Rev. T. R. Stebbing writes: 'The Fall of Man, as described in Genesis, having been shown to be a fond thing vainly invented, it follows that the redemption of man from his imaginary Fall by a Divine mediator in human form can never have occurred.'[30]

Psychoanalysis, and indeed all forms of analytical investigation, has been able to tell us a great deal about the unconscious source of all these religious concepts. The intra-psychic conflict between id and superego, originally perhaps the conflict between infant and parent, particularly when it reached the form described by Freud as the Oedipus complex, gave rise within the human psyche to such an intense degree of terrifying guilt feeling, that many of our patients, and no doubt so-called normal persons, are spending their lives trying to atone for and redeem the wrong, the feelings of which remain in their minds in the form of guilt. Every device known to analysis is used for this unconscious purpose. All the unconscious mechanisms are called into play, denial, undoing, impotence and frigidity, repudiation of sin and often sex, asceticism, super-morality, kindness and service, and, as I see daily in a middle-aged woman patient, solicitous enquiry regarding my health; (she feels unconsciously that she may have damaged or destroyed me). Not that she cares objectively whether I am alive or dead, but only in so far as I symbolize her parent and protector. She is forever begging me to say (1) that I am all right, and (2) that I love her, or at least do not dislike her. As a child this patient offered a shilling to her sister to ask her mother whether she loved her. She was afraid to ask herself because a denial would have meant death.

The reason for all this is one and the same, unconscious feelings of guilt. If mother loves her, it means either that she was not guilty after all, or that she has been forgiven and redemption is at hand. The unconscious phantasy belongs to the Oedipus level of her having destroyed her mother (in phantasy) and usurped her place with her father. Her superego (the introjected mother) will surely destroy her unless she can undo this terrible crime, get support in her denial of it, or be redeemed. Naturally most of this belongs to the period of infantile amnesia, and is strongly repressed into the unconscious. I mention it to illustrate the extraordinary dynamic power of this phantasy, with its accompanying guilt complex and the compulsions that ensue from there.

In the light of our obsession with guilt and innocence, crime and punishment, immorality and morality, damnation and salvation, it would seem that we are not very different from this woman, even perhaps as regards the intensity of the emotions connected with these early complexes. We may well regard ourselves as fortunate in having found a ready-made neurotic or psychotic system of delusion, authoritatively supported, if it mitigates our internal discomfort and enables us to achieve some respite from the tormenting combination of guilt. That the system, whether in the form of one of the ancient religions or mythologies, or any of the modern ones, will not stand up to rational or scientific testing as regards its reality or truth, may be deplored, but can be overcome by a rejection of our sanity in favour of insanity. Dean Inge says: 'Religion . . . is fundamentally irrational',[30] and Bishop Gore admits that: 'Reason is at the last resort our only instrument of truth. Thus we cannot play false to our reason, or be content with any crude antithesis between faith and reason; faith, we find, being only reason in the making.'[30]

It seems to me a pity that some of these intelligent ecclesiastics, especially those of a generation or two ago, were not fully conversant with the discoveries of psychoanalytical investigation, for then they would surely have been saved a great deal of painful puzzlement, or better still, had they subjected themselves to a course of personal analysis, they may well have found all the answers to their puzzlement and struggle within their own unconscious mind.

The Fall is obviously the sin against the Father. In the Oedipus complex of the boy, it is the murder of the father in order to usurp his place with the mother. At the dawn of infantile genital sexual organization, sex is synonymous with incest (and murder), and that is why it ever after tends to have feelings of guilt associated with it, very often irrespective of whatever form it takes. Satan is symbolical of phallic sexuality, the symbolical figure of Satan, whether in red or black, with his lithe, tall form and multiplicity of angles and sharp points, not excepting the horns and tail, is one of the most typical phallic figures which we encounter in dreams, the potent and pleasure-filled sexual symbol. In the same way as primitive man projected a multiplicity of such symbols of evil and aggressive spirits into the terrifying world around him, so in later years they have tended to become concentrated in one all-encompassing evil figure. The fact that he was once one of God's angels, or an appendage of God, and then rebelled and was cast out of Heaven, may well be some unconscious reference to the child's, or at least the boy-child's, development from a pre-Oedipus stage to a phallic stage, in which his unconscious phantasies rebelled against the frustrations of father, a stage when he wished for the forbidden gratification of the Oedipus situation. He was cast out of Heaven, and in some religions and mythologies, such as Hephaestos in Greek mythology, was lamed by the fall, a clear symbol of at least some degree of castration, but evidently not enough to allay the guilt. The result has been that we have gone through life ever since accepting the capital punishment or annihilation, and only temporarily relieved from its anxiety if the omnipotent or almighty parent forgives and blesses us.

The mythology of the Deluge, or Flood, lends itself to analytical interpretation, though at the outset it may be said that it is not confined to Christian or Hebrew cosmogony, but is found in many places. The Encyclopaedia Biblica says: 'The points of contact between it (the Babylonian story) and the Hebrew story are so striking that the view of the dependence of one of the two on the other is directly suggested even to the most cautious of students.'[30]

The generality of mythological concepts immediately suggests to the analyst a common source in intra-psychic phantasy. We know from dreams and associations of thought that water, especially still water, or water in which one can be immersed, is usually symbolical of birth or/and of death. Therefore it is tempting to suggest that the Deluge may be a symbolical psychological method of destroying (death) all those sinful acts, and subsequently being reborn (out of the water), free from this intolerable burden of guilt. Religious ceremonies of baptism and conversion, especially for instance those of the Baptists, bear out this interpretation. Original sin is as it were washed away or drowned, and the now innocent child, born again of the father, is resuscitated.

I have mentioned some of the innumerable devices which the mind adopts to mitigate the sense of guilt, however unconscious its source may be, and this apparently is an additional one, symbolically acted out. In our analytical work we encounter many instances where dirtiness is symbolical of wickedness or sin (something bad), and where cleanliness is correspondingly identified with godliness or a freedom from sin. I have mentioned the case of the girl of sixteen who was the victim of an unfamiliar sexual titillation by a man, and was subsequently discovered by her mother exhausted in a bath in which she had been scrubbing herself for two or three hours. I have mentioned also that our social habits of washing and bathing have more unconscious determinants of this nature than the socially desirable ones of which we are conscious.

Belief in immortality is naturally wrapped up with the belief in a soul, and the belief in a soul emerges very early in all mythologies and religions. Once the idea of *Mana* or magic has been entertained and believed in, belief in a soul seems inevitable. The anthropological idea that it was due to primitive man being puzzled at the difference between a dead person and a live one does not fit in clearly with psychoanalytical evidence. It seems to the analyst more likely that the infant's belief in his own omnipotence would naturally include a belief in his imperishability, and when he came to see other people perish, he would have to extend his treasured concept of imperishability or immortality to them also, in order to reinforce the necessary conviction about himself, although there is evidence that each person, while able to accept the extinction of others, finds it difficult to believe in his own utter extinction. Thus he must have a soul and be immortal.

It is clear that many primitive men, such as the Neolithic man, and the ancient Egyptians, were so certain of the immortality of the soul that they made a great fuss about the corpse and even put food, weapons, etc. in his cave or grave. It is not much good to have immortality unless there is some happy place to go to when we are forced to relinquish this earth.

With regard to the concept of salvation, there is obviously in every psyche some dim or repressed memory of a wonderful guilt-free life like the Garden of Eden, never since encountered. Much of our activity may be motivated in part at least by attempts to recover this elysium, possibly it was in the womb or during the occasions of breast-feeding. Failing to re-enter this sublime state of mind, it is only natural that we should invent it as a promised land to offset the intolerable possibility of annihilation, or what the Rev. A. Wakefield Slaten believes to be 'a cessation of consciousness'.[30]

With regard to its objective reality, Forsyth says: 'the various religions are by no means agreed among themselves as to the kind of place that heaven is. The Christian conception of it is a place of angels, and singing. The Moslem paradise is provided with black-eyed houris, seventy-two of them for each believer. The Red Indian has his Happy Hunting-Ground. But in one notable respect the different religions are agreed, and that is in the firm conviction of each of the reality of its own heaven, and the falsity of the others. To the student who is interested in learning about not one but all religions, two deductions suggest themselves here. First, it seems evident that the intensity of the conviction with which a religious belief is held can be no measure of the truth of it. Secondly, it is very difficult for him not to conclude that all these heavens are equally figments of the imagination.'[10]

A practical consideration from a sociological point of view may be that in so far as people are looking for comfort and happiness in the after-life, this may detract from their incentive to try to build a heaven upon earth, or to mitigate the hardships of this life. The Rev. T. R. Stebbing says: 'All those attributes and qualities which fit a human being for a limited term of existence on this globe are ridiculously inappropriate to an ethereal heaven.'[30]

The mythological concept of Hell is less firmly held on to, and for very understandable reasons. We do not want punishment—unless it be for others, or unless we are masochists, for admittedly there are some persons so overweighed with guilt that they must at least have a purgatory if not a hell to absolve them. However, such persons usually succeed in creating one for themselves on this earth. Perhaps for most of us capital punishment would be enough without an eternity of torment.

The main value of the hell phantasy is of course for the satisfaction of our unrelieved sadism, beautifully expressed by certain classical writers such as Dante and Milton. As we cannot massacre heretics like we used to do in mediaeval times, for instance the Turks and Saracens at the Crusades, we can, so long as we have a hell, at least consign them in phantasy to an eternity of hell-fire.

Canon B. H. Streeter says: 'Scientific discovery, historical criticism, and subtle change—for the better I would suggest—in the mental outlook of the race have made the mediaeval idea of Hell appear to the majority as both ridiculous and immoral.'[30]

Delusions or false beliefs which are characteristic of psychosis are, as the symptomatology of this book purports to show, so general and widespread both in the history of man and right up to the present day that it is difficult anywhere to introduce the term 'normal' as denoting anything more 'normal' than the equivalent of *folie à deux*, or the participation in a mass psychosis.

It might be argued that it is only natural for people to have differences of opinion, which indicate that one or other or both parties to the difference must be mistaken or deluded, and that it is similarly natural for some 'normal' people to share the same opinion, erroneous or otherwise, and thus invite the allegation of being

victims of some degree of delusion or psychosis. Now this book is
pointing out very much more than this. It is pointing out that in our
most important thoughts and beliefs, the very things on which we
found our way of thinking, our habits, our customs and our rituals,
including our social habits, institutions and the structure of our
lives . . . the very basis of it all is emotionally determined belief or
phantasy, in which there is no evidence of any objective reality. One
can only say that if this is the yardstick of what is called normal,
or the normal being, sanity must be grossly abnormal or non-
existent.

But let us leave our psychopathological deliberations for the time
being, and investigate what further symptomatology the apparently
ineradicable burden of guilt, born of the Oedipus complex or earlier,
compels us to elaborate. Knowing that ontogeny repeats phylogeny,
we may assume that the history of man goes through similar stages
to that of the mental history of the individual from babyhood onwards.
Babies and infants may not be so weighed down with guilt as the
individual appears to be when his overgrown superego is fully
developed. Similarly we find that primitive peoples, are terrified of
all the evil with which they have peopled their external world and
are certainly not free from symptomatic behaviour indicative of an
attempt to deal with guilt. Nevertheless they do not appear to be so
compulsively and obsessionally or exclusively driven by the atonement and redemption motive, as we become when more civilized.
Correspondingly we may detect in some of the more intelligent
mythologies plenty of crime and punishment, but not such an
exclusive preoccupation with the need for redemption. Thus, as
humanity grew into an older, more mature or more civilized community, the old id freedoms or 'sins' became more forbidden and
repressed, and the need to eradicate the guilt connected with them
became greater. It is perhaps for this reason that we may detect in
many ancient religions a growing need for more evidence of a
benevolent god, of more reassurance of his benevolence, and even a
growing need for direct guidance and instruction by him. This need
begins to be met by prophesies of a coming Messiah, a teacher
inspired by God.

The story which is most familiar to us, and a terrifically stirring one
it is, is that contained in the New Testament. There is the charm of
folklore, and as in many religions, the prophecy of the coming
Messiah. The hope is that we shall then know better how we stand in
relation to God, be reassured and have our anxiety regarding everlasting punishment or annihilation, mitigated.

In this way there becomes implanted upon the old mythologies,
which were good enough for our forbears, a new element in keeping

with the more advanced stage of human development. Perhaps the delusional system was becoming a little vague for us, and we were developing a need for its reinforcement and confirmation. The wish is father to the thought . . . or to the further delusion. The expectation of a Messiah grows in strength until it must reach its gratification. Prophets represent minor degrees of this achievement until such time as we can acclaim the consummation of the real thing.

The enormous emotional appeal of these mental movements, and everything connected with them, characteristically sweeps aside the relatively feeble faculties of objective judgement and reasoning, but if we could calmly or in cold blood reflect upon it, we might come to the conclusion that the strength of these emotions are not proof or evidence of the truth of the resulting belief, on the contrary, evidence of its overwhelmingly strong emotional determinant.

Nothing could be more wonderfully stirring than the phantasy of God coming to earth amongst us as a little baby, born of a virgin . . . *and* with the prospect of this burden of guilt with which we have struggled everlastingly being finally removed by God himself a miraculous atonement and our miraculous redemption. In view of the agonizing mental state in which we live and labour, it may seem that this simply *had* to be invented.

As one might expect, such a fundamental emotional reactive pattern, reactive to our original (Oedipus) guilt feelings, is not confined to Hebrew mythology, but has its corresponding patterns wherever mankind has developed sufficiently to feel this need.

We have endeavoured to give a curious twist to the old situation by alleging that this (our) God came from God, or indeed was himself God in human form, who has taken our burden of guilt upon his own innocent shoulders, and suffered the extreme atonement of our behaviour so as to redeem our guilt. In other words, the sacrifice of Himself was His own doing, and not ours. He did it out of love for us. Thus we should know that the omnipotent parent figure by this token loves us, and so either we are not so guilty as we supposed, or if we are guilty, the guilt has all been washed away by the Redeemer's blood, a curious mixture of the concept of sacrifice and purification of (dirt)-guilt being removed by washing.

However, the matter of making us on better terms with God, or more like him, does not end with this supreme sacrifice. As in the pagan days of human sacrifice, of which Frazer tells us so much, the victim has to be incorporated to complete the magic. Admittedly the ancient sacrificial figures were largely 'eaten' indirectly by using their bodies to fertilize the soil, so that hungering humanity could eat the fruits thereof, but at the cannibal stage particularly, direct eating was a common practice. By incorporating the flesh, the body and blood, the superstition has always been that we incorporate the qualities of the person eaten. If this person is Christ, the very God-head, we obviously become like Him, perhaps identical with Him, and therefore obviously most acceptable by the almighty Father. We are no longer guilt-ridden, sin is no more and we can rejoin the happy family as before, or long before our stage of Oedipus develop-ment. It is a phantasy of back to the Garden of Eden, back to mother's breast or mother's womb, loved and accepted without any conflict or opposition by the authoritative figures, loved forever more in an everlasting life: Heaven indeed.

At any rate, this is the aim. Unfortunately, or fortunately, the conflict of these phantasies with the vestige of sanity that remains to us, and that we cannot entirely shake off in spite of all our endeavours, somewhat spoils our permanent residence in Paradise. There is always a struggle throughout our lives between phantasy and reality; we never did like the latter.

As we have seen in Chapter III ('Mythology, Cosmogony, and Comparative Religion'), there is much in Christianity, including the rite of communion, that far from being original was merely a con-tinuation of long-established religious and pagan practices. Archibald Robertson says: 'The Dead Sea scrolls prove that before the Christian era, at a date which can be fixed within a few years of the Roman conquest of Palestine, there was a sect of Jews to whom the idea of a Messiah triumphant over suffering and death was quite familiar. The evidence points to the identity of this sect with the Essenes mentioned by Josephus. Here, therefore, we have an Essene writer of the first century B.C. speaking of a dead leader of his sect in terms indis-tinguishable from those in which many early Christians spoke of Jesus. Two possibilities arise. . . . One is that the Gospel story has somehow or other been post-dated by about a century. The other is that the thing happened twice . . .

'The Dead Sea scrolls, if we accept the majority verdict as to their date, point to the execution of an Essene Messiah by Aristobulus as one source of the Christian legend. The resemblance between the earliest Christians and the Essenes is too close to be accidental. Their resemblance leaps to the eye more than ever now that we know that the Essenes, besides despising riches and pooling their possessions, also venerated a martyred leader whom they expected to come again with glory to judge the nations. As Professor Dupont-Sommer says, if there was borrowing, it was on the part of Christianity.'[29]

Whatever the details of the historical chronology may be, the close similarity between the religion of the Essenes, particularly their ethics, and the teaching of Jesus (for instance the Sermon on the Mount), rather inclines one to the view that He may Himself have been an Essene, or have had sufficient knowledge of their doctrines to be able to formulate His message in the terms which they were also using, and propagating. If this is so, it would suggest that Christ's teaching was less original than it was a final finished product.

We are told that: 'the reality of Our Lord's Incarnation . . . is the central truth of the Christian faith.'[31] But the Encyclopaedia Biblica tells us that in: 'the whole birth and childhood story of Matthew, in its every detail, it is possible to trace a pagan substratum.'[30] Bishop Gore reminds us: 'The Virgin Birth was certainly not part of the original Apostolic message.'[30]

Many ecclesiastical scholars have come to the conclusion that 'the record of a birth in full wedlock had been changed by about A.D. 70 into the record of a Virgin Birth'.[31] Thus it would seem that the Virgin Birth idea of incarnation, like so much of the material of the New Testament, was introduced at a very much later date than that of the first recordings. We will remember that in all the ancient mythologies, including Greek and Roman, gods even of lesser orders are not usually born in the ordinary physiological manner. The apparent willingness on the part of some theologians to waive the Virgin Birth element of the incarnation is most probably nothing more or less than a reluctant concession to science and popular incredulity.

How thoroughly Christianity influences our social, political and economic life, our art, our recreation, our philosophy, and sometimes even our science (but most markedly our social life), has to be discerned to be believed. Part of the object of this book is to draw attention to the magnitude, extent and ramifications of these irrational influences (cf. superstition, magic and mythology).

I have mentioned the development of a psychological need for a Messiah, or better still an emissary of God, or God himself on earth, who would lend a very necessary aid to the alleviation of the intolerable burden of guilt. In the case of Christianity it seems to me principally that Christ (or God) is used to atone for our crimes and reduce our guilt feelings. Ingeborg Flugel tells us that: 'The ambivalent attitude in the Communion service is revealed by the doctrine that, whereas participation in the Communion is highly beneficial to the pious, it is full of danger if we partake of it unworthily, for then "we are guilty of the body and blood of Christ, Our Saviour (i.e. become His murderers) and drink our own damnation".'[23]

Religious beliefs, like every other mental symptom, including the thoughts and activities of the obsessional neurotic, show a therapeutic element. The individual neurotic or psychotic commonly has to invent his own system of symptomatic relief, but in the case of religion, social behaviour and beliefs, the symptomatic pattern has been invented for us, and is ready to hand. Perhaps on this account it has been alleged by various people, including some psychologists and psychotherapists, that this ready-made psychosis is a valuable (even invaluable) therapeutic weapon. With this I most strongly disagree.

Dr Suttie says: 'Though it is hardly correct to say that religion is a neurosis (unless we remember that neurosis itself represents an attempt at cure), it is true from the nature of the case that religion tends to fall into the hands of neurotics.'[32]

This reminds me of a clinical episode of a neurotic patient of mine whose most tormenting symptom was a paralysing inhibition preventing him from doing public speaking, which he was particularly desirous of enjoying. Just before his session he had been listening to an evangelical sermon in which the preacher had almost hypnotized his audience with his oratory and his emotionally charged rampagings about hellfire. He himself had been entranced and lying on the settee he expostulated: 'If I could talk like than man, if I could stir a congregation as he did, if I could believe everything he believed . . . by jove, doctor, there would be nothing the matter with me, I would be perfectly well.'

His voice and gestures had reached a climax, and he then lay motionless on the settee. After about ten minutes' silence, he expressed in soliloquy what he had been thinking: '*Or would that be a more serious mental illness ?*'

Of course it would be a more serious mental illness, for a psychosis (to believe all that emotionally charged nonsense) is more serious than a neurosis.

In the light of the remarks of so many of my colleagues that religious beliefs can have some therapeutic value, I think we ought to distinguish between the 'therapeutic' effect of the formation of a symptom and the effects of this symptom upon our behaviour, our environment, and its repercussions upon those with whom we or the symptom come in contact.

Perhaps it is not always possible to differentiate between the direct effect of a delusional belief, mythological or religious, and collateral behaviour determined by equivalent unrealistic, or superstitious attitudes of mind. Are we to say that such social practices as the mutilation of the adolescent's genitals, male and female, mis-called circumcision, the cruelty of the restrictions placed upon menstruating virgins, and innumerable cruelties culminating perhaps in human sacrifice and cannibalism, are collateral to the religious beliefs of that time, or were causally related to them. It seems to me that to anyone reading details of the innumerable cruelties from which whole populations suffered in the name of the religious belief of the time, they could hardly be grouped under the heading of 'the therapeutic value of religion'!

If we should wish to argue that these were barbarous practices of primitive times, and very foreign to the effects (therapeutic or otherwise) of religion on civilized communities, we will find plenty to contradict this view in our own history, from the time of the Crusades, with their extermination of hundreds of thousands of disbelievers—a practice perpetrated by almost every modern religion at some period of its existence—to the indescribable cruelties of the Inquisition, and the even more recent witch-huntings and burnings.

It should not be forgotten that such florid examples of the antithesis of therapeutic value are apt to mask from us the fact that in every nook and cranny of our social life, religious or delusional belief appears on investigation to have in varying degrees an injurious effect. For instance, through the many hundreds of years which are now referred to as the Dark Ages, this indoctrination halted scientific and social progress, which meant in practice that the whole community continued to suffer the inconveniences and torments which they would otherwise, by virtue of their capacity for intellectual and scientific development, have long since overcome. These included up to recent times such practices as infant and child labour, and many other things which we would nowadays stigmatize as diabolical cruelties.

But the instances of the psychologically and physically injurious effects of erroneous beliefs extend to even the most superficial inconveniences and injuries of children and adults. For instance, a Scottish patient of mine tells me that when he was a boy he was on Sundays not permitted to play any game whatever, and games were the very pulse of his life. Instead each Sunday is still remembered by him as a protracted torture of stiff collar, best clothes and the going to Church service and Sunday school, and perhaps worst of all, the utter and complete boredom in between. He still feels that the injury of this one day a week stayed with him until its awful recurrence seven days later. I am reminded by this story of the fact until the end of the Second World War, the playing fields in our recreation grounds and parks, and many potential playing fields, were desert places, whereas now, with some relenting of religious 'authority', they are crowded with happy youngsters and adolescents, enjoying health-giving activities.

But the injurious effects of delusional beliefs extend into much more covert and hidden places than these. Flugel reminds us that 'religion . . . can exercise a severe crippling and inhibiting effect upon the human mind, by fostering irrational anxiety, and guilt, and by hampering the free play of the intellect'. He continues: 'In this respect religion mirrors the evil effects of the primitive internal superego, and in the long run even an increase in individual neurosis may not be too high a price to pay for the removal of the restrictions it imposes.'[24]

A certain proportion of mentally ill people appear to have had their breakdown caused and maintained by their reactions to what can be an excessively guilt-producing indoctrination. Admittedly the formation of the symptom which I am calling erroneous belief, or religion, may well be an attempt on the part of the mind to reduce its overload of guilt, but seemingly it is a two-edged sword, and instead of reducing the guilt, in many cases it appears to enhance it to a degree that results in mental breakdown, and this is by no means an exceptional or very unusual occurrence.

Perhaps it may be said that every nervous breakdown is precipitated by *frustration*, no doubt analogous to the original frustration of the infant's automatic natural attempts to relieve his tensions being frustrated by parents and reality. When in later life undue frustration is again encountered, the id impulses (libidinal and aggressive) which had advanced to that point of perhaps adult forms of satisfaction, being again blocked by frustration, tend to regress or go backwards along the path of their pre-adult development. This regression is an interesting concept, for in most cases we can see that fixation points, finally overcome in the course of our development, are again activated, and, as it were, the old struggles renewed. But perhaps the most important of all fixation points is that of the Oedipus complex belonging to the period of infantile amnesia. In other words, incestuous desires for mother are aroused, together with their subsequent and accompanying exaggerated horror, due to the phantasies of annihilation.

I may here mention that a patient told me of a very vivid phantasy which he had had just before the climax of his nervous breakdown. He said: 'I was sitting in church when I had the phantasy. The phantasy was that I was sitting there naked and my mother, also naked, was sitting on my lap, facing the same way. Perhaps incest was going on, I cannot tell you. What I do remember is that I found the whole idea so repugnant and disgusting that I wanted to rush out of the church, and nearly did so. *Actually* my mother was sitting beside me in church when I had this phantasy.'

The fact that this phantasy of incest was experienced while the patient was in church may suggest that 'church' or religion had something to do with one side of the conflict, and by contrary association may have stimulated the other side, a mechanism with which one is fairly familiar.

One may detect also that once the natural movement of life has been stopped, for instance by attempts at purity and asexual 'perfection', and consequentially the libido has regressed to an Oedipus level of conflict, involving incest, the victim's superego (introjected mother and father) will institute the utmost opposition, accompanied by feelings of anxiety and guilt.

Religion, though an elaborate attempt to dramatize all these things and to alleviate guilt by its system of phantasies and delusions, can, as we see, have the opposite effect, namely that of underlining and reinforcing and even rationalizing the irrational guilt emanating largely from the Oedipus complex (which the individual has to bear). The direst punishments instituted by the superego may follow, ranging from actual suicide to every degree of partial 'suicide', mental, nervous, or/and physical breakdown, psychosomatic illness and serious and even fatal, organic disease.

Religion offers us the love of an all-important father in exchange for the surrender of our sexual instinct—an everlasting life if we will overcome the impulse to enjoy the sexual life of the moment—or as some would say if we overcome the life of the moment. In this connection it is noteworthy that in celibate religious orders the initiates (munks or nuns) have the funeral service read over them when they take their final vows. On reflection it would appear that all they are giving up is sexuality, which religion thereby tacitly recognizes as 'all'.

Another patient, speaking of her devotion to religion, of the consolation she received from it, and of the pleasures with which it provided her said: 'What I like best in life is being in church and though for some reason which I do not understand I am a little ashamed to admit it, I enjoy most of all taking part in the singing. There are occasions when I am singing psalms in church when I get a most extraordinary sensation. It is usually when I have got very worked up with the singing and the music. Suddenly an extraordinary thrill takes possession of me, travels over my whole body right down to my very finger tips.' If anything further was needed to convince one that this was the experience of an unsuspected sexual orgasm, it is the fact that she admitted to finding genital moisture when she returned home after such an event.

The complex or basic conflict which emerged on further analysis does not particularly concern us here. Enough to say that it was an Oedipus fixation to the father-image. This was responsible for her symptoms, in that, one, the unconscious incest taboo was naturally too powerful to permit orgasm, or even sexual feeling, when natural intercourse took place, and two, the religion and superego sanctioned singing to Father, permitted the desired union to be consummated, provided there was no detection on the part of prohibiting forces, and this absence of detection was ensured under the guise of religious esctasy.

I have given this as an instance to show that with the total repression of the primitive sexual pattern, sexuality including its orgasm nevertheless finds an expression, an outlet, no matter what conscious content of mind it has to use for the purpose, even that content which is supposed to be antithetical to sexuality. So much for the apparent or alleged absence of sexuality in any person, and so much for its supposed absence from our social order, institutions and habits, for it is seen to invade even those such as religion, which might have been regarded as the most antithetical to it.

Ernest Jones[33] says that in common with mythology, fairy-tales, folk-lore and superstition, religion 'is a product of human fantasy, the investigation of which has been one of the main tasks of psychoanalysis. . . . The psychoanalysis of myths shows clearly that they represent in a disguised way the most primitive wishes and fears of mankind. The mechanism of the disguise, as also the motive for it, is extremely similar to that of dreams, and, indeed, many mythologists before Freud had pointed out the far-going resemblances between dreams and myths. The energies that could not be transmuted into the real tasks and interests of life were expressed in the wishfulfilments of myths, and still more openly in that of fairy-tales.'

'All religion is founded on the idea of sin, i.e. the sense of guilt at not reaching a prescribed standard. Without this idea religion loses all meaning. All sin can be expressed in terms of disobedience to the Father (or even rebellion against Him), or else desecration of the Mother (and her attributes or substitutes). Now these are the two components of the primal oedipus complex of childhood; incidentally, the Protestant and Catholic types of mind correspond with the component on which the accent falls. The subject of guilt has had to be investigated by psychoanalysis in very great detail, for it plays an important part in every individual analysis. . . . One can only say here that the lofty sense of spiritual value attaching to religious feeling and beliefs owes much of its importance to the fact that these at the same time fulfill the deepest cravings of the human mind and afford some appeasement to the unconscious moral tension . . .

'The other important element of religious beliefs, namely, that in an after-life, displays the feature of wishfulfillment more prominently than that just considered. Salvation betokens a joyful reunion with the parents against whom the unconscious sinful thoughts were directed. Heaven is the reward of that "at-one-ment". All the unsatisfactoriness, hardships, and injustices of this life will find their due compensation there. And it is fitting that the symbolism of heaven should contain endless allusions to the unconscious identification of this reward with the notion of recapturing a form of bliss that we once possessed (hence the idea of the Fall), of returning to "that imperial palace whence we came".

'To sum up: religious beliefs, whether savage, mythological or Christian, may or may not be true—in their nature thay are not capable of proof or disproof—but it is highly probable that they would have arisen in their identical forms whether they were true or not; the genesis of them can be adequately accounted for without invoking any external (supernatural) agency.'[33]

In other words, Ernest Jones is saying in this last paragraph that, one, from what we know of the unconscious mind, it is highly probable that religious beliefs would have arisen in their present form and, two, which he is not stressing, that there is no other evidence for them whatsoever.

CHAPTER XVI

'TREATMENT' AND EGO DEVELOPMENT

If we are going to insist, as I expect most people will insist, that the ego takes a hand in the amelioration of our psychosis, (an ego sickness), then we had best begin with a differentiation of the early pleasure ego and the recently developed reality ego. It is this latter only which I regard as deserving the name of Ego (cf. reality principle).

The Reality with which the Ego or Reason has to cope must be regarded as at least twofold—in a sense threefold. First, there is the external reality or the real world outside ourselves, so far as we are capable of appreciating it. This may be called environmental reality. Secondly there is an internal 'reality', a world of real forces within ourselves which has nothing to do with reason or necessarily with consciousness. To adjust this internal world with the external world of reality is the essential function of the ego. One of the ego's difficulties may be that it finds it even more difficult to become adequately aware of the nature of this internal reality than it does to arrive at an adequate appreciation of external reality. *In so far as the ego is able to become cognisant of this internal reality, to obtain insight into it, and to appreciate the respects in which it is powerless to alter it, it behoves the ego to treat it with as much consideration as it has treated the inexorable forces of Nature outside itself.*

What do we know of this internal reality? We know that it comprises forces which for descriptive convenience can be divided into two more or less separate camps. The first group of these forces we label primitive *id* drives or impulses. The so-called life instinct and death-instinct would belong here. The ego, to be an adequate ego, must do something about these, and to approximate to perfection, the ego must do the most perfect thing possible about these. That most perfect thing is *not* to attempt to incarcerate them in a strong-room or dungeon—the only successful or practical effort in that direction would be incarceration in a tomb with the corpse—and certainly not to adopt the ostrich policy of ignoring their existence.

Most of the symptoms of neurosis and of civilization bear witness to the failure of this attempt to ignore or incarcerate the forces of the id. They are the forces of life itself, and *will* come out in some form or other. The business of the ego is, or should be, to let them out where they are not in conflict with other (e.g. environmental) reality, and where they *are* in conflict, to *modify* them in such a way that their swords shall be turned to ploughshares.

But the matter is not so simple as all that. There is another group of forces forming as it were a rival camp within the realm of this internal reality. This camp represents the efforts of the primitive and infantile ego to deal with those same original id drives or instincts. The efforts of this primitive ego, the methods it employed, were very primitive and barbarous. Reason, according to our present standards, had hardly dawned. The primitive ego was created largely at the instigation of Fear (projected on to parent figures), and it employed the savage destructive weapons of the id, borrowed as it were from the id, in order to do battle against this id-menace to its existence.

The trouble is that this primitive ego (the superego), using its same out-of-date weapons, is still rampant within every one of us. It is still ready and active in attacking id impulses with its id-borrowed savagery and unreason, whenever and wherever it should detect them or think it detects them.

Not content with this unconscious activity, the superego endeavours, and with an enormous measure of success, to enlist the services of the ego and even to browbeat the ego into stupidity and assent.

Whereas the 'madness' of the raving maniac may be attributed to the ego becoming overwhelmed by the id, the 'madness' of sane persons and of civilization may be attributed to the ego becoming overwhelmed by the primitive ego or superego, or else to the ego never having freed itself from the domination of this savage unconscious conscience (superego).

To be sane, to evolve a better world, it is necessary that the adult ego should take into consideration the forces of its superego as a part of internal reality, as well as the forces of the id. To be in a position to do this the first step is obviously that the ego should become cognisant of the forces of its superego, and should be able to distinguish them from itself, from reason. The point I wish to make here is this: the EGO having become cognisant of these superego forces, *in so far as it is unable to destroy them or modify them,* must take them into consideration as an internal reality in its attempt to make the best possible adjustments between the realities, external, and internal, with which it has to deal. For example: if your ego tells you it is foolish to have a bath, and yet your superego is not satisfied with your reasonable conduct in not bathing, it is better to bath than to suffer the torments of intrapsychic conflict. Similarly if your id *and your ego* are both in favour of a particular sexual act, but your superego is likely to slay you for it, it behoves your ego to make the best possible adjustment between the contending forces with due consideration of their relative power. It may be considered to be more reasonable to live 'unreasonably' than to die for 'reason'.

The trouble with 'normal' man is this: he behaves towards his id forces very much in the way that his superego behaves towards them: so long as they are not disguised or handed over to the angels, he is apt to regard them as devils within—and this quite irrespective of whether their immediate tendency is destructive or constructive.

On the other hand, the *same* forces or impulses of *unreason*, in so far as they have been handed over to the superego (unconscious conscience), are usually regarded by the ego as though they were, a higher moral self. Thus he can indulge in sadism—so long as it is sadism towards the malefactor. In fact he usually fails to recognize that these so-called moral or righteous forces within him are devoid of reason, and in consequence much of his judgements and conduct are devoid of reason, and to a comparatively reasonable person have the mark of the brute.

If this consideration of the madness of mankind is to teach us anything, it is these two things: one, that the changes necessary to establish a better and a happier world are psychological changes in the individuals who comprise the world, and two, that these changes are *not* to be brought about by a mere tightening up of the dictatorship of Reason.

Reason must make allowances, further allowances than it is at present making, for the inexorable and unchangeable forces or instincts within the id, since these forces are the drive of life itself. Whereas it is necessary to deal (either by repression or preferably modification) with these forces when they would run counter to external or even unalterable superego 'realities', it is unnecessary and unreasonable for the ego to deny these forces an outlet merely because they are detected as belonging to the primitive self, and when their expression would not conflict with other reality considerations. Thus there is no need to suffer from constipation either of the bowels, the bladder, the seminal vesicles, the speech or the mind.

Repressions of id forces commonly lead to an escape of these same forces under the flag of the superego, with an equal amount of savagery, aggression, or cruelty, levied either against the self or against other persons. Further, they influence or control the ego in the direction of unreason.

How can reasonable psychological changes be brought about? Apart from the psychological analysis of adults, probably the only way is by a fundamental change in our upbringing of children. These pages may help us to recognize that we are mad, or partly so, that our standards and criteria are largely mad standards and criteria. If we recognize this we may be less dogmatic in our attempts to force our children to adopt these standards. Though we may recognize as we now do that our children are wrong, we may be less confident and less autocratic in forcing them to abandon their behaviour in favour of our behaviour. We may recognize that their methods of getting relief from their id tensions are not necessarily very much worse than our methods for getting relief from our id tensions. If Freddie wants to play buses with the cushions in the drawing-room, we may recognize that this is not necessarily more unreasonable than our predilection for tidiness and cleanliness of that same drawing-room. We may recognize that our impulse to punish him with hand or cane is no better than his (perhaps fear-repressed) aggressive rage at our interference. We may thus avoid sowing the seeds of future war and bloodshed.

In general a fundamental and far-reaching change in our up-bringing of children will be the first practical step in the direction of modifying the savagery of unconscious superego forces in the next generation. We will learn to allow harmless id-impulses to obtain freedom under infantile ego supervision. We will strengthen an ego of reason instead of a superego of unreason. (For instance, harmless though perverted sex impulses will be allowed).

If what I am saying has any merit, it lies in this: Hitherto attempts to achieve a better world have focussed attention exclusively upon manipulation of *external* reality, the objective world. My thesis is that improvement depends upon manipulation of *internal* reality. I have stated that this internal reality consists of two subdivisions, the id and the superego. Of these the superego, though responsible for so much of the madness of civilization has, in contradistinction to the id, two attributes of practical importance. One is that it is to some degree modifiable, in the adult at least, by psychological analysis, and that it is not wholly innate, but is subject to developmental influences and modifications from babyhood to infancy. It is with this last point, the encouragement of ego (reason) development and a simultaneous discouragement of superego development with which we are dealing.

For example, if you tell an infant that he must not do so-and-so because it is naughty, you may be encouraging superego (fear-aggression—unreason) development. Whereas if, utilizing his positive love feeling towards yourself, you explain to him that *if* he does so-and-so the consequences will be disagreeable either to himself (e.g. stomach-ache), or else to you, on account of your limited abilities to bear hardship, and nevertheless allow him to try out the experiment, you may be encouraging the development of his ego (reality-appreciation and reason).

It may be that no harder task could be set for any adult, in his present state of ego-limitation, mental chaos or madness. But what is difficult for the adult is even more difficult for the child; and the child of today is normally presented with an impossible task, that of enduring the misguided interference of 'mad' adults. It is small wonder that his mental equipment cracks up under the impossible strain and he grows up to perpetuate a world of madmen.

If in the course of many generations the superego almost disappears as an important mental force, having given place to a relatively greater ego development, we must turn our attention to that other internal reality which *is* innate and inexorable. What is the ego to do about this other great source of unreason? The *Id* has been said to comprise two great primal forces: the life-instinct or libido, and the death-instinct or aggression. Some psycho-analysts, with Freud, believe that there exists a primary instinct deserving of the name of Death-instinct; an equally strong body of psychoanalysts feel that this so-called instinct is largely if not entirely a secondary product resulting from the thwarting (to some extend *inevitable* thwarting) of the life-instinct in its pursuit of pleasure or gratification.

In any case, there can be no doubt that the aggressive instinct is enormously enhanced, if not called into being, by any and every frustration of primary libidinal urges (life-instinct). Also it may be said that a free expression in the real world of aggressive impulses (death-instinct) as such, is very difficult to achieve without the most drastic challenge to reality values—without the most flagrant madness (e.g. murder, war, punishment, etc.). The best that can be done with them is a rather precarious sublimation, such as struggle for existence, competitive sports, or the writing of an aggressive book on all the world being mad.

If, however, these aggressive instincts are called into being simply by frustration of libidinal (or life) instincts, the obvious way of dealing with them is to prevent their birth (or at least their further growth) by removing every possible frustration of libidinal instincts in so far as this is compatible with a due regard for other realities. Is the reason of mankind, is the ego of the individual, doing everything that is possible in this direction? The answer is that the ego seems to be paralytic or non-existent when it is faced with any such work. It is notoriously impossible for the average person's ego to take a reasonable attitude with regard to sexual matters, and often, an extension of this, to almost any matters in which sensuality or pleasure is the stake at issue. It is here that the superego seems to step in and almost entirely usurp the functions of the ego. This is not very surprising when one reflects that it was out of these id urges (libido, etc.), that the primitive ego came into existence, and its chief function was to do something about these urges, by hook or by crook. The *early* ego was in such a weak position that it, aided and abetted by the unreason and fear of adult retribution, assumed tyrannical measures, enlisting all it could of the worst qualities (aggression) of the id to defend its weak or desperate position against the id.

In this respect the adult rarely remembers that he has grown up, or should have grown up; and that he should have an ego or reason to call upon both in his individual adjustment and in the upbringing of his progeny. There is no longer any necessity for the ego to get scared out of its reason whenever it detects a libidinous or id impulse clamouring for freedom. If we cannot help it in ourselves, it is necessary that we should make some sacrifice to save the next generation from developing our own peculiar madness.

There are innumerable libidinal urges of babyhood and infancy that could be allowed a much greater degree of freedom without any more disastrous consequence than the retardation of aggressiveness and, ultimately, the bankruptcy of armament factories.

We are still wise enough, or fortunately blind enough, to permit the newly-born baby to suck the nipple or the teat; we may even allow it to suck its fingers or its toes without inflicting our ignorant interference. But its early paradise is short-lived; we see to that. When a little later on it begins to pick its nose, or continues unduly to obey the behests of its loaded bowels or bladder, it soon discovers that the erstwhile gratifying environment, parents or nurses, is not a world of good and lovable objects after all. It discovers that the world is peopled with enemies—enemies or bad objects are those that frustrate or interfere with gratifying impulses—and lo! there has begun the process that ends in bloody death on Armageddon. If the baby's nose-picking annoys us, it is we that need the cure, not the baby. If its natural bowel activities conflict with our ideas of cleanliness and orderliness, it is we who need a purge for our mental constipation, and not the baby who needs a mental cork to enforce its real constipation. (The worst cases of fear-aggression neurosis or sadistic perversions with which the medical psychologist has to deal are traceable to early interferences with bowel function.)

But worse is yet to come; should the poor suffering infant in this world of enemies, finding its rage (at present) impotent, be forced back in its intolerable distress upon the great discovery of its genital organ as a source of consolation, the fat is indeed in the fire. Instead of the mother recognizing that the child once had the nipple to gratify it, and it might reasonably have expected that the mother in some shape or form would continue as she had begun, out of her love to gratify it, and that she having turned traitor, it has shown her her inadequacy by falling back upon its own efforts, and has in truth discovered a nipple substitute in its genital organ—instead of the mother recognizing intuitively these things, she is blinded by her own intra-psychic madness and hastens not to make amends for her failure, but to institute further frustrations, deprivations, hate feelings and intolerable distresses.

A less natural substitute for the already mentally sick condition has to be discovered by the unfortunate infant. Steadily but surely is he driven to take steps towards the universal madness. The following is a common experience at child clinics: a girl of three years is brought in by an unduly alarmed mother on account of genital masturbation. Months later the mother, now smiling and happy, tells the doctor that she has cured the terrible habit. The seated child is seen to be energetically swinging her legs. She has found an alternative method of masturbation which does not stimulate her mother's guilt feelings. The mother will be less pleased when in later life she finds a still less primitive and more 'cultured' method of consolation for her deprivations by, for example, stealing.

If, however, an infant, perhaps a little later, should make real mental progress, for example in the direction of finding an external object for his desires, a real mother-substitute, in the shape of another erotically disposed infant, it will be driven home upon him that the world consists of unreasonable enemies indeed. His character is speedily split into a portion that, divorced from the world of adult enemies, seeks and finds surreptitious, anti-social gratifications, and a superego that takes the side of these powerful and cruel beings. Then will his life be a miserable battle between these two intra-psychic forces, and his behaviour in the real world will be forever tainted with their madness.

In short, the remedy suggested is that libidinal activities in infants and children should not be allowed to provoke guilt feelings in adults, and do not call for superego interference on the part of adults. Generally they are harmless or even necessary for the child *under the circumstances*. They would not take place spontaneously were there not some adequate cause for them. They must not be removed by forcible frustration. Sublimation will occur spontaneously if the child is provided with the ordinary amenities for it.

The indignant reader may ask: do you mean to say that children should be encouraged to pick their noses, to mess themselves and even to masturbate, and to indulge in mutual erotic performances? This is too much.

My answer is quite emphatic: certainly not. No child should be *encouraged* to do any of these things. Are these things so important for you that you *cannot* let them alone? *Must* you either *encourage* or *frustrate?* If you have forces of unreason, such as libidinal urges, aggression, hate or morality, that you *must* give vent to, do it somewhere else but not in the nursery or school.

I have known as serious consequences to ensue from adult or semi-adult encouragement of masturbation in an infant, as from frustration.

Only frustration is far more often the common experience, and the madness of the world owes more to this than to encouragement. The child might stand a chance of growing up relatively sane if it were not for the unreasoned *interference* of adults.

Would you then advocate no training or discipline for the child? Are children to grow up wild, uncivilized, impossible?

The most that can be done, without paying the price of intra-psychic damage, is to use a love-transference to *encourage* the child's mind in its natural tendency to sublimation. This cannot be done by an enemy. If we incur the child's enmity, even its repressed unconscious enmity, we have lost our ability to help it, and had best disappear out of its life. We will incur its enmity if we *frustrate* its desires, its gratifications. It loves us because we gratify it, and we had best maintain that role, substituting adequate cultural gratifications for those we feel it should abandon in favour of reality.

Let us be sure that our own reality sense has not become mixed up with unreason, with our passions, libidinal, aggressive or superego, or we shall make the child as mad as we are.

CHAPTER XVII

THE MIND IS PRIMARILY A PHYSIOLOGICAL
ORGAN

The mind, when not subjected to censorship, produces the most unexpected and extraordinary revelations about itself. It shows quite clearly that it prefers not to have anything to do with reality at all. Indeed, it retreats from reality, and occupies itself almost exclusively with what Freud called the pleasure principle, together with a certain amount of equally irrational compulsions. I say that these processes are irrational because they take flight from reality, and all reality knowledge, and all reality considerations, so that the individual becomes as it were automatically immersed in a world as unreal as that of the superstitions of primitive people.

One realizes that it is very difficult to convey to people unacquainted with analysis the basic importance of the revelations discovered through this process and available only through this process. I have said that these revelations amount to a demonstration that the mind is engaged upon the process of relieving its tensions, its discomforts, by means of a repetition of early infantile phantasies, that the individual feels that he is living, truly living, only while his mind is thus engaged, that every interference with this automatic and natural movement of the mind is felt by him to be an interruption of his life, a frustration, a discomfort, something which increases the tensions within him, makes him feel discomfort and pain, or indeed as though his life process had been arrested, he hopes only temporarily. 'We are such stuff as dreams are made on.' At the first opportunity, he will return to the automatic processes in accordance with the pleasure principle and the compulsion within him to go on living his emotional life in this natural or automatic way. There is evidence that within the normal mind there is a feeling of resentment at these interferences and interruptions which the world, environment and other people impose. This resentment activates hate feelings, resistance, even anger and aggression. If it persists, illness ensues. There is a limit to the amount which any of us can stand of this impinging of an unwelcome environment upon our autonomy, omnipotence, or schizophrenia.

I shall try to give one or two excerpts from recent analytical material to illustrate what I mean by this contention. A colleague

who was retiring sent me a French lady patient of his who needed
treatment because she was so quarrelsome, vituperative and violent
on occasions towards her saintly husband, and also because she could
not bear her family, which included one or two young members, and
her motherly and domestic duties. People who did not understand
would have said she was a nasty, violent, shrewish wife, and a totally
impossible and hateful mother. The following little story will show us
why she appeared to be all these things. There was no disputing the
fact that she was a character full of fire and emotion. In the course of
free association of thought, she told me the following little remi-
niscence, perhaps for the purpose of illustrating her resentment to the
world in general, her husband and children in particular. She said:

'Several years ago, I took my little girl, then only two or three
years of age, to a beautiful hotel on the Riviera, at Aiguebelle. I grew
so tired of being tied to the infant, and my movements confined by
having to look after her, that I got a young woman to be a sort of
baby-sitter or nurse, and I went off for an afternoon's holiday. I took
a bus to Lavandou, and proceeded to walk home. It was a lovely
afternoon, and along the road by the bays, I was delighted with the
beautiful scenery, the sunshine, the trees and the flowers. I felt I was
walking on air, it was like a paradise.'

Then she revealed the interesting fact that her late analyst had told
her that he had lived at that very town as a boy. She had never outgrown her extraordinary transference to this elderly analyst, now
retired, and I strongly suspected that it was 'holy ground' she was
walking on, the ground that this 'god' of hers had walked upon forty
or more years ago. Perhaps this is what made it paradise. He was the
only man to whom she had ever had a real positive transference, one
might call it a grand passion. At least, he was the only man to whom
she could remember having such a passion, for analytical evidence
revealed that she had a similar passion as a small infant or baby for
her father. Both passions had of course never been consummated or
gratified in actuality or instinctually, they were of course confined to
romance, dreamings and imaginings, and feelings of paradise.

After she had strolled along for an hour or two, revelling in everything, the adventure turned into a misadventure. A motorist stopped
at her side and offered her a lift. She refused. The same man repeated
his request a few hundred yards further along the road. Again she
refused, saying she preferred to walk. A few hundred yards still
further, she found him on foot, asking her if he could accompany her
on the walk. She flew at him, screaming 'Don't pester me!' and he
was off—and she never saw him again.

Nevertheless, this little incident changed her happiness into unhappiness. She said: 'I walked the rest of the way home crying.' Then
she added: 'No, it was not the man, he was nothing. It was the

association. The association was to my husband. I was walking home to my husband, the frustrator of all my happiness in life. I was enjoying a wonderful romance if you like, I do not know exactly what the dream was, but it was all happiness, eternal happiness. If there is no romance in life, one is better dead. One can't live without it, any more than one can live without air.'

She continued: 'It is not that that man destroyed my romance. That man made me think of my husband. Reality is my husband, and that is something that I can't forget, my husband, and the duties of motherhood and wifehood.

'When I was engaged all those many, many years ago, it must be understood that I was not in love, but I thought: "He is a good man, they all want me to marry him. He is a good man. Why not, I may be happy".'

It may here be pointed out that the good man, the kind man, the saintly man, the man who does not interfere with a woman's way of life would be welcomed as a husband by the majority of women. We like people like this because they are so passive and we can go on dreaming our dreams or living our own lives as it were, having our own phantasies, without their interference. They do not interfere, perhaps they are living their own phantasy-lives, consciously or unconsciously. But in this woman's case it did not work out like that. It seems that even the good man, when he becomes reality, destroys the romance.

I pointed out to her that the poetry of this walk was really something in herself, and had nothing to do with her present-day environment, either of husband or children. I said to her: 'The poetry, what you call the loveliness, is in you, and any reality evidently spoils it.'

She said: 'It's sad that it should be like this, perhaps I will get you to understand why I attack my husband, why I hate him, why I don't want the children.'

Further analysis will reveal in due course that this phantasy, this paradise in which the patient lives is nothing more or less than some early imaginings accompanied by the dawn of feelings of a pleasureable nature, probably including sexual feelings, which began in childhood, in infancy, and were wrapped up with her parents. Indeed, the phantasy in which she is living and which gave her so much pleasure, which she declares is her whole life, although she does not know the contents of it, is the familiar infantile Oedipus phantasy, a love-phantasy that lives on inside her and seems to be the only thing that keeps her alive or makes her life worth living. Reality, why reality is just an intolerable interference. As for any capacity to accept reality objectively, why, it is beyond one's wildest dreams.

A man patient of mine is restless and agitated, moving about most of the time, he can hardly keep still, he cannot do a job on this very account. Though normal in many respects, and appreciative of the opposite sex, he is inclined to be unduly aggressive to nearly all males. He raises his voice, shouts at them, and some people may think him objectionable, though of course he can usually be very well-mannered, concealing all these tendencies of his.

Now why this patient behaves as he does, has the symptoms which he has, and indeed the character, nature and reactive patterns which are very conspicuous, cannot be appreciated at all until one gets some knowledge of his unconscious phantasy. Everything is explained once one understands the unconscious phantasy of any person, and nothing is explained until one does understand this unconscious phantasy. The job of analysis is to bring the repressed unconscious to consciousness, and that is how it comes about that the analyst knows more of these things than do other people.

Now this patient had the following little dream or nightmare: he says he was on a stage. There was a play going on. He was in a dark corridor. There was an aperture through which the actors and actresses came. A beautiful actress came through this aperture. He said, very significantly: 'She looked like my mother'. There was a slight act of recognition between them. He said: 'It was then I came to know that an evil man would appear and go on to the stage. He would appear out of this aperture.' Suddenly this otherwise interesting dream became a nightmare. He said: 'Suddenly the whole thing became real instead of a play, and I became somehow aware that there was a real man standing at the back of me, in the dark, in this aperture. I sensed that his hands were coming towards me in the dark. He was going to throttle me. I knew it would be the end if I didn't do something about it. I couldn't turn, but I shouted, I yelled at the top of my voice and he vanished, and I awoke.' Presently he added: 'Now perhaps you can understand, doctor, why I have to jump off the settee, and go across the room and sit in a chair facing you.'

It was not long before he and I understood a good many other things also. We understood why he could not sit still anywhere, why he raised his voice in argument, why he was on the verge of being aggressive all the time, and certainly on the alert in case anybody, put out his arms to throttle him. It is interesting that the throttling item in the nightmare occurred while this man was anticipating enjoyment, looking after the attractive actress in the dream. The patient later told me that he was dimly aware of a large number of phantasies resembling the one that emerged in his dream. He said:

'I always feel that there is somebody just behind me, going to tap me on the shoulder, and say: "You're wanted—you're wanted outside". It must be something guilty in my subconscious, to do with a crime that I've done. I think it's some sexual crime, like that girl passing, that actress in the dream.'

This patient is obviously on the defensive against repressed anxiety. Later he goes on to say: 'I suppose I am enjoying myself, or trying to enjoy myself all the time, always with the feeling that there is this man at the back of me, wanting to get me for some crime, which I know I haven't really committed.'

Well now, the dream gives us a distinct hint as to what the crime was, because the person whom he saw, the actress, who emerged from the aperture, he immediately associated with his mother. Of course, one does not jump to conclusions on such flimsy evidence, but I may say that we have innumerable quantities of evidence, circumstantial evidence galore, indicating quite clearly that the crime in this man's unconscious phantasy is nothing less than incest. Incest in phantasy is a crime that involves opposition, rebellion, to mother and father, to the superego, and with this rebellion comes murder, in phantasy of course, and in consequence fears of punishment, of being murdered or liquidated for it.

That is why this man has to be on the move all the time, physical exertion is the only thing that keeps his anxiety at bay. He is on the run. In his unconscious phantasy he has committed these crimes to gratify his instinct and he is wanted, he is guilty, somebody is after him, the throttling hand, the executioner. While he is on the move the anxiety is not so acute, but if you get him to sit down, well, the anxiety is just too much, he cannot bear it, he cannot keep still. He went on to say that all the people around who go about doing jobs and being active are just anxiety-driven without knowing that they are. They get their anxieties organized somehow into some so-called reality purpose, and they think they are sane. They are not, they are all running about, just as I am doing, propelled by anxiety.

'I think I am the one that has got the mental strength, which they haven't got, because I come to analysis and stick it through, coming face to face with all these horrors in my unconscious. But I will say this, that *unless one is acting out these phantasies of one's unconscious, it is not life, and if one is acting it out, it is not reality.*'

Now this is a most profound truth, which this patient has told us, and that is the gist of this excerpt, which purports to show that life is synonymous with living our unconscious phantasies, and our reality activities are for the most part nothing more or less than interruptions to what we feel to be life. What is more, they are often, as the excerpts even from the last patient show, intolerable interruptions, hateful interruptions, and if there are too many of them and too little of the phantasy pleasure life, then the strain is too great for us, we either get a nervous breakdown, a mental breakdown, or a physical breakdown. Anyhow, to that extent our health is impaired.

In short, the thing we are all after without knowing it, is freedom to enjoy, or at least to act out the reactive pattern, the conditioned reflex pertaining to and connected with these unconscious phantasies which accumulated during our early unreality life in the womb, at the breast, or in mother's arms, or attached by invisible cords to our parents, an attachment which continued while our instinctual patterns developed into their more mature form, long before puberty was dreamed of. Nevertheless, these immature infantile patterns continue to act themselves out and relieve our tensions while they are acting themselves out, whether we like it or not, whether we know it or not. Whether we like it or not, it is the way we live, it is the form our life takes, our mental life, and no other form brings health like this does. All other forms are a potential interference and a movement in the direction of the abandoning of life, and the onset of death.

The purpose of these clinical excerpts is just to illustrate what all the material of analysis teaches us, namely that there is a process going on in the mind which is designed not to appreciate reality, or indeed to make reality adjustments, primarily, but essentially to discharge uncomfortable tensions, and thereby it would seem to keep the body free from disturbing or life-arresting influences. After all, it is the physiology of the body which is more important than anything to do with environmental adjustment. It would seem that if the body accumulates tensions that it would normally discharge by these physiological and psychological processes, and is prevented from doing so for the sake, for instance, of reasonableness, it will then suffer a dusturbance of its life function and become uncomfortable, ill and on the way to demise. In this sense the mind and its brain could be regarded as an organ, like any other organ of the body, designed to maintain physiological, chemical, and physical movements that preserve life. All this proves to be the essence of life, whereas the things upon which we concentrate our conscious attentions, when we can, are in a sense nothing to do with life, they may have something to do with those matters which would interfere with life processes. They are, in a sense, the enemies that surround the living organism.

But the point about analytical investigation is that 't reveals the surprising fact that practically all mental activity is enga\,red in something very near to this physiological level. And when it would seem that it rises above this physiological, chemical, physical level, it is then exclusively engaged in early reactive patterns, a matter which I regard as very close to instinctual patterns.

These primitive reactive patterns are those which very early in development, about the time of birth znd immediately after birth, fill the experiences of the nervous system and mind. Some people may prefer to regard them as conditioned reflexes, but I think they go a little further than reflexes in that they have what we can call a psychological content. At their highest level they may be regarded as re-living all those pleasure-giving and, as it were, indoctrinated experiences which befell the organism in its earliest and most malleable stage of life. They were experiences largely to do with the relief of instinct tension and subsequently to do not only with the relief of instinct tension but also with the object in the immediate environment, breast, mother, father and other people who in some way became related to these reliefs of instinct tension, or indeed sometimes to the accumulation and accentuation of instinct tension.

All this is being sorted out in the deeper recesses of the mind, and the mind continues to function according to these early patterns and according to these early experiences, apparently all through its life, even at advanced years of adult life. This sort of thing is going on all the time, and what we prefer to regard as environmental reality gets indeed very little innings. It is only grudgingly admitted and usually regarded as interruptions to the more comforting and comfortable process, the, as it were, automatic process that goes on in the unconscious mind interminably, both in waking life and in sleeping life.

Now this pattern, this mental movement, fixated as it were to our earliest infancy, includes of course an endless repetition of the craziest levels of our mental functioning. All our erroneous impressions, erroneous beliefs, and emotionally determined attitudes of our earliest infancy are forever being lived within us, within our minds, to the exclusion of any capacity to appreciate reality independently of these delusions. After all, we would not expect an infant of one, two, or even three or four years of age to be what we call sane, and yet we have the psychology of this infant going on inside our minds all the time from the cradle to the grave. Is it then small wonder that we nurse all sorts of ideas which are contrary to our adult intelligence, or what should be our adult intelligence? Perhaps these considerations explain the evident fact that the individual is not only insane at the age of one or two years, but remains insane throughout his entire lifetime—not necessarily insane in relation to the other individuals around him, for they are all in the same boat and all suffering from a similar if not identical form of insanity. Thus they can bolster each other up in their common delusionary systems, while the cosmos wheels on through space, unnoticing and unnoticed.

In the same way as we have come to recognize that the individual adult is an everlasting repetition of himself when he was an infant, so we find in considering our social customs, our beliefs and everything that is us in the present day, that this entire pattern, this pattern of culture, is no more than a repetition, maybe in slightly altered form, of the infancy of humanity as a whole.

In the same way as primitive man preferred his superstitions, his anxiety-relieving beliefs of ancient times, his mythologies and cosmogonies, to any facts which were before his very eyes to observe, in the same way our modern culture prefers to cling to these old, outworn and disproved patterns of beliefs, behaviour, customs and so on, just as the individual mind evidently prefers to repeat its inanities of infancy to dwelling upon its science of today. As the individual adult is mentally a continuous repetition of the infant which he once was, so society of today is an endless repetition of the primitive society which it once was, be that several thousand years ago.

Society still clings to its unfounded superstitions, its unfounded beliefs, its unfounded moralities, its unfounded customs and ways of behaviour. When I say unfounded, I mean unfounded upon anything real, on any scientific knowledge or accuracy. It is founded upon an age when there was relatively little or no science, when everything was unknown. So environment was, as it were, created in the image of man, and of his mind and his projected phantasies and impulses. In other words, an entirely erroneous reality was postulated, believed in and clung to. The point I want to emphasize is that it has been clung to ever since, and is still being clung to. That is the reason I have for naming this book *Madkind*.

CHAPTER XVIII

A MODERN COSMOGONY

In attempting to write the case history of our psychosis, I began with what might be called symptomatology. An abundance of symptoms, chiefly paranoid or delusional, was enumerated, covering an extensive 'Family' background. One realizes that this history is only a fragmentary review, merely a selection of a few samples gathered from anthropology, mythology, religion, folk-lore and history. This approach, though more clinical than scientific, may give the reader a better immediate idea of the principle I have in mind, and perhaps help to justify the title chosen for the book as a whole. Otherwise the medical or psychiatric theory on which it is founded might be felt to have insufficient justification.

Here, I am essaying a study of aetiology in the widest (some would say wildest!) meaning of the term, and the origin and development of the mind. The aetiology of our psychosis may be regarded as inseparable from the nature of the mind and it is not irrelevant to ask, and attempt to answer, a number of questions about the so-called normal mind, which naturally presents us with this mass of delusional and psychotic symptoms. Very likely it is all bound up with the riddle of the universe, which may well be beyond the capacity of the human mind to solve, or even to formulate. The attempts at formulation reviewed under cosmogony may suggest this to us, if they suggest nothing else. But within this riddle their lies the riddle of the mind itself: where it came from, what it is for, what it does, how it works, and of course finally, what happens to it, where it goes; in short, its origin, its nature and its destiny.

To attempt the task of answering adequately these questions would of course be preposterous. Perhaps it is a recognition of this which is responsible for the fact that practically no scientist has made the attempt. Nevertheless I feel that in the absence of any scientific attempt to perform this impossible task, the world is presented again and again with some supernaturalist or evangelist coming to the 'rescue' and propounding another emotionally based delusion, comparable to my mind with those that characterize the psychotic family history we have reviewed. I would like to see an attempt based upon what knowledge we have, however inadequate, rather than attempts on the old-fashioned patterns of ignoring what we know, and being carried away by our emotional need, our need to relieve our anxiety by promoting any sort of illusion or delusion. I would rather have no 'knowledge' than false 'knowledge', particularly as one has noticed, from the sacrifice of children to Moloch to the burnings of heretics and the hangings of schizophrenics, how dangerous the latter can be.

I consider that in our present state of scientific knowledge and of ignorance, it may not be absolutely necessary to know the intricate details of atomic physics, chemistry and biology in order to understand the background out of which the mind came and the environment in which it grew to its past and present condition, but a theory of the universe which is not based on scientific principles, is worse than valueless: it is dangerous. I feel that this is due to a tendency of the mind, to which scientists are not always immune, to rush back to its emotionally gratifying addictions immediately the strict discipline of real knowledge fails it. I believe that this is due to an inherited weakness so conspicuous in the past history of this 'psychosis'. But the danger of this disease may recede in accordance with our appreciation of the incontrovertible laws of natural science. It is evident that without some appreciation of these, without some background of scientific principles, we are apt to be as blind as our primitive progenitors. It seems to me possible also that some psychological knowledge of this inherited trend (which justifies the title of this work) may be helpful in avoiding a reproduction of the worst symptoms that we have been dealing with in the early chapters, if only to reconcile us to accepting the principle that what we do not know, we do not know—yet, and letting it rest there, instead of rushing off into anxiety-relieving assumptions. Surely we should not abandon reality principles and turn in our anxiety for consolation to pleasure-principle-thinking. Can we avoid delusion in this sphere, where it is so inappropriate and potentially dangerous? In short, the question is, are we able to tolerate a recognition of ignorance without undue anxiety; are we able to tolerate anxiety without inventing delusions or psychoses as a consolation or alternative for it? It is a speculative hypothesis that *if* we know *everything* we would feel no fear; but that hypothesis itself may be an illusion. We rush into psychosis whenever our scientific investigations, research and understanding fail to explain the problems we are trying to understand.

Now this brings me to a point which has puzzled many people and been used by some in support of their emotionally biased desire or need to cling to at least the last remaining vestige of their pleasure-giving or anxiety-reducing illusion. They will point to some of our greatest scientists and say, 'Ah yes, he knew more than you did, and yet he turned to God.' Now the scientist is definitely trying to understand the nature and behaviour of these environmental 'devils', that is to say, for example, the laws which determine the behaviour of inanimate matter. In so far as he is successful he is, whether he knows it or not, reassuring himself against the anxiety of helplessness. To take an extreme view of this idea, one could say that if the scientist could understand 'everything', that is to say, the whole of the cosmos and every detail of its operation, he would conceivably then be omnipotent . . . and have nothing to fear. What happens in actual practice is this: the fact that he is a scientist—the fact that any of us are, says that we have turned to some extent from blind, childish illusion, pleasure-thinking ideas of omnipotence, or utter dependence upon some allegedly benevolent parent figure, to the idea of acquiring some degree of security by finding out the truth (reality) ourselves, and perhaps learning, or hoping to manipulate it in the way we wish. That is to say we have in a sense, or to some extent, changed our gods.

In the following pages I have conceived the idea of making an attempt to transcribe in writing the sort of universe or cosmogony that may be understood in the light of our limited scientific knowledge, and to consider whether we can become satisfied with that, in spite of limitations of the concept, without having to recreate our dead parents and take flight into being little children again.

If we can forego these emotional needs, this modern cosmogony may help us to understand our minds a little better, or in a different light. If we can consider the human mind in the light of its origin and development we may better appreciate its basic nature and its inevitable limitations. The curious position is that whilst we are looking at the cosmos as though it were an objective or environmental reality, we may come to recognize that the very mind with which we are looking at this environment is itself developmentally a part of the environment at which it is looking, is indeed no more than a specialized portion of matter developed from matter, subject to the same laws and limitations, including that of having attained only a particular stage in the process of change or evolution.

The suggestion is that scientifically our insuperable difficulties lie only at two points, the beginning and the end. Everything in between these two points, at least everything up to date, can be shown to be a natural consequence of the operation of the laws of nature. Perhaps this is saying a little too much, but only a little. Admittedly there are gaps in scientific knowledge, even between these two points, but the impression that anybody scientifically trained should gain is that enough is known about scientific principles to make the law of cause and effect inescapable, and the conclusion obvious, namely that everything we know has come about by a natural operation of these laws.

The recognition is also inescapable that the human mind does not suddenly become a totally different instrument from that which has evolved through the ages; from the instrument which developed for the primary purpose of enabling the organism to relieve its discomforts and tensions, and to gratify its physical, chemical and physiological needs, including relief of the variety of discomfort which we call anxiety.

We have seen that, when man, emerging from his pre-man or animal ancestors, first acquired enough 'reality principle' to recognize the existence of a reality that he wished to explain, he proceeded within his lights to enunciate cosmogonies to satisfy his emotional requirements. We may well ask the question whether that is not the best that we can do, even in this age.

The subject matter in the following pages is entirely due to the work of scientists and specialists in the respective spheres of study, and my selection is at the most a very fragmentary outline of a vast mass of detailed knowledge scientifically accumulated by them. The portion I have selected is relevant to my overall purpose of exposing the nature of the mind of man, particularly of its limitations and aberrations, past and present.

Astronomers are fairly sure that this planet has existed for approximately five thousand million years. It is said that the human species of animal has existed for about half a million years. Any form of articulate communication between individuals, such as speech, probably began not much more than one tenth of a million (100,000) years ago. These considerations may give us some orientation for the psychological aspects of our new cosmogony.

Perhaps it would be right to say that most of us have the impression that if there were no matter, no material existence, the only alternative would be an empty space, and that in this empty space time would go on. Many physicists would say that there are no grounds for such assumptions. Therefore we may perhaps conclude that this idea of ours reveals only the peculiar nature of our mind, a mind whose capacity for recognizing things is of course evolved from and based upon the sort of stimuli and impressions which contributed to its evolution and growth. We cannot appreciate a reality to which we have not grown accustomed. There is no knowing what there may be in reality that we cannot see, feel, hear, or know anything about. (To my mind this does not justify us in inventing it, whether we call it supernatural or not).

Eddington said that the physicist is like a student of fishes, who is catching them in a net with meshes one inch wide. After many careful experiments he concludes no fish exists shorter than one inch. The net with which we catch the phenomena of our objective environment is our senses and scientific instruments. Certainly the scientific instruments have helped to reduce the holes in the meshes of our net, but who knows how many varieties of millions of fishes may be escaping our observation.

Here, at the very outset of our endeavour to look at reality objectively, we find our attention, of necessity, deflected on to the question of the instrument with which we are endeavouring to investigate. We wish to observe what reality is and how it came about, how our minds came about, and instead we find that we must look at this mind first. Many philosophers have assured us that much of what we think we observe in nature may in fact just be some property of our own mind. They tell us that this is most probably the case when we consider the concept of timeless nothingness. They tell us that space and time have a meaning only if associated with matter. Where nothing happens there is no time. The fact is that what we call empty space, namely the region not occupied by matter, is actually the seat of forces of many kinds. Physicists tell us this space is filled with what they call 'fields', e.g. gravitational fields and electro-magnetic fields. In other words, they are occupied with something. It is not matter, that is why we think of these fields as spaces; but there is some force or energy present, so we are wrong to regard them as empty.

Einstein has told us that space and time are not distinct entities but are connected. In a universe in which everything was moving at extraordinary speeds and extraordinary variations of speed, he asks us to recognize that space and time would have a very different objective reality from that which impinges upon our limited experience. He says that they are not separate entities, there is only a certain combination of distance in space and interval in time which is the same for all observers. This last point is a consequence of the principle of relativity, which asserts that wherever one is in the universe, however one moves, the same mathematical equations must describe one's observations.

So we are again thrown back upon a consideration of the observing instrument, namely the human mind, and it seems impossible to disentangle objective reality from this bias of observation and still to understand it. Nevertheless, this is what science is endeavouring to do. This leads us to the suspicion that we discover things in the world around us, not necessarily because they are there in the form in which we see them, but because our minds are of a certain nature and work in a certain way, a nature and way which is the product of our past evolution and our very limited experience.

The quantum theory tells us that: 'The energy of a body is not continuously variable, but can take only certain determined values. In the case of an oscillating electron it must consist of a specific whole number of quanta; the energy can be taken up or given out in such quanta only. An oscillator can thus emit or absorb one, two, three,

four, etc., quanta of energy, *but no intermediate or fractional amounts.'*
(My italics).[35]

Einstein went on to show that radiation (such as light) was
'actually propagated through space in definite quanta or *photons,*
moving with the speed of light'.[35] This is connected with the fact that
an electron cannot have a continuous gradation in the distance of its
movement round a proton, *but must jump as it were from one definite unit
of distance to another definite unit.*

Thus, it would seem, it is only when the energy-time units reach a
sufficient magnitude, perhaps only when they become infinitely
large, that the space and time of current conception can have any
possible existence. Some physicists would insist that there cannot be
any space or time in a condition of nothingness, that is to say, in the
absence of anything approximating to matter or energy. It simply
happens that *in our very limited experience we have had to deal only with
'very high quantum numbers' and so our present conception of the world consists
of those entities which only take definite shape for high quantum numbers.*
Thus, as far as we can go, we may conceive of the origin of matter as
we know it and as the physicists know it, as the result of an infinitely
great increase in the energy-time quantum units.

This rather mathematical idea of the origin of reality is taken a
stage further in a later form of quantum theory. To understand this
theory at all it seems that we must first divest our minds of our
ordinary concept of matter altogether. We must regard what exists as
just a space or field. Next let us suppose that we can see some movement or some sort of oscillation or waves taking place in this field.
Let us then conceive of these waves reaching an intensity in concentration which separates that particular spot, or part of the field
from other parts in which the movement is relatively nothing, though
there may be still some movement there. When the wave reaches such
a degree of intensity and such a degree of concentration that it is
distinguishable from the relatively small intensity and absence of
concentration of its surroundings, then that point can be distinguished
from those surroundings in the same way that an electron can be
distinguished from the field in which it moves. Thus we may conceive
of all that exists as being nothing more or less than waves and concentrations of waves.

Physicists used to go so far as to say that the formulation which
must have the credit for the most far-reaching success in scientific
prediction is this formulation of the laws of propagation of waves, the
wave equation. They even go so far as to give their idea of this concept
of waves a symbolic Greek letter ψ. Perhaps one should stress in connection with this new form of the quantum theory that there is no
reason to call the quickly moving concentrations of waves 'reality' or
'matter', and the background or field in which they move 'space', or

'non-matter'. Objectively there is no standard by which one can regard the one as positive and the other as negative. It is purely optional which way we look at it. If the space were regarded as light then darkness, or black points, would be the matter, whereas if space were regarded as darkness, then we might regard light or white points as the matter, or reality.

Once we have arrived at an oscillation or wave taking place in what we, perhaps erroneously, call 'space', or in what the physicists call a 'field', we need no supernatural agency to be justified in our conclusion that a certain degree of concentration of the energy implied in this movement could result in the evolution of what might be called a 'fundamental particle'. At the moment physicists do not agree on the definition of a 'fundamental particle', and say it is a problem beyond quantum mechanics and the waves, and the number of particles that have recently been discovered and called fundamental has increased at a surprising rate. Fundamental particles are common to all kinds of matter. We know that some of them can be produced by cosmic rays, and it has been said that such particles have caused some of the genetical mutations which make possible the course of evolution; but that is another story.

The study of cosmic rays, amongst the most interesting phenomena in connection with our problem of the origin and development of matter, began as early as the beginning of this century, but it is only comparatively recently that a great deal has become known about them.

We must now pass on to a consideration of the Origin and Development of Matter.

Objective reality is described as matter, or as matter and energy. According to the principle of relativity, these two are in fact the same thing. Indeed, matter can be disintegrated into energy and it would seem that in the course of movements in 'fields', energy, oscillation or waves, naturally tend to concentrate into what might be called fundamental particles, foci of energy, protons and electrons. There is no satisfactory answer as to how this began. The suggestion that it originated by some supernatural event is incapable of scientific investigation or description. We are left with the alternatives, one, that matter has always existed or, two, what amounts to practically the same thing at this stage of our discourse (but not at every stage), that it is continuously being created all the time by a natural process. The latter view is preferred by many scientists, who regard it as inescapable, mainly because if matter were ageless, they say that the universe would by now have reached a state of equilibrium, in which no dynamic process could occur. In other words, it would by now have 'run down'.

It may be as well to begin by considering the fundamental nature of matter. So far as science knows at present, all substances existing in the universe are built up of about ninety chemical *elements*. Most substances or most matter consists of chemical compounds. Atoms can combine with each other or with other atoms to form molecules. The unit of the chemical compound is a molecule, which can be defined as resulting from the union of the atoms of two or more separate elements. Many inorganic molecules (that is to say, molecules which do not contain a carbon atom) are very simple, and contain only very few atoms, for instance the molecule of water consists of two atoms of hydrogen and one of oxygen, and is therefore written H_2O. On the other hand, most of the molecules of which living tissues are formed are extremely complicated and may contain hundreds of thousands of atoms. Atoms and molecules are the smallest part of an element or chemical compound that still keeps most of its properties. Further subdivision of an atom leads to fundamental particles, common to all kinds of matter.

To get some idea of the possible origin of matter from simpler forms, such as fundamental particles, or from cosmic rays, it may be simpler to examine the structure of an atom and, as it were, disintegrate it in the mind's eye into its fundamental units. Every atom is made up of a nucleus, which comprises several components, including at least one proton, and this nucleus contains almost the whole weight of the atom. This nucleus has a positive charge of electricity, which is always an integral multiple of a fundamental unit of electric charge. For instance, the nucleus of the simplest atom, hydrogen, has one unit, that of helium two, that of carbon six, that of iron twenty-six and so on. Around the nucleus of an atom are found a number of electrons. These are fundamental particles with one unit of electric charge each. This charge is always negative, and their total corresponds exactly to the positive charge which the nucleus of an atom always possesses. For instance, if the nucleus has one positive charge, as in hydrogen, it will have one electron associated with it, and the negative charge of the electron will neutralize the positive charge of the proton. That is how they stick together, and that is why the atom is electrically neutral. The number of electrons revolving round this nucleus is equal to the number of units of charge in the nucleus, for instance, twenty-six for iron. One may picture the electrons as rotating round the nucleus as planets round the sun, though physicists have now rejected this attractive model.

Our minds, accustomed as they are to our very limited experience of the reaction of matter upon us, can hardly realize its fundamental nature. Only special instruments and methods of scientific investigation can show us that truth is stranger than fiction, in this sphere as in all others. For instance, how could we be expected to understand it when the physicists tell us that if all the atoms constituting the almost three billion human beings living on this earth at the moment could be so compressed that no empty space remained in their atoms, all humanity would not take up any more room than a seed of corn!

The electron is directly or indirectly the cause of practically all phenomena observed on the earth (with the exception of radio-activity and a few others). Chemical binding is due to it, and so are most electric and magnetic phenomena and the production and absorption of light. As it is the cause of practically all the phenomena on earth, it is similarly the important factor responsible for all phenomena within the body and brain of man. It is directly instrumental in the electrical impulses which produce sensations and which carry orders from the brain to the muscles.

A physiological fact of interest is that some nervous functions such as reflexes have an all-or-none condition of reacting, that is to say, the reflex appears to have a threshold below which nothing happens and above which everything happens. In other words, a nervous cell is either active or not active, but of course no *exact* relationship with electrons and their habits has yet been established. This is just an instance where there is a suggestion that the 'lowest' possible level of natural reactions (electrons) and the 'highest' known level (human brain function) appear to have a similar characteristic.

Returning to the atoms, the points to remember are, then, their constitution, vaguely recalling that of the solar system, and the fact that they can exist only in certain states which can be predicted. This last property is shared by molecules and more complex organizations. By saying they can exist only in certain states it is meant that intermediate states do not exist, or rather that an infinite continuity of states does not exist. This is because the electrons go round the nucleus of the atom at a certain distance, *or* they jump to another orbit at a specified unit of distance, and cannot perform in an orbit in between these two. This is in accordance with the quantum theory.

An atom or molecule can pass from one to another of the 'allowed' states by absorbing or emitting energy. It is generally impossible to predict which transition will occur in given circumstances, but only to assign the relative probabilities of several possible transitions, since these different states correspond to different electronic configurations and motions.

One of the most important ways in which atoms can join to form molecules is through the sharing of pairs of electrons, the two electrons spinning about themselves in opposite directions. The number of electrons in an atom available to be shared in this way (those of the inner orbits are bound much too tightly to take part in this process) is equal to what the chemist calls the valency of the element. For instance, carbon, the most important element in organic chemistry, has four such electrons and it is just this four-valency which, with other factors, makes possible the great complexity of the molecules of organic chemistry on which life depends.

There are other types of forces that bind together atoms in molecules. For instance, it may happen that when two atoms come together, there is a redistribution of their electrons such that one of the atoms acquires a positive electrical charge, and the other a negative one. The two charged atoms (or ions, as they are then called) will attract each other because opposite electric charges attract each other, and they will remain bound together in a stable molecule. The nature of the chemical bond is of extreme importance in biology, that is to say, in the processes of life.

But before we go on to consider the elaboration of the fundamental units of matter into more and more complex chemical compounds, and larger and larger molecules, such as amino-acids and proteins, before we are in a position to consider a synthesis of the units of matter into long chains of amino-acid molecules and ultimately into protoplasm and the beginnings of life, it would be as well to digress slightly in order to study the wider field of the background of man's existence.

In other words, before we proceed further with the microcosm, let us devote at least a chapter to the macrocosm. This is not irrelevant as it puts mankind and the whole biosphere in their proper perspective and is, I think, and I believe most people will find it so, the most interesting of all interesting subjects. It is certainly the largest. We shall have to come back to examine our microcosm again in the light of some new considerations which shall have arisen.

CHAPTER XIX

THE MACROCOSM

Strange as it may seem, there is, according to the scientists, a good deal of very sound evidence that our Earth, the Solar System, and the Galaxy of stars of which the Solar System is a part, all started between four and five billion (5,000,000,000) years ago. However, there is the reservation that 'the scale of time may have altered from the most distant past', so that what we now may measure as five billion years was in fact a much longer interval of time.

It is now generally known that most of the stars we see, including of course the Sun, are part of a Galaxy or nebula comprising hundreds of millions of other bodies practically identical with our sun, only many larger and some smaller. The average size may be very like that of our sun.

It is said that our galaxy is of a shape somewhat resembling that of a bath bun, and that we are situated perhaps a third of the distance from the rim and perhaps a little nearer the bottom than the top. When we look into the sky towards the bottom or the top of the bun, we see relatively few stars as our galaxy is relatively thin in those directions, but when we look towards the edge of the bun, our line of vision encounters hundreds of thousands of stars belonging to our galaxy. Naturally, some of them are much further away than others, but the effect of these large numbers of stars extending to the limits of our galaxy gives the effect of a luminous cloud, known to us as the Milky Way.

All the stars which we can see in the sky, without optical aid (estimated at about three thousand), excepting luminous cloud-like wisps which are nebulae or other galaxies, belong to the Milky Way system (our own galaxy). Our galaxy is very like its neighbour Andromeda, only 700,000 to 900,000 light years away. It is a thin disk which trails away at its edges. As I have said, our solar system lies somewhere towards the edge of the disk. The disk is 60,000 light years across, and only about 10,000 light years in thickness. Like all the other galaxies it is rotating and the speed of the solar system due to this rotation is nearly a million miles an hour. In spite of this speed, the dimensions of our galaxy are such that it takes about two hundred million years to make a round trip. (In addition to these enormous speeds, there is, of course, our planet speed of 70,000 miles an hour round the sun, and also its speed of 1,000 miles an hour at the equator round its own polar axis). 'Astronomers are generally agreed that the galaxy started its life as a rotating flat disk of gas with no stars in it.'[36]

In the same way that our sun is only one of hundreds of millions of similar objects within the galaxy, our galaxy itself is only one of millions of similar galaxies, occupying the space around us. Indeed, the most powerful telescopes have already discovered about one hundred million other galaxies within their field of view, each of them containing anything between one hundred million and ten billion stars, each star, in the average, being about the size of our sun.

These discoveries have been accumulated since 1912, when Dr Slipher of the Lowell Observatory, Arizona, began investigating the velocities of thirteen spiral nebulae, and extended his observations to fainter and fainter objects.[37]

The magnitude of these galaxies is almost inconceivable. Some of them are so large that it takes light several hundreds of thousands of years to travel from one end of a single galaxy to the other, but they are only luminous specks in our most powerful telescopes because their distance from us is so great.

Do these galaxies then comprise all the matter in the universe? As we shall see, it is more than likely that there are an infinitely greater number of galaxies, infinitely greater than the one hundred million which our most powerful telescopes can detect, but these, perhaps infinite in number, will never be seen by us. They are outside our field of view, not necessarily on account of distance, but on account of the speed of their recession from us being greater than that of light.

What is perhaps not generally realized is that all the stars and galaxies put together are not very massive compared to the universe! Altogether they contain only about one thousandth part of the matter in the universe. All the rest, forms what is called the interstellar and intergalactic gas. This enormous expanse of gas is made up almost exclusively of hydrogen, the lightest chemical element. Although extremely rarefied, it occupies such a vast volume that it weighs nine hundred and ninety-nine times as much as all the galaxies put together. It is becoming more and more widely recognized as the ruler of the galaxies. It controls their birth and their growth and the motions of the stars. This intergalactic hydrogen weighs nearly one thousand times as much as the rest of matter. In addition to matter, space is occupied by radiations of many kinds.

It has been suggested that some wave motion or oscillation in space 'originally' provided energy out of which the fundamental particles of matter came into being, but I think most astronomers and perhaps even physicists are happier to begin with the assumption that initially there was this rarefied intergalactic gas. It is assumed that initially a galaxy contained only this rarefied gas and no stars. It was in the form of an immense disk rotating like a wheel. Physicists tell us that such a disk is unstable. They say that it may be proved mathematically that the attractive force of gravitation acting between all the atoms in such a disk must increase any irregularity in density that may 'casually' arise during the 'random' motion of the atoms. In consequence of this, the gas disk has then to break up into a large number of separate clouds. The conclusion is confirmed by astronomical observations which prove further that condensation takes place in each cloud, so that finally stars are formed.

The size of the stars is the result of two opposing processes: on one side the contraction that would go on indefinitely and on the other side the expansion produced by the generation of nuclear energy. As a star shrinks, its internal temperature rises, and when this temperature is sufficiently high, the hydrogen of which the star is made explodes, as in a hydrogen bomb. In the process of this explosion, it is converted into other chemical elements, chiefly helium, through nuclear transmutations. As a result of these two opposing processes, contraction and expansion, the star will acquire a certain size and temperature, as a sort of equilibrium between the two.

It is now generally thought that our universe appears to be *expanding*. Observations on the Andromeda nebula showed that the novae found in that system were about twenty-five thousand times fainter than the faintest naked-eye star, showing that it was an extremely distant object, far outside our galaxy. Finally, a series of observations with the hundred-inch telescope at the Mount Wilson Observatory established that the Andromeda nebula was nine hundred thousand light years away, and that it was a sort of island universe much greater than our galaxy.

Spectroscopic observations on the light emitted from this and from other spiral nebulae established the simple fact that they were all moving away from us at a surprisingly high speed. As early as 1925 the highest speed discovered was found to be 1,125 miles a second. Since then, more distant nebulae have been seen, and their speeds of recession have been found to be even greater.

'That does not imply that we are at the centre of the universe. At whatever point in the universe we might be placed, the same phenomenon would be observed.

'Now from the observed rates of recession, it can easily be inferred that the universe doubles its dimensions about every 1,300 million years . . .'[37]

What is of even greater interest is that the velocity of recession of any nebula is directly proportionate to its distance from us, as it would be if the whole universe were expanding uniformly. Hence the theory inescapable from this observation is equal to the theory of the expanding universe.*

There are many galaxies which are millions of light years away, and indeed many which are many thousands of millions of light years away, but the point is that according to this phenomenon of recession, on account of the fact that the further away a galaxy is, the more rapidly it travels away from us, we have the mathematically inevitable conclusion that at the distance of about two thousand million light years the rate of its recession becomes equal to the velocity of light. A galaxy which has passed that distance is receding from us with a speed greater than that of light. Although the light from it will travel on towards us, its distance from us increases more rapidly than the light can travel. In consequence, this light can never reach us. Therefore, at the distance of two thousand million light years the universe has passed an horizon beyond which we can never see. So we may come to the conclusion that so far as our observational powers are, and perhaps forever will be concerned, our universe is limited to a diameter of two thousand million light years. This does not mean that nothing exists beyond that horizon, it may be logical to assume the contrary, it merely means that it is beyond our powers of observance.

It has been calculated that the rate of creation required to maintain our universe as it is, that is to say, to compensate for the inevitable disappearance of galaxies, would be no more than 'one hydrogen atom per cubic metre per 300,000 years',[37] or one hydrogen atom every year in a volume equal to that of St Paul's Cathedral. This rate is much too small to be measured. But our observable universe is so staggeringly large that even at this apparently extremely slow rate, the amount of matter produced would be 'equivalent to about fifty thousand suns each second!'[37]

No wonder our pre-scientific progenitors constructed their cosmogonies at a much smaller and (to them) more credible scale! This is perhaps another instance confirming the dictum that truth is stranger than fiction. Fiction is phantasy based upon our limited personal and emotional observations. Fact is connected with an attempt to discount those in favour of unbiased objective observation. Presumably nobody would have the temerity to produce theories quite so 'fanciful' as these out of the imaginings of his mind. As Sir Harold Spencer-Jones points out[37] 'It will be evident that the hypothesis of continuous creation of matter requires space to be infinite in extent and for the universe to have existed for an infinite past

---

* Recently a theory called the fatigue theory of light (the photons lose energy in their long journey and thus their wavelength, which is inversely proportional to the energy, increases) has been put forward again, apparently with sound observational evidence. This may call the expansion theory in question.

time. Only under these conditions can the mean density remain constant in time, despite the continuous creation. It must follow also that the universe will exist for an infinite time in the future. We have no longer any need to concern ourselves with beginnings and endings when we picture the universe as having existed from an infinite past, up to the present, and as being destined to exist through an infinite future.

'You may ask what happens to the galaxies that have run their course, and have reached the end of their life. We do not see them, of course, for any galaxy that is born within our range of view will have passed over the observational horizon long before it reaches the end of its evolution.

'Our own galaxy is comparatively young. All the evidence points to an age not exceeding several thousand million years. By far the most abundant element in it is hydrogen, and the next most abundant is helium; as its evolution proceeds, hydrogen is being steadily converted into helium and other elements. If our galaxy were of advanced age, we should not expect to find nearly as great an abundance of hydrogen as we do. A necessary consequence of the expansion of the universe as a whole is that old galaxies cannot come from a distance into our range of view: we lose galaxies by disappearance over the observational horizon, and the galaxies that come into view are those that condense out of newly created matter.

'We have not touched upon the question of what the created matter may be. It must be electrically neutral, for if it were not the excess charge would be repelled to infinity and the principle of homogeneity would be violated. We may expect it to be matter in one of its simplest forms. The three alternatives that suggest themselves as most probable are protons and electrons, created at identical rates so as to remain electrically neutral, or neutrons, or hydrogen atoms.'[37]

In this picture, the universe is thus in a dynamic state, things are continuously happening everywhere, and yet, taking an average over a long time, it is in an immutable condition. The created gas generates new nebulae which produce new stars, with perhaps planets round them; the nebulae recede and eventually disappear for ever when their speed of recession exceeds the speed of light, and new nebulae take their place. This leads some people to speculate on what has been called the closed loop system, namely that every event, however small its probability must be everlastingly recurring.

However, I do not think that it was this speculation, or any intuition of the facts on which it is based, that led the old cosmogonists and mythologists to enunciate the theory of everlasting life.

Before leaving the subject of universe, galaxies and solar systems, it would be as well to review our perspective. Galaxies are of such enormous dimensions (sort of island 'universes') that when we speak of stars or suns, we are speaking of something relatively insignificant, and when we speak of such things as solar systems and planets, we are going, relatively speaking, from the immense to the minute.

Many scales have been used to impress these truths upon the lay reader. Hoyle appears to favour a model which reduces the sun to the size of a grapefruit. He then points out that the bulk of the planetary system going round it lies at a distance of a hundred yards or more. Apparently this is what deals 'the death blow of every theory that seeks for an origin of the planets in the sun itself',[36] but the interesting point here is that on the same scale, the nearest star would be something like two thousand miles away on this model.

An old-fashioned scale is one that placed our sun at nought on a plan, and our earth at a radius of 1/30 of an inch from it. The planets would then form a circle of little more than an inch. One then finds that to put in the next object in space, the nearest star, one would have on that scale to go 230 yards. I feel this helps to convey the disproportion between planetary and solar distances as compared with inter-stellar distances. One may add here that the nearest star is in the neighbourhood of four light years away, whereas most of the stars we see are a hundred or more light years away, and the diameter of our galaxy is sixty thousand light years. Most of the galaxies are at least over ten times this distance away from us.

'It is estimated that there are about one hundred million (galaxies) out to the distance of 500 million light-years, which is the limiting distance up to which reasonably complete surveys have as yet been made. This great number is probably an underestimate. Between us and the observable horizon are likely to be at least ten thousand million galaxies. As space continues to expand, carrying the galaxies with it, one by one they will pass beyond the observable horizon and will then be for ever lost to view.'[37]

CHAPTER XX

PROTEIN SYNTHESIS AND THE ORIGIN OF LIFE

Environment is a necessary condition of life, and life is a necessary condition for the mind in its functioning. Similarly, it is clear that man, his physical being, his liver no less than his brain, may be regarded for our purpose as essentially environment—environment no more and no less necessary to instigate and maintain mental functioning than are the suitable conditions of energy and matter, such as earth, atmosphere, temperature and pressure. Admittedly, the mental environment or habitat designated as the body (and brain) of man is more closely and intimately related to the functioning of his mind. But in a universe of such obvious interdependance where are we to draw the line between the essential nature (as regards mental functioning) of immediate and remote environments! The mind could not function, could not be there if the body (or brain) were destroyed, and likewise it could not function if the atmosphere became oxygen-less, or the temperature rose to 100 deg. centigrade. Indeed, the slightest changes whether within or without the body will surely have their repercussions upon the mind. This reveals that they are all perhaps equally essential environment, and if we are to demarcate the limits of the material basis of mind, we might as well mark it as the limits of the Cosmos, as the limits of the skin or of the brain substance. Indeed, its limits are even wider than those indicated, for as it extends spacially it also extends backwards and forwards in time. Mind is not limited to one individual lifetime. Its developmental history is an essential part of its origin and of its nature. In short, its basis is not merely three dimensional, it is four dimensional—an integral part of the time-space continuum.

To understand its nature—a full comprehension of its nature in true perspective—it is necessary not only to understand the immediate origin and physical basis (animal life) but to understand the processes which gave rise to this phenomenon of life, their nature and how they themselves came into being.

The impression hitherto created is that energy, concentrated in electrons and protons, became condensed and as it were locked up more or less within the atom which it thus created. The process evidently inherent in the nature of energy which had thus produced matter continued so that these atoms grew larger and larger incorporating within themselves increasing quantities of energy. Thus there arose in growing quantity elements of an increasing complexity and weight of atom.

In due course when an appropriately low (relatively speaking) temperature has been reached, certain of these elements, still sufficiently ionized and unstable owing to the environmental energy such as heat, combine with one another to form even more complex units called molecules. The molecule evidently comes into being through the atom finding a greater degree of stability or mutual electrical balance by means of atomic and molecular union. Thus, for instance, at a certain temperature the atoms of a mixture of hydrogen and oxygen combine with a further dissipation of energy, in the form of heat, to produce the molecule H_2O in the gaseous form of steam. If the temperature falls sufficiently this gas, like all others at their appropriate temperatures, condenses into the liquid form called water.

No doubt this process took place on a large scale on our planet, the earth, hundreds of millions of years (estimated at two thousand million) before the origin of life.

Eventually we might imagine the outermost surface of this planet completely surrounded by a dense cloud of water vapour, which in so far as it condensed further and formed droplets of water or rain, would have thus re-formed into steam even while the force of gravity was drawing them towards the lower atmospheric levels, and so again as it were hurled back to the periphery. Undoubtedly this went on for millions of years before the earth had cooled sufficiently to allow even boiling oceans to settle upon its surface. But settle they did, and in the fullness of time one of the principal natural phenomena constantly going on on the earth's surface was that of unceasing rainfall and re-vaporization. This phenomenon is, of course, still going on, but now not by means of an intrinsically hot earth, but by the radiant heat of the sun. *In passing it may interest us to reflect that the re-vaporization of the earth's water is one of the principal physical conditions of all its terrestrial life, vegetable and animal.*

With the cooling of the earth's surface there was a tendency for molecules to follow a development or evolution analagous to that of the atom and to become increasingly large and complicated.

At a sufficiently low temperature the element carbon began to enter into a most varied and multitudinous series of combinations with other elements—particularly with oxygen and hydrogen—to form not only the numerous carbohydrates with such complex molecules as $C_6H_{10}O_5$ (starch) and $C_{12}H_{22}O_{11}$ (cane sugar), but also in conjunction with almost every other known element to produce such an extensive series of combinations as to require a special branch of chemistry (called organic chemistry) reserved exclusively to their study.

The process of material evolution did not end with the production of the heavy molecules of these carbon compounds. On the surface of this earth under the appropriate physical conditions, including that of temperature, even more complicated heavier and larger molecules came about, presumably conditioned by the same processes which gave rise to matter itself in the first place, until at length there came into being the very large and complex molecule of certain carbon-containing colloid substances.

I can see no reason why we should draw any hard or fast line across the smooth continuous stream of evolutionary progress. I can see no reason to draw a line of demarcation between the evolution of the molecule of the simpler carbon compounds and the larger and more complex molecule of their nitrogenous combinations, for instance those of the amino-acids and of protein. This last nitrogenous carbon compound has a gigantic molecule containing smaller molecules of amino-acids which together contain hundreds, sometimes thousands, of atoms. There are a large variety of proteins which by analogy might be regarded as Isotropes. Their mean formula is $C_{141}H_{391}N_{65}S.O_{71n}$ but as the molecular weight exceeds 15,000, 'n' here represents a figure of not less than three and in some proteins as much as nine.

Until recently protein was a substance which could be produced only by the action of living matter, and the same opinion was held regarding the molecule of the amino-acids into which the molecule of the proteins first breaks down. But in recent years the molecule of the amino-acids, despite its enormous size and complexity, has been synthetically produced in laboratories, and it is clear that within the next few years the step between this and the molecule of the protein will be taken, and it will be found that proteins also can be synthetically produced. Protein-like substances have already been obtained. Anyway, here they are upon our planet and we may assume that they were not here when that planet was red hot.

The reason for stressing the probability that in the fullness of time we shall be able to produce protein synthetically is that protein is the principal constituent of protoplasm, the substance of which all forms of life on this earth are made, and the most complex chemical mixture in the world. Protoplasm itself consists of three-quarters or more of water, perhaps the first chemical compound to appear on this earth, and about ninety per cent of its weight is made up of only four elements, carbon, oxygen, hydrogen and nitrogen. In the remaining ten per cent almost every other known element has been found.

It should not surprise us that the flower of nature's evolutionary processes, so far as they are known to us on this earth, should have as its material basis what is undoubtedly the most complicated chemico-physical product of the substance of the earth. Protoplasm is a complex physio-chemical aggregation in which proteins, carbohydrates, fats, water dissolved gases and ions of salts form a united system. Its approximate molecular structure is $C_{450}H_{720}O_{140}S_6N_{116}$. Apparently it only required the appropriate environmental conditions for the nature of the atom (itself the product of electrical charges contained in the proton and electron), to produce these progressively more complex and heavier molecules.

Thus we may regard these more complex chemical substances as expressions of something which may still lie within the ingredients of the simplest atomic structure, of something which originally lay and still lies within the nature of electrical energy itself. Further, if we are agreed that this something was directly responsible for the development of the more complex chemical compounds, as we can see happening in the world around us today, it is only logical to assume that it was responsible also for the particularly complex molecule of proteins and protoplasm and through these for the development of those processes called mental, of which we have no evidence in the absence of this material basis.

What molecules had to be formed if life was to appear? Evidently those that are part of the metabolism of every living thing; sugars, or carbohydrates, to give them their technical name; fats, or lipides; and, most important, proteins. The first two groups are mainly to be thought of as fuel for the living machines, while the proteins are the stuff of which life itself is made. At first sight one might think that the likelihood of just such substances being formed out of the innumerable possible chemical compounds must be very small, too small in fact to happen in any significant amount even in four billion years. But an experiment carried out by Miller seems to show that this is not so.

Miller had a gaseous mixture circulating in a sealed apparatus. The mixture (methane, hydrogen, ammonia), was an attempt to reproduce the primitive atmosphere. Electric sparks were made to take place in this mixture. After a week of continuous circulation and discharges, the contents, (about one gallon) were analyzed and over one gram of organic compounds was found. Without any doubt this had been synthetized from the 'atmosphere' of methane, hydrogen and ammonia as a result of the electric discharges. What was even more sensational was that most of these organic compounds were of the type known as amino-acids. Now amino-acids are known to be the bricks out of which the edifice of the protein molecule is built up. Further experiments showed that, by altering the composition of the mixture, or the nature of the electrical stimulation, one could obtain predominantly carbohydrates. The conditions were designed to reproduce those prevailing on the primitive Earth, and would indicate that there must then have been a natural tendency to produce amino-acids. It would seem that the appearance of these substances was almost inevitable in the physical conditions prevailing at that time.

To go further, we must examine the properties of amino-acids, generally unfamiliar except to chemists, and including substances called glycocolle, glutammic acid, leucin and valin. Most chemical substances can be classified either as acids or as bases (alkalis). The amino-acids owe most of their importance to the fact that they partake of the properties of both types of substances. Treated with an alkali they behave as an acid, and treated with an acid they behave as an alkali. This occurs because one end of the molecule has the appearance of an acid and the other end the appearance of a base. Two molecules of amino-acids can be joined together, if the acid portion of one interacts with the alkaline portion of the other. In fact chains may be formed out of the same amino-acids or out of different varieties. If these substances are present in any concentration, the chains will form automatically. Now, in a protein one finds these chains perhaps with as many as a thousand links.

Thus the first step towards the formation of protein or potential living material was the formation of amino-acids from conditions which would electrically stimulate the primitive Earth's atmosphere of methane, hydrogen and ammonia. This linking up of amino-acids into chains would be the second step in the formation of the protein molecule, and in the light of what we have just considered, it would seem inevitable. All it requires is that these substances (amino-acids) should be present in sufficient concentration.

It is suggested that a stage was reached when there were present on the Earth many complex chains of amino-acids, chains which we now call proteins, chains which are an essential part of the process of the building up of proteins.

We know that every molecule does to some extent modify the chemical properties of its own environment, and has to some extent a catalytic action on certain reactions. These chains of amino-acids have this property, to a high degree and in a selective way. They seem in fact to be able to master their chemical environment and make order in it. (Of course we know of organic substances which have this property to an even more extraordinary degree, substances which we call enzymes and hormones, for instance). It was presumably this property which brought about the evolution of more and more complex structures. The selective action of the proteins explains also why certain compounds only were formed out of the innumerable variety possible—*A priori*. They probably acted at the beginning by favouring (technically catalyzing) the formation of

other chains similar to themselves. These in turn would bring about
the production of other chains, and so on, re-forming in the process
the original chain. *In this phenomenon, one has a chemical equivalent of
nutrition and reproduction.*

It should be mentioned that some even more simple molecules,
such as the famous adenosintriphosphoric acid (ATP) are life-like in
that they can replace lost parts, and therefore, in a sense 'reproduce'
themselves. To be more specific, adenosintriphosphoric acid picks up,
as it were, lost atoms from the surroundings and makes itself whole
again. Some chemists have been fanciful enough to suggest that some
of these chemicals can even stimulate sexual reproduction, in that
two of their molecules can become modified so that they can combine
with each other and with other atoms around, with the result that
the end product has four of the original molecules instead of two!

To summarize then, those compounds became more and more
abundant that had the faculty for favouring in their surroundings the
formation of compounds similar to themselves. The ultimate result of
such a process might well have been that a molecule developed which
could, in suitable chemical surroundings, in a sense reproduce itself
much in the same way that protoplasm does in favourable circumstances. Certain inorganic molecules are notoriously unstable, in
other words they tend to be constantly breaking down at some point
or another. But most of these very heavy molecules have not the power
to 'anabolize', they can only 'catabolize'. On the other hand, the
highly complex molecule of protoplasm not only catabolizes but even
anabolizes, with the help of certain protein molecules, (deoxyribonucleic acid and ribonucleic acid), and is therefore undergoing a low
degree of a process which is known as metabolism, and is characteristic of life.

It is of special interest for our purpose that, like some of the substances we have been speaking of, it is conspicuously able, in favourable chemical and physical circumstances, to anabolize or reform its
broken down molecules by means of its own chemical processes. But
living protoplasm is, in a sense, a chemical abstraction. We know of
it almost exclusively as the complex chemical entity which is the chief
ingredient of the substance of living cells. It should be here stressed
that the living cell is of course a very much higher product of evolution
than the chemical 'life' with which we are here concerned. Nevertheless, protoplasm is the physical basis of life, and it may be said that
life is the changes that occur in living protoplasm. On the other hand,
it may be that we have not to go even so far as the chemical complexity of protoplasm in order to meet with a phenomenon which is
undoubtedly one of life.

We are all apt to forget that the essence of what might be called the living process, from the lowest to the highest, from bacteria and viruses to man, vegetable and animal, under the sea and on the land, is a chemical process, a process of chemical reactions. Of course proteins differ from one another in a variety of ways, for instance in the sequence of the different amino-acids in the chain, also in the length of the chain, and also in the way the chain is folded upon itself. There are other differences also, such as what may be regarded as hangers-on to the sides of the chain, and the *way* these are folded or related to one another. There can also be conjugated proteins associated with the proteins, such as the nucleoproteins, which can alter the whole character of the protein and its activities. But it should be emphasized that the main structure of the protein molecule is this long chain or thread, which could be visualized as the 'backbone' of the whole thing.

I should mention here that other chains are linked to these, such as the chain molecules of the fats, which are of another kind and much shorter than those of the proteins. In spite of all these ingredients, it has been said that the chain molecule of a protein is only one ten-millionth of a centimetre in diameter. However, what seems to give the combination of molecules 'life' is largely the catalytic action caused by enzymes, and most of the proteins in living organisms form enzymes.

Now this problem of protein synthesis is perhaps the most important problem in the study of biochemistry, and in speculation about the origin of living substance. A substance called nucleic acid has a great deal to do with the enzyme quality of protein. Like proteins, they are molecules built up from smaller units, called nucleotides, making up what is called the nucleic acid chain, but whereas in the protein of higher animals and plants there are twenty different kinds of amino-acids forming the ordinary protein chains, there are only four different nucleotides to form the nucleic acid chain. Now one important thing about nucleotides is that they all contain sugar as part of their structure. The two main groups of nucleic acid are those that contain the sugar, called ribose, and are named ribonucleic acid, and the other group where this same sugar contains one oxygen atom less than ribose, and is therefore called deoxyribose. The resulting nucleic acid is called deoxyribonucleic acid. The latter is called DNA and the former RNA.

Now the function of these two nucleic acids on protein synthesis and on the whole process of life cannot be exaggerated, in fact they might almost be regarded as the essence of the whole process, ordinary protein being as it were under their protection, command or compulsion. Their difference in function is also of paramount interest. DNA is as it were less in quantity in living substance, but resides one might say at the top of the tree, whereas RNA is far more abundant and more widely distributed. DNA's most distinguished role is that it is found inside the nucleus of the germ cell, and forms the genes and part of the chromosome. Thus it is the commander of the reproduction of the protein, which is responsible for hereditary characteristics. It is also found in the nuclei of all cells and is in a sense the commander-in-chief of every reproductive process, apparently seeing to it that what is reproduced is chemically identical with the protein of which it is itself composed, and which surrounds it.

RNA on the other hand is distributed throughout the cells of every living creature, and resides not only in the nuclear portion, but particularly in the cytoplasm. Cells which have a lot of RNA in them make protein, that is to say, protein identical with their own, at a greater speed. Thus it would seem that RNA is a very active agent in protein synthesis. On the other hand, DNA appears to exercise an overall control over the process of protein synthesis, perhaps more obviously in connection with reproduction, the sperm head seemingly consisting of little else. These are emptied into the egg cell which responds similarly and the combined DNA nucleic acids appear to initiate the synthesis of a protein, having characteristics only of themselves.

Thus DNA appears to supervise and command the enzyme activities that will ensure protein synthesis to be exactly of their particular nature, although it does seem that RNA presently takes over a great deal of the spade work, particularly in so far as less important cells than the germ cells are concerned. As E. F. Gale so aptly puts it:[38] 'DNA is the substance that determines which proteins are made in a cell but the actual synthesis of those proteins is brought about by RNA. In other words, DNA is the architect and RNA is the builder.'

Thus we may see that every form of life, every species, every living organism or individual has a chemically determined system inside him which ensures that proteins and food material which he absorbs shall be synthesized in a specific way, to make a protein identical with those of which his protoplasm is also constructed. It occurs to one that this must be a very exact and very specific process, for it is known that nobody can take a skin graft from any other person, even from the closest relative such as a mother, father, brother or sister. Their proteins will destroy the proteins of the graft. The one exception to this rule has been found to be the case of uniovular twins, indicating that their protein is identical with each other.

One may add that a difference between DNA and RNA is that the nucleotides of the former can form endless chains, whereas the nucleotides of RNA cannot. The former is concerned with being specific, the essence of the quality of a gene.

Now there are also some sort of genetic particles in the cytoplasm of cells. These are called plasma genes. It has been shown that viruses can evolve from genes, or plasma genes, and experiments have been carried out in the vegetable world. Of course they do this by turning the protein of the cell into their own protein, exactly as viruses do. Thus the very substances which produce protein synthesis and are the activating agents of the living process, can as it were get out of hand and produce only themselves, an interesting reflection that a virus can arise from the vital ingredients of the cell it normally serves. A slight chemical change can bring about this important functional alteration, or excess. Cancer is probably always due to such a change, or a succession of such changes in the cell, and similar changes can be chemically induced in insects, causing viruses.

Darlington tells us that: 'The simpler plant and animal viruses all consist of combinations of RNA with protein. . . . Can we say the nuclear genes propagate themselves by DNA, the cytoplasmic genes by RNA? . . . when viruses arise from self-propagating particles in the nucleus or in the cytoplasm, they will keep the chemical character of the type of gene from which they have sprung.'[38]

Thus it will be seen that protein synthesis and the processes underlying life and its reactions are all based upon the chemistry of the molecule and the interaction of various complicated molecular structures. A small chemical change, and the entire process of the synthesis of a particular form of protein (such as ours) can be altered so that a chemically different protein, for instance that of a virus, can result and proceed to synthesize and grow.

The *viruses* have been regarded as border-line structures between the animate and inanimate. They appear to have the essential property of living matter, for when placed in their natural environment, they reproduce. At the same time, it has been said that their action is that of autocatalysts, for if the substrates of its formation are found in the cell it inhabits, then infection of the cell by the virus would cause production of more of the virus.

Some of the larger viruses are composed of proteins, fats and carbohydrates, and are evidently structures of considerable complexity. There is no difficulty in thinking of them as living matter. On the other hand, some of the smaller viruses consist of only a few protein molecules. These viruses have been crystallized and have retained their infective power.

Here we have, at least in some instances, a protoplasm-like substance in which there is not only no evidence of cellular structure, but which can actually be dissolved in water and crystallized, and yet not destroyed thereby, but capable of re-assuming its protoplasmic-like activities of growth and increase. We may ask what happened to any hypothetical hyaloplasm and spongioplasm during the stage of crystallization, and whether there was any living process going on in the crystal? There is every evidence that there was not; that it was as 'dead' as any other crystal, and yet its re-solution and the placing of it under appropriate conditions speedily gives us every evidence of unimpaired life.

In recent years, Stanley's experiments with viruses have shown them to be as it were a missing link between living and non-living matter, though unlike the prototropic bacteria and certain types of mould and algae, they do not synthesize inorganic or non-proteid material. Viruses are undoubtedly alive, and yet they have many of the properties of non-living matter.

It should be explained that viruses are sub-microscopic infectious entities which are capable of causing disease in man, animals, plants, insects and even in bacteria. They are responsible for instance for such diseases as measles, yellow fever, the common cold, rabies and several mosaic and yellow diseases of plants. In the past they have been characterized by their invisibility, by their ability to pass filters capable of holding back all ordinary living things, and by their inability to multiply or reproduce in the absence of living cells. However, because viruses may reproduce under certain conditions, because they are specific in that such viruses occur or cause disease only in certain plants, because they may change and adapt themselves to new conditions, and because of the lasting immunity which usually follows most virus diseases, practically all of the workers in the virus field still regard viruses as invisible living organisms.

Thus the existence of viruses may be taken to suggest that life was the outcome of evolutionary processes which began with structures something like them.

There is probably no single character by which living organisms can be distinguished from non-living, and there is no reason why there should not exist things having some of the qualities we usually associate with life and not others. Thus viruses may be intermediate between a living and a non-living substance, and those whose particles are larger show a more complete development of vital qualities than do the smaller kinds.

As knowledge of the viruses increases the gulf between the living and the inanimate must slowly but surely become less.

Living organisms, protoplasmic life proper, achieve reproduction through the so-called genes, of which chromosomes are made up, and which carry the hereditary characteristics. The exact chemical nature of the specific autoreproducing units is not known, but it is known that it is a spiral-like molecule of deoxyribonucleic acid. It is thus reasonable to suppose that the substance of the first living organism must have been a combination of an acid of such a kind with one or more proteins. The acid was the self-reproducing unit, the proteins exercising their modifying action on the ambient, by which is meant the surroundings, for instance the surrounding amino-acids.

To recapitulate: it is interesting to note that the most vital part of the living process, the substance through which hereditary characteristics are transmitted, is chemically little more than a spiral-like molecule of deoxyribonucleic acid, and that it is comparable in simplicity to the virus. Then we noted that the virus can be separated into a nucleic acid part and a protein part. As we noted, each part can be crystallized, and in the crystallization, each has non-living properties but on re-uniting them the activity of the virus reappears.

This seems to me a very strong evidence of the sporadic generation of the living process from non-living organic matter.

When we come to protoplasm, the chief ingredient of all living organisms other than the viruses, and in a sense perhaps we may add, other than the gene, we find that it is a mixture of many different substances of varying complexity, among which predominate the complex proteins. Its important behaviouristic characteristic is that it is always in a process of change, but whatever the changes which may occur, it always tends to return to a state of structural and physiological equilibrium. Not only is protoplasm complex, but it is so delicately adjusted that the very act of analysis destroys it, but although it no longer functions it is possible to determine its chief chemical constituents. The principal elements which compose protoplasm are common, and relatively few in number. Four are primary. They are carbon, hydrogen, oxygen and nitrogen. These form the bulk of all the compounds of protoplasm. In lesser quantity, but also essential, are phosphorus, potassium, iodine, sulphur, calcium, iron, magnesium, sodium and chlorine. Still others, such as boron, copper, cobalt, zinc, manganese and others are essential as trace elements in some organisms.

In protoplasm it is the combinations of these elements which are significant and characteristic and result from the capacity of carbon, hydrogen and oxygen to form the numerous complex compounds which in turn supply the basis for intimate associations with other elements. Carbon seems to be an indispensable bond which links all the other elements in organic unity. The compounds of carbon which are characteristic of protoplasm fall into three chief groups, Carbohydrates, Fats and Proteins.

Protoplasm then, is a complex chemical system in a ceaseless round of change. Since change means motion and motion takes energy, protoplasm is constantly consuming itself in order to stay alive. At the same time it is always taking in new materials in order to replace worn out parts or build new. These activities of building and destroying, storing and consuming, in short metabolism, are the very essence of life.

CHAPTER XXI

THE ORIGIN OF LIVING FORMS AND THE DEVELOPMENT OF NERVE TISSUE

Once such a complicated and unstable chemical compound as proto-plasm came into being and tended by physical laws to break into droplets, or small portions, its surface would sooner or later acquire changes in the direction of forming something comparable to the cell membrane which has been established in most forms of life.

It is well known that even the multi-cellular organism such as the human being reverts, for reproductive purposes, as it were, to its original uni-cellular form. Now if we examine the cell itself, or the fertilized ovum, or zygote, we find that inside this cell, 'cataclysmic' changes appear to take place before it embarks upon the process of cell division or reproduction. These 'cataclysmic' changes include the breaking up and splittings not only of its nucleus, but of the very chromosomes within that nucleus, and a refusion of these chromo-somes with those of the fertilizing cell. Is not this very like an actual demonstration that life does not begin with one fully developed or highly organized cell, but rather with something far more simple, namely with a chromosome or a string of genes or even in a sense with genes themselves. Now these genes in a free-living form would be practically identical with viruses, basically with the spiral-like molecule of deoxyribonucleic acid, and its attendant amino-acids. In short, does not this basic process of reproduction demonstrate to us before our very eyes, as it were, the origin of life from forms far simpler than that of the uni-cellular organisms, even perhaps from that of the large and highly complex molecule whose chemical reactions represent the essence of the activities of protoplasm?

Once the process of chemical and pre-biological evolution has reached the stage of producing that very unstable oxydizing, anabolizing and catabolizing complex substance called protoplasm it has, as it were, done its work, and initiated the process of biological evolution which in turn has led through successive stages to man, and the apparatus (mind) with which we are endeavouring to survey our history.

The simplest form of 'higher' life is, as we know, a-cellular, and it is conceivable that this may have been the state of life on this planet for an indeterminate period of time before the next evolutionary stage, the division of the protoplasm into cells to form multi-cellular organisms, took place. Now each animal and plant cell consists of a mass of protoplasm with at least one visible organ, the nucleus, differentiated from the rest of the protoplasm. It contains other organs beside its nucleus, but these other organs are often not visible to direct observation.

In view of the complexity of the living cell, it is inconceivable that life first appeared in this form; even a chromosome is so complex that it could hardly have sprung suddenly into existence. Once we get to a form of life such as cells, we can be sure that they always spring from pre-existing equivalent forms. From this fact alone I feel we should know that there is a history or story of evolution told, or waiting to be told. The fact that some cells are relatively simple and others more complex suggests that the more complex ones may have arisen in the course of evolution from the simpler ones. In the same way, the relatively complex chromosome must have arisen from the relatively simple genes, or a string of genes, equivalent to the sort of thing we get in certain bacterial forms. Eventually, something in the nature of an unprotected nucleus would be formed. If this nucleus acquired an appropriate surrounding in the form of cytoplasm, and the cytoplasm through, for instance, being oxydized or dried by the surrounding air, acquired a hardened exterior, one would have a fully formed cell with nucleus, cytoplasm and cell membrane complete.

Dealing with the cellular form of life, biologists tell us that in the earliest days of evolution an organism, probably in its unicellular state, would either have to evolve a mechanism enabling it to use sources of energy, such as light, other than those bound up within organic compounds, or it would have to evolve a mechanism for attacking the substance of other living organisms. Naturally, before there was an adequate supply of other living organisms, it would have to take the first course and manage to live by tapping the energy sources of inorganic and inanimate material. There is evidence that it did this largely with the help of energy from the sun, such as light. The process has been called photosynthesis.

On the other hand, in the early stages of the earth's evolution, it is likely 'that photosynthesis, as it is known today, had a predecessor which produced organic matter without the help of a dyestuff' (such as chlorophyll).[39]

'This proto-photosynthesis must have occurred when no oxygen was present in the atmosphere and, consequently, the ozone layer was also absent. At that time ultraviolet light could reach the surface of the earth, and the absorption of it by carbon dioxide as well as by water molecules could take place directly so that the help of the dyestuff was not needed. The organic matter formed in this way might again have been partly destroyed by ultraviolet light, were it not for the fact that the substances, once formed, would be taken up by the water and protected from destruction. This condition is probably the physical basis for the biologist's opinion that life started in the water.'[39]

The above is obviously connected with a mechanism enabling a living organism to nourish itself without the use of organic matter, in other words, with the adjustment of vegetable or plant life. Organisms which chose instead a mechanism for devouring the substance of other living organisms would be classified by us as representing animal life. Thus we have the basis laid for the two divergent paths of evolution, the animal and the plant.

In vegetable or plant life the mode of nutrition is accepted as the criterion distinguishing plants from animals because it seems to have been this which led to the evolution of the great structural differences between the two groups of organisms. Fundamental to these differences is the presence of the very firm cell wall in plants and its relative absence in animals. Cellulose is permeable to water and to solutions of all those substances which the plant requires but is a complete barrier to solids.

This difference between animals and plants has had many consequences. One is the immobility of plants. This is possible because the raw materials which they require are distributed with an almost complete uniformity through their environment. Things are different for the animal for the possession of a firm cell wall would hinder the mobility so necessary in the search for food. If animals owe their mobility to the relative nakedness of their cells they also owe to their mobility the great structural complexity which they display. The advantage of locomotion resulted in the evolution of organs like muscles and limbs. The power of locomotion also enabled the animal to take effective action, by attack or flight. The search for food or the avoidance of enemies led to the development of sense organs by which food and foes might be detected. The necessary correlation between the organs of sense and of locomotion was provided by the nervous system.

This contrast between plants and animals would suggest the existence of a sharp distinction between the two great groups of living organisms, plants being known by their holophytic nutrition and animals by their holozoic. Such a sharp difference does indeed exist between most kinds of plants and most kinds of animals but at the base of the scale of life we find the simple Flagellates which possess characteristics of both animals and plants.

The algae would definitely seem to be of the plant world, but a point to be mentioned is that in typical unicellular organisms, reproduction is by mitosis (direct cell division), whereas in some algae a sexual process is employed. The plants form special cells, the gametes, which fuse with one another. The algae show the beginnings of evolution of single cell organisms into multicellular ones.

Among the simpler creatures which reproduce by mitosis no cell is destroyed. Tissues from the bodies of animals can be made to survive in culture solutions for far longer than the natural life of the organism from which they came, and this seems to imply that cells from multicellular organisms have not lost their potential immortality, but that death is somehow the result of regimentation within the organized community of the body. Death would, of course, supervene in all cases, unicellular as well as multicellular, where *environment* failed to support that particular form of life.

Before it could survive on land, plant life had generally undergone considerable change, including an alternation of generations. In this case, one of the alternating generations was usually mobile, and in the nature of a gamete, whereas the other was the generation which produced the spore, and in that form there was a loss of mobility which made possible a conservation of energy.

All structures essential to life on dry land had to exist before the plant could venture successfully from the water. This preparatory selection probably occurred among the plants living in the tidal zones.

The first plants to colonize the land were probably Algae, whose life cycle resembled that of Spirogyra. The plants were haploid, reproduced sexually and the reproduction occurred in the zygote.

Since the land above water was completely devoid of life the first land plants were free from competition and hence would have tended to survive if well enough adapted to the conditions presented by the inanimate world.

In the evolution of land plants we see a gradual reduction in the gametophyte generation, which is dependent on water for fertilization of its gametes, and a gradual development of the sporophyte as a land plant. The fern still has a swimming sperm cell, but in the development of the selaginella the last step has been taken in the reduction of the swimming sperm cell to a mere sperm nucleus, incapable of independent movement which drifts down the pollen tube to enter the egg cell. The pollen grain and the embryo sac are male and female gametophytes held permanently within the fully established land plant which represents the now dominant sporphyte.

In animal life the nature of animal metabolism precludes the possibility that animals came first. It was among the flagellates we found the most primitive plants and there we find, too, the most primitive animals. These are the protozoa. Within its single cell, a protozoan performs all the basic animal functions which in higher animals are carried on by a variety of organs and organ systems. Its size is limited by its requirements. In the protozoa we see the basic animal pattern of metabolism. They move about in search of food. They possess structures for motion and sense organelles and co-ordinating mechanisms for directing their movements. They were the first organisms to possess a kind of metabolism that makes it possible for them to commandeer the compounds of other organisms for their own uses.

Amongst these unicellular creatures, we find the tendency of some to form colonies. Groups of cells have to appear before individual cells could specialize for limited specific functions as in the metazoans. The fact that this pattern is to be found among organisms that still exist today indicates that it must offer some advantages in the struggle for survival. Once the colonial pattern had been evolved it was almost certain that sooner of later mutations would appear which would lead to differentiation and specialization within the colony.

The simplest and most primitive real metazoans are the sponges. They probably originated from some form of colonial protozoan, and are not closely related to any higher forms of life. Simple as they are, the sponges are far more complex than the most advanced colonial organisms. Not only do they have clearly differentiated types of cells beyond the simple division between somatic and germ cells, but there are suggestions of special areas within the body and even, in rudimentary form, the beginnings of tissue layers. The adult sponge is not capable of movement.

Coming from a different group of protozoan ancestors are another group of simple metazoans, the coelenterates. The coelenterate body begins to show the basic metazoan pattern. The basic features of the coelenterate body are seen in Hydra.

Although the Hydra is considerably larger than most protozoans, its individual cells are much smaller but surprisingly specialized. The body wall contains about eight different kinds of cells in addition to its gametes.

The coelenterates also show cells for co-ordination which are fore-runners of the nervous system of higher animals. This enables hydra to function as a unified organism rather than as so many individual cells as in sponges.

There are many branches of development or of evolution which appear to reach a sort of dead end. For instance, the molluscs, soft bodied creatures without internal supporting structures, such as snails and clams. They have been perhaps the most successful of all the invertebrates, for they exist in every environment on earth capable of supporting life. Their skeleton is outside the body instead of inside, which not only makes them highly specialized but perhaps rigidly unadaptable.

Leading towards the vertebrates are two invertebrate groups, some of whose members are strikingly primitive compared to the highly evolved Molluscs and Arthropods. They are the echinoderms and chordates.

Vertebrates show a bewildering capacity for adaptability in form and size, but all of them have a basic structure which differentiates them sharply from all other creatures.

Evolution in fishes has taken many turns but they have shown very little brain development. The brain of the bony fish is indeed more highly developed than that of the cartilaginous fish but the development is restricted to those centres associated with the sense organs.

Amphibians, although not now very important in the animal kingdom as such, probably give us a clue as to how vertebrates, in the form of fishes, came to invade the land, and evolve into all the various forms of land-living vertebrates. Before they could crawl out of the water, they needed the support of a bony skeleton, limbs instead of fins and lungs instead of gills. Reproduction by eggs which developed in the water had to be changed and a skin evolved which would prevent the drying up of the body fluids in the air. Not all these characteristics were attained by the amphibians and so they have survived as a small group only. Their lungs are not adequate for their oxygen requirements when on dry land and so much of their respiration takes place by diffusion through the skin. This demands a moist glandular surface and so they are limited in their movements and cannot stray far from water. In their adult stage they are carnivorous and so the enormous potential vegetable food of the land is unattainable by them.

In spite of the fact that their ancestors were the first real land animals modern reptiles are only a remnant of what was once a dominant class. They cannot control their body heat and so they remain largely tied to tropical countries and cannot range freely over the world. The advantage given to them by the internal skeleton for an increase in size was developed by the reptiles to such an extent that it ceased to be an asset and became an encumberance. This was one of the largest contributing factors to their extinction.

Birds and mammals, alone among living things, are warm blooded. Their body temperatures remain constant in spite of external climatic conditions and this has enabled them to spread all over the world. It has given them an increase in control over their environment, for they can remain active for more than a limited portion of the year. The variations in form, colour, habits and other characteristics found in birds are inexhaustible, but the variations in the basic design are few. In the story of vertebrate evolution, they represent a branch away from the main stem. They are too highly specialized and too well adapted to be easily susceptible of great change.

In the beginning mammals were of insignificant size but they contributed to the ultimate extinction of the reptiles by feeding on their eggs. Reptiles fell an easy prey to adverse climatic conditions because they were probably already suffering from partial starvation. The smaller mammals survived the adverse climatic conditions and now there are more than three thousand living species of mammals. In no other group is there such a range in size, for among the mammals we have the tiny shrew and the giant whale. No other group has had such mastery over the whole earth, for mammals roam wherever there is life at all.

Having in the barest outline mentioned some points in the structural differentiation and evolution of the main phyla of the animal kingdom, it may be more apposite to our purpose in tracing the causes or aetiology of the human mind, its functions and disfunctions, to review similarly the evolution of the nervous or co-ordinating system in the primitive forms of life. This is very relevant to a new and proper orientation to the brain and mind of man.

In the simplest forms, in the protozoa for example, the effector organelles are in direct protoplasmic continuity. Only in certain of the higher forms are portions of the cytoplasm set aside for the function of co-ordinating their activities. In the protozoa the cytoplasm is of a sufficiently generalized nature to retain its powers of sensitivity and conduction as well as of irritability. In the metazoa, however, as a necessary corollary of increase in size, the effector structures may lie at some appreciable distance from the receptor organs, and so to overcome this difficulty a special conducting and co-ordinating system is developed. This is the simple beginning which leads in the process of evolution to all the complications of the nervous system in mammals, including the autonomic nervous system and the central nervous system, together with the brain.

In the amoeba, emphasis is laid upon simplicity and the ability of apparently undifferentiated protoplasm to perform all the necessary life activities without the aid of highly specialized structures. If the anterior end of an amoeba comes into contact with a solid object, the direction of the flow of the protoplasm is altered to make an angle with that which it had before. If only a small part of the anterior end has been stimulated, the angle is small and the effect is that the amoeba moves round the obstacle. If the obstruction is large, so that the contact is made over the whole of the ends of the advancing pseudopodia the direction of the flow turns so that the movement of the animal is practically reversed. In both cases the final result is that the obstacle is avoided. Similarly amoeba moves away from unduly hot water or any solution of unusual composition, such as acid, and will travel down a beam of light away from the source. If a pseudopodium comes into a spot of very intense light focussed up through the culture it is withdrawn, others are put out, come into contact with the light and are again withdrawn, and this goes on until there is a sudden reversal of the direction of streaming and the animal moves away from the light.

It would seem that this apparently purposeful behaviour is a physicochemical reaction, and I think we should learn from this that probably all behaviour, whether in inanimate or in animate objects, is basically (that is to say, if traced back to first causes), nothing more or less than a physicochemical reaction, though in higher animals, such as man, the complexity of the general chain may, as it may in amoeba, give the appearance of purposeful, teleological or even intelligent behaviour.

Another interesting point which may suggest to us that even physico-chemical reactions can be facilitated by experience, and that therefore there is probably no need to postulate a different principle for mental learning in man than there is for behaviour learning in the amoeba, or even in protoplasm, is this: if an amoeba is watched coming into spots of light on successive occasions, it is found that it *learns by experience,* for the number of contacts necessary for reversal progressively decreases.

One of the positive reactions of amoeba is the feeding reaction, in which two pseudopodia are put out to surround a particle of nutrient material. A further interesting point is that when an amoeba is feeding, it does not give a response to a beam of light. This fact, and the two types of reaction to contact, show that the behaviour depends not only on external stimuli but also on the internal state of the animal at the time. It reacts automatically, but it does so to the whole situation and not to an isolated element in it.

In other members of the protozoa, many specializations are possible, even within the limits of the protoplasm of a single cell, enabling the animal to carry on its activities with greater efficiency. *Paramecium,* for instance, is covered by a stiff but flexible outer covering which prevents pseudopodia formation and gives the animal a definite and permanent shape. It can move more quickly than amoeba because it has developed accessory structures. These are cilia, which are protoplasmic extensions through minute holes in the stiff surface covering. The combined effect of all the cilia, rhythmically stroking backwards, is to drive the animal forwards. The high degree of co-ordination displayed by these cilia in the swimming movements, or in food taking, suggests that some co-ordinating mechanism resembling nervous control in higher animals must be present. Such has been discovered in paramecium. Near the surface of the animal is a system of protoplasmic fibres which run longitudinally and connect the rows of small granules at the bases of the cilia. Such a system has been termed a *neuromotor apparatus.*

It should be made clear that one is not here speaking of nerve cells and nerve fibres. Indeed, paramecium itself is simply one single cell, a unicellular organism belonging to the class of protozoa which are all unicellular. There is no room in a unicellular organism for anything in the nature of nerve cells and fibres. Some nerve cells are probably bigger than the entire paramecium. What we are talking about here as a neuromotor apparatus is something far more primitive. It is indeed not the specialization of a cell to take on the functions of the nervous tissue (excitability, conductivity and correlation), but merely a modification within the protoplasm of a single cell (paramecium) of some of the protoplasmic substance itself. It is as though a portion of the protoplasm has organized itself in the form of threads or fibres running longitudinally and connecting the rows of small granules at the bases of the cilia. These fibres function like nerves, in that stimuli apparently travel along them and are therefore an interesting suggestion of a very primitive or pre-nervous apparatus.

Experiments have shown that protozoa, or unicellular animals, are limited not only in size but also in degree of specialization. Specialization in a protozoan is that of *intermingling* protoplasms, which become differentiated functionally and structurally.

With the development of a multicellular organism comes the beginning of specialization of cell function. Even sponges, for they are the most primitive of the many celled animals, have at least the rudiments of a local co-ordinating mechanism. Any sponge cell is irritable, and will react if directly affected, but the animal cannot respond as a unified whole. There are no sense cells to receive stimuli, and no nerve cells to transmit the stimuli to other parts of the sponge. Sponges are interesting because they illustrate cell differentiation without much cell co-ordination, a stage which cannot be found among the other many celled animals.

There is every degree of this sort of thing in nature. A tree for instance, can have things happening to one part of it without other parts being unduly disturbed! To my mind the mammalian body differs only in a matter of degree, and still shows many of these primitive characteristics. Even in man it is similarly possible for things to happen to certain parts of the body, without necessarily very much reaction from other parts, although, presumably by virtue of the autonomic nervous system within, the various organs scattered about the interior of the body are better synchronized, and more co-ordinated than the various parts of the sponge. In my opinion, analogies to these can be extended sociologically, some social communities being less co-ordinated and interdependent than others.

When we move from sponges to the coelenterata, which include jellyfish, anemones, corals, hydras, we find the organization of cells into tissues, with division of function. Hydra, the most successful fresh-water coelenterate, has a network of nerve cells extending through the entire animal. This nerve net is slightly more concentrated around the mouth than elsewhere, but there is very little evidence of nerve cells combined to form a specialized controlling group as in the brain of higher types. However, all the essentials of a simple nervous mechanism in a many celled animal are present in hydra, and it may be seen that the nerve net of the coelenterates contains the germ out of which has grown the central nervous system of higher forms. The nerve nets are at least components of the nervous systems of worms, molluscs, arthropods and even vertebrates where they are specially associated with the digestive tract and the circulatory system, including the heart.

It surprises one that these primitive nervous systems or co-ordinating networks are in so many respects the homologue of the autonomic nervous system in mammals such as man. It is surprising that, apart from anatomists and doctors, the educated public at large, though being cognisant of so many systems of the body, including the central nervous system, yet appears to be so ignorant of the existence of the autonomic nervous system which in a sense is even more important. It is a system of fibres connected with ganglia which automatically co-ordinates and controls all the viscera or organs of the body, including the glands even of the skin, without the co-operation of consciousness. It seems that it is in more of a direct line of descent from these very primitive nervous structures. Though connected with the central nervous system, its primary function is one of internal relationships on which health depends, rather than one of internal relationships (to environment) which are more the special, though not the exclusive, province of the central nervous system.

When we transfer our attention from the coelenterates such as hydra to the platyhelminthes, or flatworms, we have moved to a higher order. Here the animal has evolved a head end which normally travels first and collects all new stimuli and hence nervous transmission is mainly longitudinal, and so the nerve net has been rolled up to form several longitudinal nerves with frequent cross connections. These long fibres connect with a special anterior enlargement, the 'brain'. As the animal regularly crawls on its lower side, the nerves there are more numerous and larger since that side is more frequently stimulated. Nerve nets survive locally.

The brain is not necessary for the muscular co-ordination involved in locomotion, for a planarian deprived of its brain will still move along in a co-ordinated fashion. It serves chiefly as a sensory relay that receives stimuli from the sense organs and sends them on to the rest of the body. The result is a much more closely knit behaviour than is possible with the diffuse non-centralized nerve net of hydra, which lacks definite pathways and a co-ordinating centre. The nerve net does not disappear in the planarian but persists in addition to the central nervous system.

Thus we see, even on this very low level of life (flatworms) the beginnings of a differentiation of a central nervous system from what might perhaps be called a vegetative or autonomic nervous system, a process which has reached such a high degree of development in mammals such as man.

In annelids (segmented worms) the function of the brain seems to be to direct the movements in response to sensations of light and touch which it receives. If it is removed locomotion is not affected but movement is ceaseless. This suggests that the brain must inhibit many movements which would otherwise be the result of the constant stimulation. Thus we see that even on this relatively low level, one of the important functions of the brain is to inhibit reflex movements. This is conspicuously true of the mammals, including man, and diseases which interfere with controlling fibres from the brain result similarly in localized involuntary movements or reflex reactions, such as we get in *paralysis agitans,* and disseminated sclerosis, where sclerotic or neutral unfunctioning particles interpose and obstruct the conducting pathway.

In construction and function of the nervous system, there is a transition from the lower annelids to the arthropods (crabs, insects, spiders). The segmented character is obvious in both, and also its further development shows a resemblance. While in some arthropods a great number of equally large ganglia are distributed over the whole length of the ventral cord, in crabs, spiders and most insects these cell groups tend to collect in an anterior direction, suggesting a further state of brain development.

In addition to the primitive form of sensory innervation by neurosensory cells, still numerous in arthropods, a new feature, perhaps first occurring here, is seen in the innervation of special sense organs of the skin by bipolar sensory neurones which enter specialized epithelial cells, forming organs of touch. Such sense cells introduce a new step in the evolution of the nervous system, their evolutionary significance being also demonstrated by the fact that they are more frequent in vertebrates where they are characteristic constituents of the taste buds, lateral line organs, labyrinth of the ear and the complicated sense corpuscles of the skin.

Thus we see that the functions which characterize the nervous system have been derived by a process of further development from the functions of ordinary protoplasm.

When in multicellular animals certain of their cells have assumed a specialized function of co-ordination, we see that the simplest form of nervous system proper consists of a diffuse network of nerve cells and connecting fibres distributed among the other tissues of the body.

Such a nervous system is found among the jellyfish and in other parts of the sympathetic nervous system of higher animals. Animals which possess only this diffuse type of nervous system can perform only very simple acts, chiefly total movements of the whole body or general movements of large parts of it, with relatively small capacity for refined activities requiring the co-operation of many different organs. But even the lowest animals which possess nerves show a tendency for the nervous net to be condensed in some regions for the general control of the activities of the different parts of the body. By a further development of this process arose the central nervous system.

In the segmented worms the central nervous system consists of a chain of ganglia connected by a longitudinal cord along the ventral wall of the body. Each of these ganglia is connected by means of peripheral nerves with the skin and muscles of its own segment, and each joint of the body with its contained ganglion has a certain measure of physiological independence so that it can act as a unit. This is a typical segmented nervous system.

It is probably not adequately recognized that the human body, like that of all mammals, is also basically segmented, or at least shows the equivalent of this early segmentation. The vertebrae themselves clearly show the structural basis of this. From each segment there issues a pair of nerves which supply a portion of the body, dividing it up into its segments, corresponding to the segments of the spinal cord and vertebral column. As regards the internal parts, including the organs, this segmentation persists, although spacially some of the organs have changed their position to a limited extent, carrying the nerve supply connected with their original segment with them. As one would expect, if one thinks of the human body development, the nervous innervation of the perineum, the lower end of the bowel, the bladder and sexual organs, comes from a lower segment than that of the muscles of the legs. This fact is naturally in keeping with evolution and development.

But perhaps we should not lose sight of the fact that the autonomic nervous system in vertebrates, including man and all mammals, the more obvious successor in this early heritage, is in fact ventrally placed in so far as its main ganglia and nervous connections lie on the ventral side of the vertebral column, within the cavity of the body. The fact that body tissue has developed around it still more ventrally does not hide from the anatomist its basic ventral character.

However, vertebrate animals are characterized by having developed in addition to vertebrae a hollow tube of nervous tissue which extends within these vertebrae along the dorsal wall of the body and constitutes the spinal cord and brain. The cavity of this tube extends throughout the entire length of the central nervous system. It forms the central canal of the spinal cord and enlarges into fluid-containing cavities in the brain substances called the ventricles of the brain.

Most of the types of nervous systems found in the animal kingdom are represented in these two distinct and divergent lines of evolution, one adapted especially well for the reflex and instinctive mode of life and found in the worms, insects and their allies, and the other found in the vertebrates and culminating in the human brain with its capacity for individually acquired and conscious functions.

The invertebrate animals, insects and their allies possess a bodily organization which favours the performance of relatively few move-ments in a very perfect fashion. Their reflexes and instincts are very perfectly performed but the number of such reactions which the animal can make is rather sharply limited and fixed by the inherited bodily structure. Their behaviour is dominated by invariable and innate factors and they cannot readily adapt themselves to unusual conditions. The vertebrates also have many elements of their be-haviour which are similarly fixed or stereotyped in their organization. I do not think it is adequately realized what a very large proportion of the activities of even such a higher vertebrate as man are fixed or stereotyped. The behaviour of his internal organs, even the pupils of his eye and the functions of his skin are obviously predetermined, as it were, apart from conscious direction. What he does not realize is that nearly all his behaviour and even his thinking is similarly determined. In addition to this, he has a certain very limited capacity for individual modifiability in behaviour and in thought, or at least it appears to be so by comparison with lesser brethren. Also there is some relative variability here as between one race and another and one individual and another. Very primitive races sometimes astonish us by their relative unmodifiability. But higher cultures make for their own particular variety of unmodifiability.

These two branches of the animal kingdom have therefore during the more recent evolutionary epochs diverged further from each other, and now, in their highly differentiated conditions, neither type could be derived from the other. This does not mean that at a very early stage of evolution, before anything approaching the specialization of the insects arose, both vertebrates and invertebrates diverged from a common stem.

The jointed animals, or arthropods (crabs, insects, spiders) developed from the lower worms (as can be seen in their life cycle), and this branch of the animal kingdom culminates in the insects. The vertebrates were probably developed from similar lowly wormlike forms along an independent line of evolution and this branch of the animal kingdom culminates in the human race.

It may be asked why, if it is the aetiology of man or the emergence of his ego which I am trying to describe, I should choose to select the simpler forms of life and to dwell upon them.

I feel that it is the simpler forms of life which, being nearer to life's origin, show more clearly its essential nature and ingredients, its relevant physicochemical basis. Once we have arrived at the stage of vertebrates, we may have lost the simple essence of the meaning of life, and once we have arrived at mammals, we have practically arrived at man, *and with that arrival, reached our habitual blindness to our basic nature.*

I feel that the longer we study biology, the greater will be the possibility of our acquiring a new orientation to the life of man, the more probability there will be of our seeing the truth about ourselves and of appreciating the degree to which in our thinking and our attitudes, we have turned away from the truth, evidently preferring to ignore it and even frequently to deny it, evidently preferring our mental system of misrepresentation, illusion and delusion. It would seem that our pleasure lies away from the truth, not towards it—perhaps in the direction of some megalomania. I have heard people say, even in this allegedly enlightened age, 'But we are not animals!' One feels inclined to ask 'What are we then?' Every fibre of our being is animal, literally so. We have the same bony structure as other vertebrates, the same organs as other mammals, placed in similar positions, even to the minutest detail, even the same hair follicles and the same hair. We were the original eaters of other forms of life (and at one stage or perhaps at many stages, even of our own form of life, witness our cannibal ancestors). Indeed, our inheritance goes back even earlier to the valencies (cf. appetites) of elements and chemicals and before this to the nature of immaterial energy itself. It is surely some compulsion (cf. appetite) inherent in the nature of this force which is the cause of the production of our environment and of ourselves, including our reluctance to relinquish even in part our preference for the pleasure-principle and including our resistance only gradually being abandoned to the admission of reality and truth.

CHAPTER XXII

OUTLINE OF EVOLUTION

Not only the anatomical structure of man but even more plainly the study of embryology, the development of the foetus in utero, shows the story of man's life history from the unicellular animalcules.

It is certain that all human races are descended from a single species of ancestor, which no doubt goes back to a common stock from which all mammals have descended. This stock in turn descended from the reptiles from which it is said to have broken off perhaps some fifty million years ago. According to some authorities the insect-eating and tree-living tarsier, with its keen-sighted goggly eyes and no larger than a rat, is merely a small step away from the line of man's direct ancestry. It was some close relative of this little animal that was the progenitor of the monkey family which, there is evidence to suggest, first arose in North America and subsequently spread to the warmer regions of the sun of Africa, to give rise finally to the greater apes, the baboon, orang-outang, chimpanzee and gorilla. The progenitor of man was another branch of the same family.

Somatic development was primarily a response to the needs of an animal or species, the chief need being survival. Those species of mammal who learnt to survive by running and developing hooves had perhaps found an easy way which did not require so much brain development. On the other hand, many animals apparently survived by developing a high degree of physical strength. We might even include the giant gorilla in this category, but in general of course monkeys found safety in their tree-climbing apparatus. This led to an ability to investigate things by handling or feeling and may have stimulated inquisitiveness and intelligence as an aid to survival. However, it seems likely that about the time of the last Ice Age, when forests tended to disappear, our ancestors took to living on the ground, and thereafter to using their hands to break off branches of trees, and perhaps to use stones as defensive weapons, and eventually for utilitarian purposes. By the Miocene epoch, fifteen million years ago, many varieties of large ape lived on the earth, undoubtedly ancestors of the chimpanzee and gorilla as well as of man.

Man's body (as well as his mind) carries innumerable structures and vestiges showing its origin from a very primitive and even pre-mammalian form. Even as far back as the lizards there are finger bones corresponding to our own. Vestigial structures in human anatomy are innumerable, and in most cases the only explanation of their existence is their presence and utility at an earlier stage of evolution.

The tubercle of the external ear or auricle, the so-called Darwin's tubercle, has been pointed to in this connection. It is usually present on the inner edge of the outermost fold of the pinna (external ear), about a quarter or a third of the way down, and is a vestige of the pointed ear of certain other mammals, such as the barbary ape, where it is of course at the top. Indeed, it is present in every human foetus at a certain stage of development exactly in this position, before the outer fold of the ear turns inwards and the tip moves downwards to leave only this vestige. Similarly, practically every part of the human body has its signs of an early ancestry. Indeed, to my mind it is questionable whether not only many of our muscles (such as the five unfunctioning muscles in the skin of this same outer ear, each of whose nerve supplies can still be traced in the form of fibre cords) in every part of our body, but also whether the greater part of our anatomical structure, bones, organs and even hair might not be classed as inessential vestiges. Certainly we no longer require all that highly sensitive mechanism for fight or flight which was at one time so essential for preserving the individual's life, and is now chiefly responsible, in civilized man, for giving him neurotic symptoms, diabetes, thyrotoxicosis, and gastric ulcer. Adaptation to a new environment is not without its casualties.

A study of the embryological development of the human baby reveals all the stages of development, even from the unicellular animal. Later stages in its development can often be traced with exactitude, for instance, it can be shown that the auditory ossicles, or little bones between the eardrum and the internal ear have been developed from a comparable bone in the lizard's jaws. Embryological development shows a series of gill clefts corresponding to those of fishes.

What is not generally realized is that we still spend our 'infancy' in the 'water', for the growth of the human foetus begins and ends in water, namely in what is called the amniotic fluid, which is encased in a water-tight membrane the amniotic sac within the uterus. What is more, the human foetus, perhaps fully formed within three months, continues to live in this 'water' until it is nine months old.

Haldane considers that the first great step in evolution was the hingeing of one gill arch to form a lower jaw. Subsequently a second gill arch was added to strengthen the lower jaw. Everything points to our origin from fishes. Haldane considers that man is 'rather a primitive mammal anatomically'.[40] By this he evidently means that we have not specialized nearly as much as some of our relatives. We still keep most of our primitive attributes. We have not even developed hooves or wings.

On the other hand we have developed precision movements of our hands, and we have developed our brains. In this connection Huxley says 'man differs less from the chimpanzee or the orang than these do from monkeys, and the difference between the brains of the chimpanzee and of man is almost insignificant when compared with the difference between the chimpanzee brain and that of a lemur'.[41]

With the advance of science, the links between physics and chemistry seem to be complete, the frontier there having practically disappeared. In the light of these considerations, it seems extraordinary that the link between non-living matter and life as we generally recognize it, a-cellular, unicellular or multicellular, should still seem to many people inadequate. I suspect that this is in part at least due to a bias in favour of believing that life, properly so-called, must have some special quality which cannot be explained as chemical or physical. This is comparable to the bias which wishes to preserve the illusion that there is a very large and unbridgeable gap between *homo sapiens* and other mammals. Both these biases are determined by the wish for human (i.e. self) aggrandizement at the expense of truth and objective assessment. They remind one of the centuries-long bias in favour of believing that the entire universe revolved around this planet, and indeed the opposition, amounting to violence, that assailed the pioneers of evidence to the contrary.

The bias in favour of believing that there is some supernatural process responsible for the phenomenon of life has been called the theory of vitalism. I suspect that this emotionally based belief is really directed towards an attempt to separate us personally as it were from chemicophysical laws and natural processes in general. It is the old supernaturalism and belief in magic creeping back in a pseudo-scientific guise.

In pursuing the question as to how and where life originated, it is very relevant to consider the following facts, however familiar, elecited from Ernest Baldwin's 'Comparative Biochemistry':[42] 'If we compare the relative proportions of the different ions (that is, salts) present in the blood of a number of different animals, we find that there exists between them a very remarkable similarity. Had we taken random samples of different inorganic instead of biological materials, we should have been considerably surprised if there had been any particular resemblance between them; and if any marked similarity were noticed we should probably conclude that they were in some way related and perhaps even had a common origin. The series of data (given in Baldwin's table) show that the blood of widely different animals are very like each other and closely similar to sea water. On account of their general resemblance to sea water it has been suggested by Macallum that the circulating fluids of all the animals originally came from the sea water of millions of years ago. In other words, that our own blood is nothing more or less than a modified sea water. This does indeed seem reasonable if as we believe life really originated in the sea.

'Indeed Macallum says that life began in the ocean millions of years ago, that the blood systems of different groups of animals closed off at different times, and that the composition of the blood of their descendants has remained practically unmodified ever since.'

The above also suggests the further reflection in keeping with Bastian's theory: namely that life did not simply arise once and for all at a specific period of the Earth's history resulting through evolution in some of the original unicellular animals becoming advanced vertebrates, and at the same time in other descendants throughout the ages remaining in their original unicellular form, but that on the contrary there was and is a successive repetitive and continuous 'spontaneous generation' of life which still occurs at the present day, and that the simple forms of life today originated at a comparatively late period.

These and other evidences bring us to the conclusion that the living protoplasm of which our bodies are composed originated in the Eovertebrate ocean, in water which had come to contain the dissolved elements of both rock and air, for geology has shown that living things came into being only after the igneous rocks had been deposited as the earth cooled, and that their primal forms were marine. Apparently this chemical solution was the first essential condition in forming living things of every kind.

The point is that there is no natural line of demarcation between non-living and living substances. It is inherent in the nature of matter that larger and heavier and more complex molecules are constantly arising from cosmic energy, until they reach that degree of complexity and size which is the greatest possible for the prevailing conditions of temperature and pressure. In the conditions which prevail upon the earth's surface, the presence of air and of solar radiation, the largest and most complex chemical molecules (e.g. protoplasm) are necessarily unstable. If they are constantly breaking down they are also constantly being formed, with, or perhaps without, the appropriate catalyctic agents.

The primordial protoplasmic slime can only be regarded as the most complex substance with the largest molecule resulting from this inevitable natural process, evidently inherent in the nature of the atom itself. All living creatures upon this earth, viruses, ultra microscopic entities, moulds, algae, amoebae, metazoa, bacteria and all

varieties and forms of plant and animal life inevitably follow. All must
be a result of some property of energy inherent in the atom itself.

Dr David Forsyth, late consulting physician to Charing Cross
Hospital, took the view that the purpose of life from a biological point
of view is essentially that of preserving the germ-cell ('the sex cell'),
and ensuring that it at any rate has everlasting life. Everything connected with the functions and the structure of the body is only
accessory to this purpose. He says:[43] 'Must we not infer that each of
the bodily forms and functions is a specialization on behalf of this
germ? The conclusion seems irresistible to me. And this brings us
back to our original question, what is the body for? Our answer must
be—to house the sex-cell. All the complicated details of the human
frame are united in the single purpose of serving this tiny particle
within it. They contribute to its healthy existence, and without them
it cannot mature, or even survive . . .' When he says 'We must
envisage a germ producing a succession of bodies', the suggestion that
occurs to us is, is not this precisely what has happened in the millions
of years of the evolutionary process since desoxyribonucleic acid first
led to the formation of viruses or genes?

It may be suggested in extension of this that perhaps we could
regard human environment, in so far as it is the result of human
activity, including civilization and institutions, as a further extension
and reflection of the nature of the germ-cell, they, like the human
body, being as it were all its own work. Forsyth says love, as manifest
in social life, is an elaborated function of the same primitive cells. In
each of the differentiated germ-cells, male and female, there is a
'quantity of physico-chemical energy—when they fuse, their metabolic activity is instantly quickened, even several thousandfold, as has
been shown electrically and chemically. We know also that a new
soma starts growing only after the germ-cells of opposite sexes have
come together. This would suggest that the energy contained in them
is of two sorts, which are complementary to each other; and that each
needs to be supplemented by the other.'

He compares this to negative and positive charges of electricity,
and suggests that mutual fascination of the sexes is another form of
the physico-chemical (? electrical) attraction of male and female
germ-cells. He even goes so far as to suggest that 'an adult male and
female in their behaviour to each other, carry out the behests of the
sperm and ovum within them'.[43]

So are we driven by extensions of the same natural forces which
brought the original unicellular animal into existence! The germ-
plasm might be regarded as one long, continuous growth, shall we
suggest permeating the entire biosphere, and not subject to death.
Thus our habit of dividing life into individuals (i.e. spacial limitations) and into generations, (i.e. temporal limitations), would be

illusionary. The concept emerging is that life is synonymous with germ-plasm, all the apparent aspects of life being merely signs of its endeavour to build an environment which will enable it to preserve itself indefinitely. Thus we would have the continuity only apparently, but not really, broken by the phenomenon of reproduction and somatic death.

Another interesting conception of Forsyth's is the idea that all living things on the earth's surface, plants and animals, 'carry on activities which are interdependent: and they function in the biosphere much as somatic cells do in an organism'.

One is tempted to speculate as to whether the evolution of inorganic matter into organic, the origin of life and the evolution of man, may be all part of the same principle of the 'economy of energy', and as to whether the very cooling of matter, for instance by radiation of heat, may similarly be expressing an unalterable law of the line of least resistance, identical with the principle of the economy of energy. Here again, one thinks of Herbert Spencer's *First Principles*, and of his formula of the evolutionary process. ('. . . matter passes from an indefinite, incoherent homogeniety, to a definite, coherent heterogeneity . . .').[44] Whether or not these theories, like that of relativity, will stand the test of time and investigation, remains to be seen, but in my opinion we do know enough to have no doubt that it is nothing more or less than a physical process behind all visible phenomena from the evolution of galaxies to the origin of life and the evolution of man.

Biologists have told us that all inheritable factors are contained within the chromosomes; or rather the genes, of the germ-cell, and presumably are therefore immune to the influence of environment; that is to say they are totally unaffected by environment or by any acquired character of the individual. He is only as it were the carrier of the germ-plasm, and whatever adaptation he, and presumably his successors, may make to their environment, the germ-plasm will go on reproducing itself in a succession of individuals, totally unaffected by the experience of the succession of somatoplasms or bodies which have carried it, and to which it gave rise.

According to modern biology, evolution is brought about primarily by the 'mutation' of individual genes, and by fresh combinations of genes, the only other important factor being the Darwinian principle of Natural Selection, whereby the resulting variant, which the environment or nature favours, survives and continues to reproduce, whereas those variants which are unfavourable sooner or later become extinct. Accordingly, this is the only way in which 'adaptation to environment' as a long-term or inheritable quality can take place.

To my mind, we could not support the concept of evolution at all without regarding it as essentially a *progressive* process of adaptation to environment. This is the very essence of the preservation of life, the essence of the activities of all living organisms. It is the one thing that ensures their survival. I know it will be said that this Lamarckian theory* is out of date since Darwin (indeed, it was never given very much notice even before Darwin). Admitting that in science authority proves nothing (as Galileo demonstrated before the Aristotle-worshipping authorities at Pisa), it may nevertheless be worth mentioning that a host of intelligent men, literary and scientific, from Bernard Shaw to Freud, implicitly, though not always explicitly, assume the truth of Lamarckism in their theories and writings. Even Julian Huxley himself, the great modern opponent of Lamarckism, though explicitly attacking it, implicitly, to my mind, accepts it in a lot of his pronouncements. For instance, with reference to the adaptation of fishes to land, he says: 'They could survive by getting from one pool to another in case of need. In those which adopted this method, the air-bladder became a little more of a lung; their fins became better able to support their weight when out of water.'[41]

Does not this imply that the improved adaptation to land was progressively increased through the passing on of it to progeny? He continues: 'By means of minor further improvements their fins could become walking legs, and their air-bladders could become nothing but lungs.' How could this progress be maintained and improved except through the progeny having the advantage of what was acquired by their ancestors and continuing to improve it? Of birds, Huxley says: 'Their fore-limbs are so thoroughly specialized as flying organs that they *have become* unusable for any other function.' (The italics are mine).

He says of Man: 'He has developed a *new method* of evolution: the transmission of organized experience by way of tradition, which supplements and largely overrides the automatic process of natural selection as the agency of change in the human phase.' (The italics are mine). This new method, Huxley tells us, operates 'by cultural transmission'. Thus he has capitulated in favour of Lamarckism—but only where it operates in a manner too evident to be ignored or denied 'through the various media of cultural inheritance'.

I have of necessity dealt with this subject inadequately, but I hope my critics will not use it as a red herring when discussing this book. I may say that Lamarckism is essential for my entire philosophy of the mechanism of the central portion of this continuous chain which comprises the known portion of the riddle of the universe, namely the

---

* Jean-Baptiste de Lamarck's theory in his own words was: 'The environment affects the shape and organization of animals: frequent continuous use develops and enlarges any organ, while by permanent disuse it weakens until it finally disappears: all acquisitions or losses wrought through influence of the environment and hence through use and disuse are preserved by reproduction.'

portion between the origin of energy and the destiny of mind. I confessed to this Lamarckian theory in my book *Clinical Psychology* when
I quoted the great scientist C. S. Myers as writing: 'There are not a
few who think that sufficiently prolonged genetic research is in time
likely somehow to bridge the present apparently impassable gulf
between Lamarckism and neo-Darwinism. Without *some* form of
Lamarckism, it is hard to understand the evolution of mind, including
that of instincts. The closer study of instincts may enable us to
determine whether instincts are merely and always the outcome of
chance variations in the germ plasm, perpetuated *ab initio* by heredity
and by the operation of natural selection; or whether they have not
also been evoked by the interests, needs and efforts of the organism
itself, assisted by, if not also assisting, inheritable changes in the germ
plasm.'

I am convinced that the failure of biologists to see the essential
truth of Lamarckism and their insistence on the counter-claims of
chance mutations and natural selection, is an instance of the common
occurrence of scientists being so taken up with the *mechanisms* that they
fail to see the general principle, and is also due to a more fundamental
failure to see the 'identity' of organism and environment together
with the 'identity' of individual and species. Only thus could one
discount the obvious fact that adaptation to environment is the
essential condition for the continuance of life, the essential characteristic of living matter, and the essential element in the evolutionary
process—a process which is nothing more or less than an extension of
the principle of individual adaptation, and its application to the
species as a whole. I am convinced that if environment did not affect
living organisms in a more than temporary, individual manner,
affecting at the most merely changes in the somatoplasm and leaving
hereditary proclivities totally unaffected, *there would be no such process
as evolution with its essential ingredient of adaptation to environment.*

Admittedly germ-plasm changes may lag behind, possibly generations behind, somatic alterations in function and in structure. *The
anti-Lamarckian experiments of biology have proved nothing more than this.* On
the other hand the whole biosphere and the highest product of the
earliest stages of its evolutionary process, namely man and his mind,
are conclusive evidence of a world-wide 'experiment' proving nothing
more or less than the inheritance of acquired characters, however
complicated and indirect (e.g. via gene changes or so-called mutations) may be the process whereby these changes are transmitted.

I realize that I cannot do justice to my Lamarckian views in these
brief pages. My theory of evolution is, of course, larger than the
biological field; it is based on interaction of energy upon energy, of
atom on atom—in short, on cause and effect.

As this matter is of such overwhelming importance for my whole theory, and I may add for every not-meaningless theory of life and mind, and as it is impracticable to itemize here the limitless evidence in its favour, I will endeavour to re-state it with greater clarity: the essence of evolution, as indeed of life itself, is a progressive adaptation to environment. The fact of development (for instance the fact that we develop an air-breathing apparatus having had at an earlier stage of life *in utero* only gill-clefts) proves that adaptations acquired in the past are passed on to the progeny; in other words, that acquired characters are inherited. Progressive adaptation is not arrested by the basic life-process of growth; reproduction is growth, and, whether by *mitosis* or by *meosis,* is not a barrier but a facilitation to further adaptation of the adaptations already acquired. All biological (and psychological) evolution has this meaning above all others. To deny these concepts of evolution and development is to show that one has not correctly assessed the overwhelming data of observation. Admittedly the term environment should be regarded as including the soma, the body, by the same token as I (following Forsyth) have suggested that environment, even the Earth, should be regarded as an *extension* of the soma. We may remember that the egg, the germ cell, still carries around itself a sample, as it were, of that salt-water 'pond' in which it grew originally some thousand million years ago. The concentrations of salt approximate to the original seas of that age rather than to present ones. *The soma inevitably affects the germ cells it carries in the same way as a penicillin environment affects staphylococci.*

In conclusion I should like to summarize my theory regarding this vexed question of the hypotheses of congenital and acquired factors in evolution, and in the causation of an individual's or species' attributes, anatomical and psychological, reactive patterns, behaviour and beliefs. My theory is that the antithesis is illusionary, and is encouraged by what is, to my mind, the erroneous attitude of biologists in assuming that longer-term attributes embodied in the gene are alone transmissible, and that any acquired characteristics including acquired patterns of behaviour, however long established, never become transmissible.

I am convinced that our characteristics, including instinct, *like species,* were not created separately—not even by the indirect independent-of-environment or magical process of mutations. Throughout an individual's life adjustments to environment are being formed. Inherited attributes, including instincts, are being modified however slightly, and new reactive patterns are developing. This is a process of reactive adaptation to environment and I am convinced that this is the way that new attributes are coming into being, including modifications of old instincts and the evolution of new instincts. Changes are in the process of being brought about, however gradually and imperceptibly, throughout the ages. I am convinced that this is not simply a question of acquired characteristics in anti-thesis to inherited ones; this is *how* the inherited ones were originally acquired, and how fresh attributes, such as patterns of reaction, are being acquired, and new modifications and new instincts evolved. To my mind *this* is evolution.*

* The University of Michigan has now (1961) published conclusive evidence of these Lamarckian theories with its experiments on the flatworm *(Planaria Tigrina)*.

CHAPTER XXIII

GROWTH AND STRUCTURE OF THE MIND

The mind, like every other phenomenon of life, is best understood by a study of its evolution and development. To focus one's attention as we commonly do upon the conscious mind as a starting point, is comparable to taking the most recent event in history and expecting to understand it without reference to previous events.

The meaning of things lies in their historical development in the same way that the meaning of effects, in so far as we can glean it, lies in a study of their causes. The 'conscious' mind is only a final emergent —a late synthesis—of what, for want of a better name, we might call the 'cell mind'.

In a sense we may say that there are a succession or series of 'minds' throughout any multicellular living body. For instance, the 'behaviour' of the stomach and the intestines is largely controlled by a conglomeration of nerve cells and fibres situated in what is called the *coeliac plexus* which lies in the abdominal region in front of the backbone. Of course, we do not ordinarily dignify the function of groups of nerve ganglia by the name of 'mind' any more than we attribute mind to such a low animal as the earthworm, but both the earthworm and the stomach and intestines of man *behave*. Who are we to say that some function at least analogous to that of mind is not present, and controlling or partly controlling that behaviour? The fact remains that the human organism embodies within it a series of autonomous functions comparable with that of the *coeliac plexus*, some lower and simpler and some higher and more complex.

Man, the most highly developed creature, incorporates within his body and nervous system (or, more accurately, various nervous systems) every degree of simplicity and complexity of nervous structure through which he has passed during his previous evolutionary stages from unicellular animal to his present form.

In the course of his individual development from an actual unicellular animal, or fertilized egg, to maturity, he repeats approximately, in abbreviated form, the whole of his evolutionary history. (This fact is expressed in the dictum: ontogeny repeats phylogeny). His nervous tissues develop from the simplest reflex arcs to the most complicated and difficult-to-disentangle structures. Nevertheless, within his central nervous system and within his body he still incorporates every one of the stages of his evolution and development.

Thus he has, as it were, an enormous mass of nerve fibres and ganglia pervading every inch of his body and brain. They include not only what we know as the Central Nervous System with its peripheral ramifications, but also what seems to be less well known, the Vegetative, or Autonomic Nervous System. This latter is a more primitive structure which presides more especially over those operations and functions of his body and its organs which are carried out without conscious effort on his part, for example, the beating of his heart.

Nevertheless, although these various structures have their own cell collections and, as it were, 'local governments', they all have some connection, however slight and remote, with the Central Nervous System. This in turn has connections with the cerebral cortex, that part of the brain where is the presumed seat of conscious mental functioning.

The point I want to emphasize is that the many functions of the body are largely under the immediate control of various outlying or local 'minds' right up to an extraordinarily high level of the Central Nervous System. The characteristic of these various local 'minds' is that they are often as little in full knowledge of and agreement with one another as are the various nations. It is only at the relatively minute level of *conscious* mental functioning that we begin to get anything which can be regarded as approximating to comprehensive organization. Even here contradictions exist and live side by side, though at this level there is a tendency to integrate, or to cancel out, opposites, to find a compromise. Just below this conscious level of mental functioning the clinical psychologist is accustomed to meet the most diametrically opposed desires and wishes and contradictions in purpose—primitive loves and hates, all living, as it were, side by side in the same house without any knowledge on the part of the one of the existence of the other.

Admittedly, the conscious mind can and does have its influence upon other mental levels and even upon the body itself, but those who are unaware of deeper mental levels are naturally apt to overrate the degree to which the conscious mind can influence the body in health or in disease. The theory that emerges from increasing study of the nature of mind is rather the reverse of this assumption. It is namely that *the conscious mind is itself a product of the deeper levels* and is itself subject, even in the formation of its judgements, to forces which arise in those deeper levels. Thus the facts are, particularly if 'mind' is equated with consciousness, more in favour of the theory of matter over mind than that of mind over matter, however much we may prefer to think the latter.

On reflection this view should not surprise us, for we will recognize that the mind was brought into being, created and developed by matter without the mind's knowledge or co-operation, indeed, before we can presume the existence of a conscious mind to know or to co-operate. It is surprising how often one has to remind an anxious patient of this fact. There seems to be a tendency, promoted by anxiety, to believe that disaster will overtake us unless we succeed in some hypothetical *control* of our nature, our functions and even our thoughts. Very often the only thing that will happen will be health, in place of anxiety and illness!

This brings me to the question of what we inherit mentally and nervously in comparison with what we acquire in the course of our individual lifetime. It is generally and rightly assumed that we inherit our instincts. In fact, by definition instincts are *innate* (i.e. inherited) urges to react to a stimulus in a particular manner. It should not surprise us to learn also that the major instincts serve the purpose of preserving and perpetuating life. A creature born without them would be the last link in his particular evolutionary chain and after him, his type would be heard of no more.

Bearing this in mind, it is rather a curious reflection that so many of us should seem to spend the greater part of our life and energies in trying to oppose our inherited or instinctual tendencies, thereby giving ourselves a great deal of unnecessary toil and sweat, not to speak of nervous and physical breakdowns.

The explanation of why any sort of conscious struggle against the simple gratification of instinct should have come into being is that we are passing through a further stage of evolutionary progress, a stage in which the original biological principles of each for himself is giving place to an organization of living individuals into social, national and international units. Conceivably, in the depths of biological speculation, we may suggest that individual cells had at one time to surrender some portion of their instinctual individuality in favour of mutual co-operation and division of labour, thereby enabling the multi-cellular organism to come into being.

From a biological point of view the primary attribute of all living matter, virus, plant or animal, is that of *growth*. When it ceases to grow as an individual organism it buds off or grows seeds, and the seeds (or fertilized eggs) continue the process of growth. To do this, life is for ever making inroads upon its environment, converting that environment, as it were, into its own particular living substance.

Modern psychology extends this essentially *dynamic* quality of life to its concept of the living mind. Life, including mental life, is nothing if it is not 'alive'. Thus we speak of '*psychic energy*'—for ever accumulating and for ever compulsively striving for expression or discharge. It is only when this normal process is interfered with or arrested that symptom, illness or death results.

In the case of the more complex levels of the central nervous system, tensions accumulated by myriads of nerve cells are not necessarily discharged immediately. Various resistances and inhibiting mechanisms (similar in structure to that of the reflex arc) have been built up so that discharge is postponed and a considerable quantity of tension may be retained for a considerable time. This is the source of psychic energy.

The accumulated tension is for ever discharging some of its energy in a variety of activities from simple reflex actions to elaborate unconscious mental activities; and some of it gives rise to the phenomenon of consciousness and itself becomes conscious in the form of impulses and desires.

Now in addition to very primitive nervous mechanisms some of the main forms of discharge for accumulated tension are the more complicated mechanisms laid down by our biological ancestry and inherited by us in the form of *instincts*. They could be regarded as a series of very complicated reflex arcs or similar mechanisms, possessing a sort of hereditary priority for the discharge of tension. They safeguarded the preservation and perpetuation of our lives long before 'we' (that is, our conscious egos) came into the picture to aid or to interfere.

Thus it may be said that in the *mental economy* of a highly complicated multicellular organism, such as man, psychic energy would tend to discharge itself along the instinct paths already laid down phylogenetically and ontogenetically (by evolution and by development). This would normally keep psychic tension at an optimum level, and nervous and bodily health should result.

Now, if something (such as fear) prevents instinct-discharge, tensions will accumulate above the optimum level. Fear, itself an instinct, is the most potent cause of the deferment or arrest of normal instinct discharge, but it may be brought into play by a large variety of causes. It can be stimulated by external or internal (intrapsychic) causes. Threats or imagined threats, especially those occurring in our earliest infancy, can be, as it were, incorporated in a hypothetical part of the mind called the 'superego' and can function years later in spite of their frequent inconsistancy with our reason. The growing infant learning to fear its own aggression and similar instincts can project these on to others (e.g. imagine they belong to its parents) and in that form fear them! It can also project them on to things, and thus people the world with terrifying objects (cf. as in the animistic stage of human development). Subsequently it can 'introject' these imaginary monsters into its own mind to build up a fear-provoking superego. But I shall avoid going further into these complicated mechanisms for the production of fear and the inhibition of pleasure-giving instincts.

Another force which can oppose the natural process of instinct-discharge of tension, is the ideology of the ego. We would call this ideology true if it is a correct assessment of reality—in that case we could say that 'reality' was frustrating the instinct—and false if it is a mistaken view of reality.

Enough has been said to indicate that various activities of the mind, both conscious and unconscious, can institute (usually in the form of fear) opposition to the natural discharge of instinct-tension. These activities, of course, themselves absorb a certain amount of psychic energy though they commonly obstruct the discharge of a similar amount.

All this is probably the price we are paying for current evolutionary modifications—a part of the phenomenon of 'growth'.

The point I wished to come to is this: whatever may be the cause (rational or otherwise) of instinct frustration or inhibition, the process results in the accumulation of tension within the psyche. When this tension reaches an intolerable degree of intensity, discharge will take place automatically—in spite of ego or other resistances. Nevertheless, the resistances do commonly affect the *form* in which the discharge takes place. They may succeed in obstructing it from taking its usual instinct form, but discharge itself it will, one way or another.

When control is brushed aside by this natural force the ego commonly experiences the most acute anxiety. With or without this the accumulated tension discharges itself along such alternative paths (alternative to that of the frustrated instinct) as emotional disturbances, bodily innervations or intra-psychic functions.

The first include every variety of anxiety attack, from palpitations, tremors and sweatings, to collapse and panic. The second include hysterical conversion symptoms such as bodily spasms, paralyses and pains; and the last include mental illnesses.

This is the process of symptom-formation. It will be seen that its energy is derived from accumulated psychic tension. Insofar as it provides a means of outlet for this tension it can be regarded as an attempt at 'cure'—a cure for the intolerable, but otherwise hidden, mental stress. But insofar as it is contrary to ego (e.g. conscious) wishes it is a bad adaptation—a nervous or mental illness.

The *form* it takes may be an unreasonable instinct-expression but more often it is an *alternative* to instinct-expression *forced* upon the psychic energy by the forces opposing its more direct instinct-expression. This form, chosen by the psychic energy when its instinct-expression is denied it, is the one next most easily available. This will be determined by the past instinctual or libidinal development of the particular individual and the *fixations* of her pleasure pattern to various epochs of her past emotional development, and the phantasies related to them. The frustrated energy is said to *regress* to these earlier patterns.

The morbid process may be initiated by a current or 'actual' cause of instinct frustration.

The trouble is that there may be within us a tendency to imagine or even to create frustrations, and thereby to precipitate the nervous illness even when these frustrations do not exist in the real world outside. This is a tendency which requires psychotherapy or analysis for its exposure and relief. But apart from such neurotic trends, the normal individual is habitually safe-guarding himself by endeavouring to overcome, to avoid or to circumvent the precipitating factors of illness, namely frustrations in his current environment. This last is therefore the practical point.

Our lives generally, in so far as they are attempts to make ourselves happy and to satisfy our needs, instinctual and ideational (what a host of complications that implies!) are, consciously and unconsciously, striving after the avoidance of illness and the maintenance of health.

The purpose of this book is to show, and to leave no shadow of doubt, that the 'normal' human mind in striving to achieve and maintain somatic health, develops relatively little equipment for actual reality observation and assessment. It is so developed that it misrepresents or sacrifices reality, the truth and logic, in favour of maintaining freedom from anxiety and consequent bodily health *at the expense of mental 'health' or sanity.*

I have endeavoured to show that the development and evolution of man, of his nervous system, his brain and his mind, were as inevitable and as consequential, purely from the natural laws of cause and effect, as are all the phenomena in nature, physical, chemical and biological, upon which they are not only based but of which they are a part, and with which they are identical. It was a physicochemically based change consequent upon metabolism that caused living matter to behave in a specific manner; instinctual behaviour, directed towards instinctual gratification, is only an elaborate instance of this, with identical physicochemical causation and similarly directed towards further physicochemical changes, such as neutralization of those which arise through metabolism. Gratification in chemical language spells neutralization of unstable (or 'uncomfortable') chemical changes which have arisen in the course of metabolism. Reactions of all living matter from the amoeba upwards are basically no different from the reactions of inanimate matter, physically and chemically. But with protoplasm and living organisms, behaviour gradually becomes a little more complicated.

We might suggest that the behaviour of the amoeba is directed primarily to relieving 'discomforts' which arise either from its environment or from its internal metabolic processes, and restoring a state of gratification or comfort which may amount to a physical or chemical resumption of its previous state. We may assume that if such a reactive pattern ceased to operate, death and extinction would ensue. The living protoplasm would revert to its previous inanimate state and the complicated large molecules would break down to their simpler constituent components. Thus, these reactions, whether we call them physical, chemical, vital or instinctual, are essential to the preservation of life.

This is being stressed because I wish to suggest that from the amoeba to man, including the operations of his mind, there is no need to postulate the introduction of any new principle. The same determinants hold good throughout the biosphere—and the cosmosphere. It is only some physicochemical interference from without and from within (e.g. metabolism) that stimulates reactive behaviour, namely that of eliminating the stimulus or neutralizing conditions provoked by it.

At a higher level of life, such as in insects, we may suggest that the instincts are only a more elaborate pattern of behaviour directed towards this same end. Probably no living creature wishes to develop, evolve, to become 'higher' or more complicated. All it 'wishes' to do is to relieve pain or discomfort and to become or remain comfortable. At the same time, one of the characteristics of living material, even at virus level, is the reaction upon its environment apparently directed towards building itself up, increasing its substance, at the expense of that environment. Maybe it is only by such a process that it can implement its 'pleasure-principle' of removing discomfort and maintaining comfort. It assimilates matter and it grows. Of course the process is chemically conditioned and probably not different in principle from chemical processes in general. All living processes are chemically conditioned, including that of mental function.

The question arises 'what is this mental functioning?' It would seem that for many millions of years, living matter got along as much of it does today, without any attribute that could be called mind, and indeed without any nervous system or physical basis of mind.

My contention is that when nervous structure and ultimately mind begin to develop, they serve the primary purpose of facilitating automatic or pleasure processes which result in growth, and of overcoming frustrations that lie between the organism and this purpose. I would emphasize that under the term growth, I would include reproduction.

It would seem that the original function of nervous tissue was simply co-ordination of the different parts of the multi-cellular animal (cf. the neuro-motor strands co-ordinating cilia of the uni-cellular animal). So long as life went smoothly, either at this stage or before it, there would be no demand for any further specialization or more complicated development.

It may be that the answer to the riddle of why evolution takes place is that the process of life never does go entirely smoothly. Perhaps the nature of life implies a struggle against inanimate matter, if against nothing else, in order to, as it were, get the better of it, ingest it, and grow at its expense. Perhaps life is always in some sense 'uncomfortable'.

I think it should be said that man has had more difficulties to overcome and has naturally therefore developed more ability to overcome them. But the reason he has had more difficulties to overcome is essentially because he has lived longer. If a superabundance of difficulties arose at an unduly early stage of development, the animal, or rather the entire species, would fail to overcome them and would become extinct. That happened to the majority of reptiles, and no doubt to innumerable other specialized species, including many varieties of insect. The difficulties have to accumulate co-incidentally with the ability of the developing animal to deal with them, and to survive, that is to say for its species to survive.

I am suggesting that until the extremely recent times when social adaptation introduced a slightly new factor, or rather an increase of emphasis upon an old factor, certainly no new principle of adaptation necessarily came into play. Man's evolution depended and depends upon precisely the same laws or actions and reactions as does that of every other living animal. Therefore it should not be too difficult to trace why and how the principal psychological attributes of man developed to their present degree of importance in his psychological make-up.

It is necessary to stress the identity of evolution and indeed of the life process itself with adaptation to environment, to enable us to understand the nature of our instinctual emotional and mental attributes, including that of the emergence of what might be called our diminutive ego, or reality principle. To my mind, nothing that we know about the structure and the functions of the body and the mind, makes any sense or can have any natural explanation without an acceptance of this reactive and adaptive principle, and of its at least facilitating some equivalent tendency in the offspring in due course. Life reacts to the difficulties it encounters in order to remain alive. Generally speaking, it does not go in for reactions which are in excess of those demanded by the compulsive (physicochemically based) principles of the life process. What is more, it will probably tend to lose its acquired achievements and degenerate into something more simple if these faculties are no longer required for survival, although admittedly biologically such movements might conceivably require hundreds of thousands of years.

How did all the various attributes of the human mind come into being? Now to begin with, the compulsion of life, be it hunger or anything else, endows the life process of any and every living creature with what we might call a certain degree of self-assertiveness, or a compulsion to act upon its environment, inert or otherwise, to gratify its hunger.

Frustration is all a matter of degree, but we can well imagine that if the living creature's consuming activities are unduly frustrated, whether by undue inertia, or undue activity, on the part of its food, it will naturally summon its reserves of energy to overcome the frustration and to gratify its instincts. Thus we may get something a little more than self-assertiveness upon the object of its hunger desire. Its attack upon that object may necessarily acquire an *aggressive* quality.

Aggression, however highly stimulated, may not always prove to be adequate to overcoming environmental frustration, and in order to survive the animal must learn to be able to do something better than this. If, in spite of summoning up its reserves of energy and all its aggression it still cannot overcome the frustration which would deny it life, it has either to succumb or make some other attempt at over-coming its obstacles in order to survive. Sooner or later this attempt would be in the nature of recognizing that there was something out-side itself, something unco-operative, and of being compelled to turn its attention, within the limits of its capacity, to that frustrating some-thing for the sake of dealing appropriately with it.

We may call this the beginning of 'science', but subjectively, in so far as it implies the development of a faculty in the mind for recogniz-ing the existence of a reality outside itself, this may be regarded as the early, perhaps the first stage of the development of an ego (reality principle, or reason). I think it has been assumed by most psychologists that the recognition of *anything* outside oneself implies the existence of an ego.

Gratification, whether achieved by the aid of objects or otherwise, is accepted by the baby and possibly by all primitive creatures as an unneeded confirmation of its conviction of its own omnipotence. The psychoanalytical theory is that the baby has a tendency to regard all gratifying objects as part of itself, and only the frustrating or grati-fication-withholding objects, even if they are actually internal, as something that is 'not-me'. Thus I think that I have some grounds for suggesting that it may only be environmental frustrations which cause a living organism to take cognisance of a 'not-me', that is to say, of a reality, and thus begin the development of an ego or reality principle.

The ego is born of frustration in an atmosphere of consequent anxiety, and it develops gradually as the perception of frustrating environment increases, both quantitatively and in regard to its degree of acuity of conscious awareness. The latter, like the emotion of anxiety, is also subject to infinite degrees of intensity.

As psychotherapists and psychiatrists we know that the intolerable discomfort of anxiety (originally frustrated gratification) if not rapidly relieved can lead and does lead to cumulative psychoneurotic, functional and organic disturbances and illnesses, a movement on the way to death. Similarly anxiety and the other discomforts inherent in the inevitable frustrations to gratification and to the life process, may lead the sufferer gratefully to embrace illusions, phantasies, aberrations of behaviour and belief which afford him, or which he hopes will afford him, some respite, however illusionary, however much he may be distorting reality in order to cling to this relatively consoling and reassuring world of delusion. *To my mind a great deal has been built up in this direction, a great deal, indeed almost the whole of our culture and civilization, including not only our habits but our very beliefs and our cast of mind in general.*

With a higher degree of development, the organism has apparently learnt to forego immediate relief of tension, to endure a temporary discomfort in order to achieve a better, more satisfying and more enduring relief as a reward. In short, it may be no more than a matter of having become longer-sighted. It is only since yesterday that the species *homo* has become sufficiently long-sighted to sow his grain seed rather than eating immediately what he had in hand.

The most basic concept of mind on an instinct level, before it develops to a structural level, when it may be regarded as consisting (theoretically) of all id (or instinct reservoir), before the emergence of ego and superego, is the psychoanalytical concept of conflict between two primal instincts, the life-instinct and the death-instinct. For instance the life instinct lies behind the force called the libido, sometimes defined as 'the energy of the sexual instinct' which is characteristic of all the appetites, desires, lusts and pleasures of the living process. It passes through many vicissitudes and reveals itself in almost all bodily and physical functions in the activities associated with life and with everything that is pleasurable and gratifying.

The death instinct, on the other hand, besides being responsible eventually for the movement towards the inanimate source from which life came, is said to supply the energy for all non-libidinal processes, such as the repetitive compulsion, destructive and sometimes aggressive impulses. Conflict appears to be inseparable from mental processes, as its very life and the simplest form of conflict (but a form with which the psychotherapist is primarily concerned) is said to be that between the life instinct and the death instinct. Indeed, Melanie Klein and many of the child analysts go so far as to say that the psychotherapeutically most important effect of anxiety is primarily due to a fear the organism or its ego has of its own death instinct. Evidently the fear is that this internal and unconscious death instinct will get the better of its life instinct with which the ego has identified itself.

These may be regarded as theories of the structure of a deep level of the mind. However, there are perhaps simpler instances of the antithesis between various clinical manifestations of the libidinal (or life) instincts on the one hand and the death instinct on the other, such, for instance, as the conflict between love and hate. It may be even more readily acceptable that manifestations emanating from these instincts can even combine instead of conflict, and that such a combination is commonly seen in the form of what is called sadism, that is to say, pleasure or gratification achieved by the exercise of destructive or aggressive power. Nevertheless, the theory of this early level of mental development would be that these antithetical instincts are not always necessarily either in conflict or in combination, for the instinct reservoir of the mind (called the id) is in itself so *unorganized* that opposites can exist side by side in it as dissociated systems.

Still on this primitive or unorganized level of mental development, we may entertain the concept of the processes of *introjection* and *projection* as early mental mechanisms, very often as defensive mechanisms operating already at this stage of development. They are said to correspond to the physiological processes of the ingestion of food and expulsion of residue and waste products. It would seem that the primitive mind tends as it were to incorporate good or gratifying food equivalents from its environment, and feels as though they were part of itself. At the same time it expels or 'projects' ungratifying food equivalents, such as pain, from out of itself and regards them as belonging to an inimical or hostile world around. In other words the primitive mind is not competent to distinguish between its own organic body and its environment.

This psychoanalytical theory of introjection and projection as early mental processes is very well established. Therefore it may not be out of place here to suggest that it is the source of animistic and animatistic beliefs, such as are so conspicuous in primitive man, the peopling of the world around him chiefly with devils, projected bad objects, in the endeavour to bring into a good relationship with himself, at least to partly introject, good concepts such as omnipotence.

To clarify the general principles of mental functioning, both in health and in illness, it became necessary for those studying and investigating the mind to postulate the development of different functional levels in the mental apparatus. In short, to conceive of the mind as having developed what might be called '*structure*', the different functional levels having as it were specialized in different functions, like parts of any multicellular animal have specialized in their various functions. Nevertheless, the division between these different structural levels is not always (though it is sometimes) very clear-cut, and it should be remembered that they have all developed from the original unorganized base (called the id), the seat of the most primitive form of instinct and reflex operation before anything which we would call mind evolved.

To summarize the most important current theory of the structure of the mind: starting with the concept of the energy, libidinal and destructive (life instinct and death instinct) of the primitive instinct reservoir of the mind (id), we can divide this structure theoretically into a three-fold system, consisting of the *id,* or reservoir of the instincts, relatively unorganized and capable of containing opposite and potentially conflicting elements, a *superego* system borrowing its energy from the first and chiefly concerned (like the parents in infancy) in the regulation and control of the instincts, and an *ego* system, or reality principle, directed towards manipulating the environment and controlling the relationship of instinct to it. Control is achieved by the *behaviour of energy* between the various systems.

It should here be said that though the idea of conflict between instincts may still be accepted, the basic nature of conflict is generally regarded as being between the various systems of the mind, principally as a reaction of the ego, often combined with the superego, against the primitive instinctual impulses of the id. It is the various *opposing energies* within a conflict which commonly express themselves in the form of *symptoms* and *symptomatic behaviour.*

The earliest aspects of ego development and their continuation for perhaps some years is, in relation not to the world of reality as such, but essentially in relation to the parents or parent figures. Therefore it would seem that the developing infant re-lives a succession of inherited tendencies, in perhaps chronological order. These are both of a physical and of a nervous, emotional and mental nature. The whole of one's phylogenetic history of course is not repeated *in utero.* The more recently acquired portions of it develop after birth, and even some of them a considerable time after birth, for example the loss of the so-called milk teeth and the growing of the second or permanent teeth, and still later the development of the gonads at puberty, and so on.

It is easy to see these things at a physical level. They are all part of growth, the process of growing in the image of the stock from which one sprung in accordance with Mendelian laws. What is not so easy to see is that psychological constellation of reactive patterns, conflicts and complexes, unconscious and invisible, similarly develop chronologically in accordance with one's racial or phylogenetic history, come to bud, flower, shed their petals and turn to seed or leave some other residue just as they did in the past history of the race. The point about these complexes, albeit unconscious, is that they have their influence in an unseen way upon the cast of the mind, its way of thinking and its way of behaving and even upon the perverted way in which it sees, or thinks it sees reality, and upon the whole of the construction of society, custom and civilization.

Amongst these phylogenetically entrenched complexes, the one which is perhaps the most difficult to understand, and at the same time the most far-reaching and all-pervasive in its effects, even to the extent of being responsible for some of our most important cultural institutionalizations, is the complex which Freud discovered and named as the Oedipus Complex. It is not difficult for the analyst, or even perhaps for the anthropologist, to discover innumerable signs of the effect of this complex on beliefs, religions and behaviour, for instance the practically world-wide rite of initiation, including usually circumcision ceremonies, are an off-shoot of nothing more or less than this complex, and probably the prohibitions of non-consanguineous marital relationships, such as many of those even in the modern prayer book, owe their origin to primitive incest taboos having so much of the emotional force of this complex behind them, that they in many cases extended to the entire tribe.

Whatever exists in the mind of man, structurally or not structurally, id, superego or ego, emotionally-charged complex or reaction patterns, all obtain their dynamic energy from the same source, and at one stage of mental development that source had been loosely constructed into what might be called a bundle of instincts, or the instinct reservoir, to which the term id is applied. In other words, the energy, both of the superego and of the ego, emanates from the id, for they are nothing more or less than developmental modifications in the form of the id, upon which, as it were, they grew. Complexes such as the Oedipus complex can be regarded as a constellation which derives elements from more than one structural level, such as id, superego and ego in conflict with each other, or two of them in conflict with the other, a conflict holding in itself a considerable amount of dynamic emotional energy, and then undergoing total repression from consciousness.

Although they are repressed and unconscious, such complexes, being highly charged emotionally, 'leak' as it were into the other departments of the mind, and have considerable effect upon their functioning, upon their relationship to one another and upon their relationship to reality. In a sense, these unconscious emotionally charged complexes can be said to have some mitigating effect upon the relationship of the ego to reality, leading to unjustifiable beliefs as well as to otherwise incomprehensible behaviour. They are something like what I choose to call emotional reactive patterns which we have accumulated in our forgotten infancy and which unbeknown to us influence our psychological reactions and attitudes, and even the environment which we construct for ourselves throughout our lives.

However, it is not enough to consider primitive levels of mental operation without taking into account the nature of the *ego-organization* controlling them and its degree of reality-sense development. In other words, analytical theory has now become much more a theory of the psyche as a whole, or, as it has been called, the 'total personality'.

The foregoing is a very brief summarization of the psycho-analytical concepts; and it may be said that practically all analytical work can be subsumed under one or other of these concepts. The above conception of the mind, derived essentially from clinical studies, inevitably leads to a new insight into not only the symptomatic behaviour of people, but also into the 'symptoms' of society as a whole. As the mind of the baby and of primitive people projects its hunger or pain and so forms the concept of a bad, or persecuting, environment, so one can see the tendency to similar mechanisms even in the most cultured person and in social institutions and practices. One sees also that much of the phenomenal world of man, observed phenomena and those which fill the history books, appear to have no explanation, so long as the unconscious phantasies and the early stages of mental development from which they spring are left out of account. The same applies to present-day activities and beliefs.

Thus we are forced to come back from abstract psychology to an examination of behaviour, including social behaviour, in the light of the new insight which we have gained. Only then may we see that the energy surrounding intra-psychic conflicts, such as the Oedipus complex, is so strong that it has forced us to institutionalize it in human society in customs, laws and beliefs. The institution of matrimony, with its rituals and taboos, is essentially designed to deal with unconscious Oedipus guilt.

The mind of man, operating as does the infant's mind when tension is too great to be contained, relieves itself by some expression such as the formation of symptoms; in the same way the tension of society as a whole is relieved or expressed in the construction of its social habits and institutions. As the individual constructs symptoms, so society constructs customs, institutions and beliefs.

It is clear that at the stage of evolution represented by animatistic and animistic beliefs, man was representing the external world, even that of inanimate objects, in accordance with his internal tensions and conflicts, very much in the same way as infants and dogs can be seen to be doing today. A psychoanalyst (Brierley) has written: 'The more irrational aspects of human life and behaviour, e.g. the sphere of beliefs and values, not to mention politics, are largely dominated by animistic thinking, and rational thinking is far more influenced by it than is generally recognized.'[45]

The interesting thing about this study as a whole, is that we may find that all the customs, rituals, institutions, behaviours and beliefs of humanity throughout the ages can be shown in the light of psychological insight without exception to be symptomatic manifestations of latent and unconscious complexes, designed to relieve their emotional pressure and to assuage the discomforts of anxiety and guilt feelings, and in many cases to help us to regain the feeling of security, of which the necessary condition was and is the belief or illusion that the omnipotent world around, originally in the shape of mother and father, loves us, and will always do so.

CHAPTER XXIV

TREATMENT, PROGNOSIS, UNTRUTH AND TRUTH, AND THE FEELING-TONE OF LIFE

Having said so much about the symptomatology of madkind, what I have to say about 'treatment' may seem to the reader extraordinarily meagre or limited. It may seem that I have little desire to 'cure' this universal psychosis, or shall we say, to try to rob madkind of his enormous construction of symptomatic relief. My clinical experience may teach me to say: 'Let him go on repeating his infantile reactive patterns. Why ever not? That is the only way he feels tolerably well, or indeed that he feels he is living. Take even a modicum of these away from him, and he begins to feel less well. Take more away and he feels ill. Why should one want to make the 'patient' feel ill for the sake of an alleged increase of sanity? Even if it were possible to do so.'

Well, in treating individual patients we find that they will only surrender little bits of their insanity and reactive patterns in, as it were, very small doses, and only in so far as there is something equally gratifying to offer them.

It should here be noted that although our unconscious phantasy life is certainly a repetitive pattern, a repetitive pattern is *not necessarily a happy pattern*. Perhaps it is this factor more than any other which makes the patient endure the analytical process, however gentle, and perhaps it is this factor which induces people in general to try to 'improve their minds', or to read such literature as this. Another point is that there appears to be something about the ego that makes us seem to want to act out our unconscious phantasies in reality. Here we may encounter great difficulties, so great in fact we mostly invent a 'reality' that will conform better to such acting out, hence my examination of religious beliefs. But this distortion of reality is certainly not limited to religious beliefs.

I hope that enough has been said about social life and other aspects of our 'reality' behaviour to show that it is something in the nature of the emotional unrealities of the infancy of man which is still the main driving force in all our behaviour and beliefs. Now, as then, the world (i.e. man) is largely driven by primitive phantasies and their attendant anxieties, rather than by any reality appreciation. Now, as then, the world is ruled by superstition, our belief in magic. For instance, in our relationship to one another, such as in our obedience to another, we function only in accordance with the '*mana*' which we attribute to the other person, such as to our leaders. Admittedly this is largely borrowed from similar *mana*-based superstitions of our infancy, in relation to the adults around us. Whenever we find ourselves in an environment resembling our early environment, we tend to regress to the period of that environment. For instance, if you are with an older, wiser, bigger and stronger man, you tend, however unconsciously, to identify him with father, and the emotional patterns formed in childhood in relationship to father are restimulated. You may, consciously or unconsciously, feel like a little boy again before his father. If you were in the habit of being afraid of him, you are again afraid, and so on. If you were afraid of siblings, for instance in school, you will feel fear when you get up to make a speech in front of a gathering of your colleagues. And probably you will not choose Parliament as a career, nor one of the fighting services. Perhaps this is also an instance of repetitive patterns not necessarily being happy patterns, but in any case, happy or unhappy, it tends to be compulsive. We are driven by the forces within us, including the reactive patterns acquired early in life.

Similarly, people in general and society at large are driven by reactive patterns, the early equivalents of which may be seen in the behaviour and beliefs of primitive societies, which we may regard as the infancy of our present-day social order and civilization. Unconscious belief in *mana* still prevails.

Those who feel that my assault upon normal civilized life, its customs and institutions, is sufficiently serious to merit consideration, may nevertheless deprecate the destructive service I have attempted, unless I can say that my object was not essentially destructive. I may well be challenged in terms such as these: 'We have read your book and listened to your criticisms (perhaps even admitted that there was something in what you had to say). We have done this in the hope or assumption that you were merely preparing the ground for extensive new building operations. We now have a right to insist that you will reveal your secret, or at least show us the foundations of the Utopia which you have implicitly promised to build.'

I daresay I should put forward a detailed schedule of enlightened beliefs and behaviour, designed to avoid all the pitfalls, including war, which result from our psychosis and its displacements. Reformers, politicians, statesmen, philosophers and even some psychologist-reformers are never tired of putting forward such improved, if not Utopian, plans.

Such an attempt on my part would have the advantage of assuaging the anxiety of my readers, and bringing them the satisfaction of a blue-print for sanity. Some degree of at least temporary complacency would be achieved. I suppose the benefit would in part be due to the fact that I was doling out the expected medicine. For instance, if in reply to the hypothetical question above enunciated . . . 'we have a right to expect that you will reveal your secret, or at least show us the foundations of the Utopia which you have implicitly promised to build', I asked the questioner 'what are the general principles upon which *you* would expect this mental or material millennium to be built?', the obvious reply which I would expect is that we should take further and more stringent steps to control the bursting forth of our mad impulses. The function of the ego should be reinforced. Reason should be enthroned as dictator . . . and so on.

Curiously enough, every neurotic patient whose symptoms and illness are directly attributable to a failure of his ego or repressing forces to deal adequately with id impulses, decides upon an exactly identical process for the purpose of regaining health. I said 'decides upon', but this is not quite correct. It is more true to say that this 'decision' existed from the outset, perhaps from the age of a few months. It is axiomatic. He has endeavoured *throughout his life* to 'cure' his illness by tightening up the dictatorship of his ego. He has come for treatment *because this process has failed*. He naively *expects* that 'treatment' will consist in the strong personality of the doctor in the role of mentor, dictator or magistrate, reinforcing the dictatorship of his ego. Patients have said: 'I have come to you with every confidence that you will help me to *control* myself', and so the reader naively proposes the same process.

It would seem that we, having repressed all knowledge of our unconscious, are so limited to conscious operations, that it is largely to ego operation, that we are incapable of thinking of any other process, and yet this is the process which is responsible for neurotic disease, and again by superego dictatorship, the madness of all the world. In other words, in our insistence upon being 'sane', i.e. ego dominated (really superego dominated), and for this purpose having repressed our instinct heritage, we have left our psyche no other course but to relieve its tensions through symptomatic behaviour and beliefs. Our idea of cure is to reinforce this process. In so far as we could let our tensions out more freely by less unnecessary control, by more *harmless* madness, we would be more comfortable and less *seriously* mad, because our ego would be more free to deal with reality instead of using up its energy reinforcing our superego, to hold back the infantile bogies of which we are still so needlessly terrified. Perhaps this is the foundation of my constructive endeavour.

However, it should be mentioned that not only harmless id urges, or id urges in so far as they can find a harmless form of expression, but also superego demands must be catered for by the ego, if we are going to have peace of mind. It would seem that we must *humour* the madman, that is our primitive self, so long as we can do so harmlessly. If this humouring of the id and superego demands does not take place, the inhibited forces modify the ego and lead to character changes. It is those character changes which are the individual basis of our psychosis, individual and social.

Naturally non-analysts have to go on trying what psychotherapy has long since largely (but perhaps not entirely) abandoned, namely attempts to modify people's conduct and thoughts by influencing them on a purely ego level. It may be that the modicum of success, however small, achieved by these methods, is due to an unwitting and discredited subconscious influence, as I have endeavoured to point out in *The First Interview*. . . . It is inevitable that this should be so, though the method used can range from purely symptomatic behaviour to every degree of misguided ego endeavour. I alleged a little earlier that it was these very attempts at undue ego control, 'sanity' or idealism, which commonly drove the patient into the very disease (neurotic or psychotic), which he wanted cured by a reinforcement of these methods. Perhaps the most symptomatic of these 'therapeutic' endeavours are those where an attempt is made to reinforce some ideal idol or something which appears to be the antithesis of the thing we want to control or get rid of.

Thousands of instances of this form of symptomatic behaviour and belief could be enumerated, from such obvious ones as mob-rule, lynching the malefactor, or murdering the murderer, to less crude and obvious instances, such as those of the adolescent rushing to conversion to reinforce the struggle against masturbation, and indeed the general principle of embracing religious and moral ideals to reinforce the struggle against sin and evil. They do not succeed. They are the expression of one side of a conflict, the superego side, it having expressed itself (cf. confession) leaving the other side perhaps more free to express *itself*.

That is perhaps one reason for Flugel saying: 'Christianity (like the other great religions) has been in most respects a failure.' It has sometimes been said that if the compulsive pervert could be converted, this would be the most reliable cure for his perversion . . . and this in the face of the fact that perversions are at least as common amongst the clergy themselves (who presumably have been converted), as in any other walk of life. It may not be too much to say that it is notorious that high moral principles on the one hand, however genuine, are only one end of the see-saw, on the other end of which sits the Devil himself! For instance, it is well known that the famous French moral reformer, Jean-Jacques Rousseau, at the time when he was reforming the morals of the entire French nation, and most eloquently persuading mothers to nurse their own babies, was at the same time writing to a foundling hospital about his own illegitimate children.

This emphasises that ego attempts at 'therapy' may be regarded, like all other human behaviour and beliefs, as the mere symptomatic expression of unconscious conflicts. This is what the unanalyzed reader is asking me to tabulate for his guidance under the heading of treatment, the only concept of treatment which he can form, albeit the treatment which was and is responsible for human neurosis and psychosis.

If you tell your dream to a non-analyst without insight, he will naturally 'deal' only with the manifest content (the form), and so of course nobody will understand anything, and you will get nowhere. As we know, the *meaning* of the dream lies in its latent content, not in the form it assumes, and it is only by knowing the latent content that you can begin to understand it. The same applies to all symptoms, and to all our expressions.

Now there are, or have been, psychologist-reformers who may be regarded as having attempted a combination of the ordinary 'practical' methods of changing our insanity (e.g. war) into sanity, together with a utilization of their knowledge of the unconscious determinants of the symptom we were trying to cure. Dr J. C. Flugel has attempted to do this in his book *Man, Morals and Society,* particularly in its concluding chapters. For instance he says on page 316 that the source of our loyalty to the State is that it is a father-mother symbol, and that the State being a father-mother symbol for our guidance, directs or commands, the provision of our needs, our security and protection (!) a step towards therapy (presumably in connection with war) could be achieved if we would transfer this need of ours *in toto* to some such body as the United Nations. I could not agree more.

Of course similar schedules, based upon unconscious determinants could be drawn up for the improvement or greater sanity of our behaviour and beliefs, in every field of human life and thought, and lead to considerable improvement in our individual and group welfare. As I have said, this method has the advantage of taking into consideration, or not entirely neglecting, the repressed emotional determinants. Indeed, many volumes of social, political and international reform could be compiled along these lines, and in a practical sense would be an advance upon the more familiar and more superficial endeavours. But my own feeling is that although they may affect the advantages of a more orderly ward in the asylum, they do not really get to the roots of the disease. It seems to me that they are more like telling the psychotic to displace his affection a step further, for instance telling a Fascist of the 1930's to transfer his allegiance from Mussolini to Hitler, and become a good Nazi, or like persuading the heathen to be converted to Christianity.

It would indeed be presumptuous to pretend that any of us can effect anything approaching a 'cure', but perhaps it would not be out of place, if only to correct misconception and attempts at malpractice, to outline something of the therapeutic process attempted in the case of the individual who is mentally ill or troubled. In the case of psychosis, with which term I have stigmatized the universal disease, we consider the patient to have made an important step towards amelioration in so far as he obtains some *insight* into his delusional system, and into himself and his illness. Perhaps my attempt in this entire work is to endeavour to promote a little insight.

I may say, however, that the method adopted, the technique used is not the most up-to-date one when analyzing the individual sufferer, or deluded person. Nevertheless, it may be some slight advance upon the methods commonly adopted in the history of man. I would say that these methods, emotionally determined as they are, and commonly expressed in the form of acting out these emotions, could be compared with the old *abreaction* therapy in which the patient is encouraged to 'blow-off' his feelings (usually related to a traumatic experience) without acquiring insight or other psychological re-adjustment. The trouble about this is that he needs to repeat the emotional cataclysm periodically again and again, and does not necessarily become any saner. We might roast people alive for generations, and have a succession of wars, resulting simply in a number of periods of exhaustion until we accumulated enough emotional and dynamic energy to repeat the holocaust. No doubt by this 'abreactive method' a temporary modicum of relief is achieved, but not necessarily any insight or amelioration of our insanity.

The next advance in analytical therapy may be called the interpretative method. Here the process was to interpret the patient's manifestations, symptomatic and associative, so as to bring the unconscious phantasies from which they emanate into consciousness. It has been belittled as the equivalent to 'Taking rabbits out of a hat', but this metaphor does it less than justice. Indeed, it is still used, but with rather a different strategical purpose than originally. It is now used as an aid to the main therapeutic technique which is that of exposing, analyzing and overcoming the *resistances* in the patient's mind. These are constructions of his superego and ego and indoctrinations from the outside world, which together form the repressive forces acting as a barrier to his insight into his own unconscious. A metaphor occurs to me: if the patient is symbolized by a castle with defensive walls, drawbridge and moat, the interpretative method would be like extracting pieces of the contents of the castle, for instance by a helicopter to show what was there, whereas the dissolving of resistances would be like removing the moat and the walls.

We can well imagine that the mind automatically exercises its best endeavours to maintain its defences (or resistances) intact, despite the fact that it may be rather uncomfortable inside. However, it is the physician's business to induce a willingness on the part of the patient to relax these defences. He will probably only do so in so far as he is emboldened by a positive transference towards the analyst, that is to say, when he feels trust or even love and therefore no need to be on guard. This situation will only be adequately achieved after he has overcome the reluctance to expressing his 'bad' nature, his hate, and got over the fear of being hated in return.

These two elements in his relationship to the analyst, love and hate, are another example of the compulsion to repeat our early reactive patterns, though they are nothing more or less than the reactive patterns he felt towards his parents in infancy and childhood. Analysis shows that every person's relationship to his parents or parent images was ambivalent, that is to say a combination of love and hate. The hate is repressed and until it is brought to the surface and thrashed out in analysis, defences against surrender of the mind will remain. We cannot surrender to a 'bad' object, or any object which we think may have badness in it, bad here meaning inimical to us, and liable to cause us damage. The ideal result of analytical therapy is that the patient should discover that his hate is unfounded and unnecessary.

It is evident from a study of our social order that society at large has certainly not discovered anything of this sort. We are still in our international relationships acting out the most dangerous ambivalence, like patients in the throes of the most difficult and dangerous stage of an analytical transference. While the nations meet to talk peace, bombers fly in circles round their airfields, each carrying an atom or hydrogen bomb, so that if the enemy, protesting love or good fellowship or agreement, should decide to atom-bomb every airfield simultaneously, there would still be enough bombers in the air to return the compliment immediately. Is this a universal psychosis, or a reality adaptation? Or is it a reality adaptation to a state of affairs brought about by a universal psychosis, and where lies the treatment and the cure?

It is hardly necessary that I should emphasize to what a pass the projection and dramatization of our intrapsychic conflict has brought us. In the meantime the world of man, dramatizing its anxiety-aggression, remains largely impoverished with regard to the vast amenities of life which would otherwise be available for it to enjoy.

If there is any practical treatment for this state of affairs, it must be directed to the period when the mind is psychologically malleable, that is to say, treatment must begin in babyhood and infancy, and be continued throughout childhood. This does not mean that I am an advocate of infant or child psychoanalysis, but rather enough

analysis of those who have to do with babies, infants and children for
them not to contaminate the growing mind with their own disease.
This is precisely what is taking place at the present time, though
there is some improvement from the few generations ago when
children were regarded as the least amongst us, and even sold as
slaves. We should not be too pleased with our recent improvements
in regard to the treatment of children, when we still seem to think our
most important function regarding them is to indoctrinate them
with as much as possible of our most obvious psychoses.

As Flugel says: 'Religion . . . can exercise a severe crippling and
inhibiting effect upon the human mind, by fostering irrational
anxiety and guilt, and by hampering the free play of the intellect.'[24]

The insanity of war and death or destruction and annihilation sink
into insignificance. The child has enough insanity of its own without
being indoctrinated by ours. Perhaps it should be allowed to enjoy
its own insanity, its own phantasies, and if we presume to interfere at
all, surely such interference should be in the interests of love and the
building up of a reality (not a psychotic) ego.

Even so, it might be many generations before 'treatment' reached
a stage when life was relatively sane and secure.

To proceed to the prognosis: I do not think we need be unduly
pessimistic, because there is an impression that in spite of everything
some developmental progress, though only a little, can be seen to have
already taken place in this direction.

There are many forces in the nature of things and of the universe,
tangible and intangible, which must influence the future of man,
irrespective of man's own agency and the state of his mind, forces
that are beyond his control. After all, it was such forces that brought
us into existence, and caused us to evolve to our present stage of
development, and not only us, but a 'series' of biological species, some
of which, such as the giant reptiles, it subsequently caused to dissolve.
There seems to be little doubt that if we are destined as individuals to
disintegrate as we are, there is no logical assurance that we should
survive everlastingly as a species. We have struggled very hard to do
so, and so far have succeeded, or perhaps more than succeeded in that
we have populated, or over-populated, practically the whole surface
of the world, to the disadvantage of our competitors.

Now there is an important element in the prognosis of human life
which is commonly overlooked by all and sundry, in spite of the fact
that many scientists and philosophers are never tired of pointing it
out and regarding it as the matter of primary importance. I am
referring to the problem of over-population. Many scientists have
shown us that populations tend to increase up to the limit of their
food supply. The problem concerning the nations of the world at

large is that they tend to increase beyond this supply, therefore they are commonly faced with starvation, famine, or infiltration or conquest by neighbouring countries. It is said, I do not know how truly, that the British handed India back because it found itself unable to cope with an annual increase in population of five million people. The consequent famines and riots would have been too much.

On the other hand, if the food supply is increased to avoid famine, the matter is not solved, for the population and the problems connected with its growth soon catch up, and are redoubled. Attempts at birth control, though effective at the highest cultural and intellectual levels, are usually of little or no value amongst primitive peoples, who would thereby tend to overcrowd the world, reducing the others to non-existence, infiltrating or overwhelming them.

However, this prognostic problem, though placed first by many scientists, is at least one which is potentially under some degree of human determination or control. Therefore perhaps I should have placed first the factor in the prognosis of man's survival which is entirely independent of anything he can do or is likely to be able to do about it. I am referring to what might be called the 'cosmological' prognosis. We know that the heavenly bodies, not only planets but even suns with their entire planetary system, are not static or permanent structures, nor necessarily does such a quality apply to entire galaxies. Therefore physicists and astronomers would have no doubt that the existence of man on this planet (or perhaps anywhere else), and indeed of any and every form of life, can at the best be merely a temporary cosmological and biological phenomenon. Of course in all probability we can do no more about this than we could about the origin and development of our lives, therefore perhaps we have little difficulty in ignoring the matter and putting it out of our minds.

In spheres other than the cosmological, man has a varying degree of potential control over the exterminating forces of nature. As we have seen, he has learnt to grow so much food that he has multiplied to a degree that itself causes a menace. At the same time he wages a constant war against biological invasion, viruses, bacteria, etc., and appears so far to have proved master of the situation. It may be that there is no guarantee that he will forever continue to be master. The plague of London made the local people at least think differently at one time, and what would happen in the event of bacteriological warfare?

There is little doubt that the progress in nuclear weapons must make war, at least on a large scale, less easily available (more ego-inhibited) as a means of or the expression of our intrapsychic aggression and anxiety-ridden conflicts. Long since have gone the days when the 'Western Mountaineer' could rush 'with bare bosom on the spear' (Marmion). But it is noteworthy that although war for many generations has provided little prospect of such emotional exhilaration, and infinitely greater prospect of sweat, blood and death, it has not on this account disappeared. At the present time the knowledge of inevitable annihilation of all parties to the conflict, aggressor and aggressed alike, has caused a change of symptomatology to the extent of confining conflicts to the old weapons, or at least to the non-nuclear ones. At the same time, the belligerents and the neutral onlookers alike know full well that this decisive means of extermination is being held back, perhaps impatiently.

Is it worthwhile, or will it prove worthwhile to approach so near to the brink of irrevocable and irreversible disaster?

The lesson of history, which is perhaps all we have to go upon, may not be conclusive, but it is unfortunately very suggestive. Periodically people have sent others rushing into war, and even rushed in themselves, in spite of gun powder, cannon, the blasting of ships, machine guns, barbed wire, and high explosives. Even certain death appears to be no reliable deterrent. It almost seems that, swept along in the emotional vortex, people do not know or cannot believe in death—at least for themselves. The current deterrent for a global war is alleged to be 'the knowledge of inevitable annihilation', and we may ask the question, will everybody *know* this? Knowledge is of many levels, some who 'know' it may succeed in not knowing it . . . for long enough never to find out. Will the nuclear bomb be the means whereby our alleged death instinct will prove itself larger than our life instinct, and solve our conflicts for ever?

Freud has said: 'The less a man knows of the past and the present the more unreliable must his judgment of the future prove.'[28] And I think we have at least a hint from the recent past and perhaps the present to suggest to us that the tendency has been for man, in recent times at least, to emerge into a greater reality sense, or some development of his reality ego. This is shown most clearly in the advancement of science. The pity of it is that he still carries this great load of animistic delusions about with him at the same time. For instance, one feels that so much of our potential emotional energy is in the form of hysteria connecting itself with the Biblical story, this heart-breaking Christ story (that, I am inclined to add, is not so very different from millions like it), that our energy is not only to some extent emotionally depleted by it, but we are intellectually impoverished.

My particular branch of science being psychiatry, I feel it is more in my province to endeavour to point out these brakes upon the progress of our reality sense which is so all-important if we are going either to meet our fate as relatively sane people, or by dint of an unimaginable degree of scientific knowledge and reality-development-ego, again succeed in rising above it. I am convinced that we will not rise above it by taking refuge in phantasy or in any form of unreality or untruth. To my mind this is comparable to schizophrenia, and must render us increasingly helpless in the face of the reality contingencies, with which we should cope in order to be sane and survive.

However dear some of our untruths may be to us, we are surely resistant to the idea that we must always be children or schizophrenics, taking refuge from reality and what ability we have to know it and the truths it can teach us.

But it may be that in my role of a physician, this enthronement of truth and sanity at all costs becomes less single-minded. I see people, individuals, who *feel* different from their more fortunate brethren. I see almost every shade of *feeling-tone* from one person to another. This is difficult for even the doctor and psychiatrist to understand or appreciate, and therefore I expect the majority of people give it no consideration whatsoever. They make such remarks as: 'Buck up, keep your chin up', and all that utter nonsense. They might as well try that technique on a corpse. I see people with internal feelings of such a kind that life to them is a protracted agony, and their only incentive in continuing to live is to seek and find at least temporary alleviation. One cannot care about sanity or anything else unless one's feeling-tone in life is a healthy one, in line with the pleasure principle.

In the light of the study of a large variety of unfortunate sufferers, one's attention is drawn to the fact that the so-called fortunate majority may not be altogether so fortunate as they suppose. Observation shows that they are forever *wanting* things on both a physical and mental plane. On a physical plane the air must be right, the temperature must be right, the humidity must be right, their clothes must fit, they must have their tea, they must have their food at frequent intervals, very many of them must have their cocktails or beer. They must have their proper hours of sleep. On a psychological plane they must have their friends, their relatives, their intimate companions, their mate, their group, their party, their royal family, their religion . . . in fact there is no end to what they must have. Maybe they are only in this enviable state of feeling well and having a good or pleasureable feeling-tone in life by virtue of a gratification of all these endless needs, physical and mental. They are fortunate in that their needs can be brought in line with the needs of the majority, and are therefore adequately or appropriately catered for.

There are of course many forms of symptomatic behaviour, including the relatively rare one of crime, and the relatively common one of promiscuity, which are motivated by intolerable internal pressures of one sort or another. Amongst these we should of course include every neurotic and psychotic symptom. In the light of this, one is tempted to say, let the poor patient have his delusions, paranoid or otherwise, or even his drugs, if they make tolerable for him a life which would otherwise be intolerable. If he is very bad, he may be of little or no value in the social machine. And then we can reflect that if the social machine is itself so deluded and paranoid, is it for the sake of a more comfortable or tolerable existence? The phenomenon of war rather cuts across this indulgent reflection, and in so far as the symptoms of every disease, neurosis and psychosis are inter-dependent and perhaps mutually determined, one is again forced back to what would seem to be the obvious deduction that 'in the long run reality thinking constitutes the line of progress'.[24]

In other words, the conclusion is that we must aim at the truth, no matter what sacrifices it costs us. If the sacrifices are too great and in consequence we become ill, to embrace a psychosis would only be to embrace an equally bad if not a worse 'illness', no matter if the whole community shares the delusion. Perhaps the whole community only gives us an illusion of security after all. If the truth costs us too much as regards our happiness, or our feeling of well-being, if our inner feeling-tone breaks down under the strain of sanity, then we are sick people and in the long run it is better to have the sane help, such as it is, that science can provide, than to embrace delusions or systems of delusions which may lead us to external as well as internal distress.

As Flugel says:[24] 'The great weakness of Christianity would seem to be that it had indicated neither a suitable outlet for the energies of aggressive extraverted individuals nor an adequate and positive goal for social and political endeavour.'

In so far as every mythology and religion is based upon emotional needs and unconscious phantasies, without reality observation and rational thought they must be regarded as symptoms of a psychotic nature, and it seems to me that we must be rather hard-pressed if we look for symptoms and psychoses to solve our problems and relieve our troubles. Are such people the great 'healthy' majority, to be judged objectively as in better health than the relatively sane drug addict? Whatever the latter has tormenting him, there is always the possibility of it having some germinal, physical or physiological source, at any rate he is trying physical rather than psychological means for its alleviation.

The conclusion that emerges from these deliberations is the one that is inescapable in the light of all the material contained in this book. It is that like the rest of the universe, we are mechanistically evolved from some attribute contained in the nature of energy, and the molecular forms it assumes. Like the cosmos in general, we have developed in accordance with the basic interactions of energy, atoms, molecules, matter and its interaction with its environment, until such times as protein and protoplasm came into being and evolved by its natural physicochemical reaction upon its environment, to form all that is contained in the biosphere. The process was never static, is not static today, and presumably never will be static.

The evolution of an increasingly large central nervous system with its brain and the development of what we call mind, are all developmental products brought into being by these primary physical and biological forces. I have endeavoured to show that the mind of man is not essentially different from that of any other living creature, earthworm or insect, in so far as its essential function is that of presiding over the physiological health of the organism. Such presiding naturally includes the adjustment of environment to organism and organism to environment, but the essential feature of that adjustment is to keep the organism free from tensions and metabolic changes that will be injurious to it physiologically, and cause its death. Anxiety is evidently an expression of some maladjustment, and in itself if excessive can cause serious repercussions in physiological function.

Therefore it may well be that the mind of the organism should be and is primarily concerned to reduce this injurious tension, perhaps immediately. For this purpose, it is not necessarily at the moment concerned with truth or untruth, but rather with exercising the old familiar patterns which have brought it relief in its past experience. The frightened or anxiety-ridden child does not necessarily examine the question as to whether mother is sufficiently omnipotent to give it the security it needs immediately. It prefers to believe automatically that she is, and is concerned only to rush into her arms.

Mythology and religion are the phantasy-created successors of these much-needed omnipotent persons. At a certain state of our evolution they come into being perhaps because they are needed for the necessary relief of tension, which would otherwise create injurious physico-chemical changes in the organism, with their injurious repercussions.

To paraphrase Freud's remark previously quoted in this chapter, we may say that the more we know of the past, the more reliable must be our judgment of the present. In this connection I would remind the reader that it has recently been discovered in greater detail than before that the molecule of DNA, and the molecule of protein, are the physical basis from which spring all the physical attributes of life and all its functioning, not excepting the behaviour of every organism, unicellular and multicellular, small and large, primitive and 'civilized', and not only behaviour but what probably follows behaviour, namely belief. Thus like every object that exists, we are as it were descended from the molecule and it in turn from local concentrations of cosmic energy, the whole thing being physico-chemically determined, no less than the behaviour of amino-acids and their action upon one another. However elaborate, it is all a physico-chemical compulsion, like the compulsion of any other chemical and physical reaction (such as oxygen combining with hydrogen, fire, and the explosion of gunpowder).

Why I am stressing this platitude is because I am convinced that this compulsion prevails throughout nature, *not excluding psychological processes such as the behaviour and beliefs of man, and the construction of social institutions, civilization and war.* In this light we may see the mind as a physiological organ concerned primarily with what might be called some degree of homeostasis necessary for healthy functioning and survival.

Perhaps it has only very recently developed an additional faculty (no less compulsive), one which we may call reason, and may hope will be capable of some degree of 'objective' evaluation of our environment and ourselves.

Thus, having tried to produce a survey of this psychosis of mankind, including its case-history with family history and symptomatology, I have found myself discussing its pathology or psychopathology and discussing its prognosis and treatment. In spite of the last named, my presumption will be unrealistic unless I stress in conclusion that treatment begins at the birth of the individual, if not before, and any attempts to alter the reactive patterns once infancy has been passed are progressively less effective. The patterns of anxiety will also have been laid down, and also the reactive pattern of innumerable inadequately effective modes of trying to deal with it. Only super-ficial changes can be made once the earthenware has been hardened in the furnace. In this connection, it should be remembered that the earth began about five thousand million years ago, and that life began on the earth some hundreds of millions of years ago. Throughout all that time, the 'pot', the human body and the human mind, have not only been in the process of being formed, but have also been in the process of being baked in the furnace. Not being able to recreate the universe, either by a reality or on a mythological plane, the most we can do is to learn to deal appropriately with our relatively unformed individuals—babies and infants. But even in this task we are ham-pered to a much greater extent than we can realize by our own unrealistic psyche with its inherent psychotic id and possibly still worse, psychotic superego. Our ego, or reality principle, is struggling painfully to emerge from this cosmic chaos. We do not realize what a small and relatively insignificant structure it is, but in it, to my mind, lies our only hope.

BIBLIOGRAPHY

1. *General Anthropology*, Edited by FRANZ BOAS; Heath & Co., New York and London, 1938.
2. *Superstition and Society*, MONEY-KYRLE; Hogarth Press, London, 1939.
3. *The Golden Bough*, SIR JAMES FRAZER; Macmillan & Co., London, 1949.
4. *Mitsinari*, ANDRÉ DUPEYRAT; Staples Press, London, 1954.
5. *The Dark Child*, CAMERA LAYE; Collins, London, 1955.
6. *Totem and Taboo*, SIGMUND FREUD; Moffat, Yard & Co., New York, 1918.
7. *Folklore in the Old Testament*, SIR JAMES FRAZER.
8. *Mythology*, BULFINCH; The Bodley Head.
9. *Seven Years in Tibet*, HEINRICH HARRAR; Hart Davies, London, 1953.
10. *Psychology and Religion*, DAVID FORSYTH; Watts & Co., London, 1935.
11. *Encyclopaedia of Religion and Ethics*, Edited by J. HASTINGS and others.
12. *The History of the Inquisition of Spain*, D. JUAN ANTONIO LLORENTE; Geo. B. Whittaker, London, 1827.
13. *Are We Civilised?* ROBERT LOWIE; George Routledge & Sons Ltd., London, 1929.
14. *Developments in Psycho-Analysis*, MELANIE KLIEN, PAULA HEIMANN, SUSAN ISAACS, JOAN RIVIERE; The Hogarth Press, London, 1952.
15. *The Psychoanalytic Theory of Neurosis*, OTTO FENICHEL; Kegan Paul, Trench, Trubner & Co. Ltd., London, 1946.
16. *The Ego and the Id*, SIGMUND FREUD; Hogarth Press, London, 1927.
17. *Psychiatric Dictionary*, HINSIE and SHATZKY; Oxford Univ. Press, New York, 1940.
18. *Annual Survey of Psychoanalysis* Vol. II, Edited by JOHN FROSCH; International Universities Press, New York, 1951.
19. *New Directions in Psychoanalysis*, MELANIE KLEIN, PAULA HEIMANN, R. MONEY-KYRLE; Tavistock Publications, London, 1955.
20. *Collected Papers* Vol. IV, SIGMUND FREUD; Hogarth Press, London, 1925.

21. *The Unconscious Motives of War*, ALIX STRACHEY; Allen & Unwin, London, 1957.
22. *Games*, ADRIAN STOKES; International Journal of Psychoanalysis, March-June, 1956.
23. *Men and Their Motives*, J. C. FLUGEL; Kegan Paul, Trench, Trubner & Co. Ltd., London, 1934.
24. *Man, Morals and Society*, J. C. FLUGEL; Duckworth, London, 1945.
25. *Civilisation, War and Death*, SIGMUND FREUD.
26. *War, Sadism and Pacifism*, EDWARD GLOVER; Allen & Unwin, London, 1933.
27. *Yearbook of Psycho-Analysis*, Vol. II; International Universities Press, New York, 1946.
28. *Future of an Illusion*, SIGMUND FREUD; Hogarth Press, London, 1953.
29. *Rationalism in Theory and Practice*, A. ROBERTSON; Watts & Co., London, 1954.
30. *A Note-Book for Christians*, CHARLES GORHAM; Watts & Co., London, 1929.
31. *Comparative Religion*, A. C. BOUQUET; Penguin Books, London, 1956.
32. *The Origins of Love and Hate*, IAN SUTTIE; Kegan Paul, Trench, Trubner & Co. Ltd., London, 1935.
33. *What is Psychoanalysis*, ERNEST JONES; Allen & Unwin Ltd., London, 1949.
34. *Primitive Culture*, SIR EDWARD BURNETT TYLOR. Quoted from 'Animism' Encylo. Brit. 14th Edition.
35. *Sourcebook of Atomic Energy*, SAMUEL GLASSTONE; Macmillan & Co., London, 1952.
36. *The Nature of the Universe*, FRED HOYLE; Blackwell, Oxford, 1950.
37. *Continuous Creation*, SIR HAROLD SPENCER-JONES; Science News No. 32, Penguin Books London, 1954.
38. *The Chemical Basis of Life*, Series of Lectures on the BBC published in 'The Listener', 1957.
39. *Science in Progress*, Edited by GEORGE BAITSELL; Yale University Press, New Haven, U.S.A., 1942.
40. *Science Advances*, HALDANE; Allen & Unwin, London, 1947.
41. *Evolution in Action*, JULIAN HUXLEY; Chatto & Windus, London, 1953.
42. *Comparative Biochemistry*, ERNEST BALDWIN.
43. *How Life Began*, DAVID FORSYTH; Heinemann Ltd., London, 1939.
44. *First Principles*, HERBERT SPENCER; Williams & Norgate, London, 1860.
45. *Trends in Psychoanalysis*, MARJORIE BRIERLEY; Hogarth Press, London, 1951.

INDEX

Abortion, 91
Abreaction Therapy, 260
Acquired Characters, 235, 237–9
Adam, 23, 156–8
Adenosintriphosphoric acid (ATP), 210
Adolescence, 55, 57, 89
  Adolescents, 86
Adonis, 25
Advent, Second, 27
Aetiology, 1, 189, 222, 228
  Aetiological explanation, 15
Africa, 12, 13, 83, 230
Alcoholism, 134
Alexander the Great, 21
Algae, 214, 218, 219, 233
All Souls, 26
Ambisexuality, 114
Ambyna, 11
America, North, 230
Amino acids, 198, 207–9, 211, 215, 216, 267
Ammonia, 208, 209
Amoeba, 222, 223, 233, 245, 246
Amniotic fluid, 231
  Amniotic sac, 231
Amphibians, 221
Anatomists, 225
Andromeda, 199, 201
Anemones, 224
Animatism, 7
Animatistic, 250, 253
Animism, 7, 80, 147, 154
Animistic delusions, 264
Annelids, 226
Anorexia Nervosa, 40
Anthropology, 7, 41
Anthropologists, 75, 189, 202
Anthropomorphic God, 154
Anthropomorphism, 34
Anxiety, 33–7, 42–4, 52, 57, 69, 71, 73, 79, 81, 89, 90, 104–7, 114, 131, 138, 141–8, 151–3, 160, 163, 169, 185, 190–3, 242, 244, 248, 249, 254, 256, 261, 262, 267, 268
Apes, 230, 231
Apollo, 150
Arabs, 21
Aristobulus, 165
Aristotle, 141, 236

Arizona, 200
Armageddon, 178
Arthropods, 221, 225, 226, 228
Ascension, 27
Asia, Western, 21
Astarte, 26
Astronomers, 192, 200
Assumption of the Virgin, 26
Atoms, 196–8, 201, 205, 206, 208, 233
Atom bomb, 119, 261
Attis, 25, 26
Auditory ossicles, 231
Australia, 12, 16
Australian aborigine, 8, 9, 24
Australian tribes, 101
Autocatalysts, 213
Autonomic Nervous System 222, 224–7, 241
Aztecs, 26

Baal, Phoenician, 23
Baby, 72, 74, 77, 80, 81, 102, 112, 119, 120, 152, 164, 178, 231, 248, 253, 262, 268
Baby feeding, 75
Babies, 150
Babyhood, 33, 78, 79, 80, 141, 156, 163, 176, 178, 261
Babylonians, 21
Bacteria, 211, 214, 233
Bacteriological warfare, 263
Baldwin, Ernest, 232
Baptism, 39, 160
Baptists, 160
Bards, 24
Barnes, 131, 158
Bastian's theory, 233
Be'al, 23
Belsen, 19
Beltane, 23
Benedict, 7, 8
Bible, 11, 27, 264
Biochemistry, 211
Biology, 190, 198, 229, 238
Biologists, 217, 235, 237, 238
Biosphere, 198, 234, 235, 237, 246, 267
Birch, return of, 131
Birds, 221
Birth control, 263

Birthrate, 111
Blood sport, 99
Boas, Franz, 20
Bohemia, 125
Boron, 215
Borneo, 9
Bowel function, 178
Brahma, 22, 156
Brierley, M., 253
Bruno Giordana, 29
Buddha, 22
Buddhism, 22
Bulfinch, 22
Bull fighting, 100
Burmese, 24
Burrows, 50

Caesar, 41
Calcium, 215
Calvary, 18
Cancer, 79, 213
Cannibal Ancestors, 229
Cannibals, 25, 29, 41, 138, 164
Cannibalism, 7, 17–19, 24, 29, 35, 40,
    41, 60, 137, 139, 149, 151, 167
Carbohydrates, 206, 208, 213, 215
Carbon, 197, 215
Castrate, 94
Castration, 41, 47, 58, 59, 62, 63, 83, 85,
    86, 88, 93, 94, 115, 117, 121, 125,
    133, 153, 160
Cathedral, St. Paul's, 202
Catholic Church, 30, 171
Catholic Religion, 152, 158
Cell membrane, 216, 217
Celtic nations, 23
Central Celebes, 24
Central Nervous System, 222, 225–7,
    241, 243, 267
Cerebral cortex, 241
Charms, 28
Chemist, 197, 209
Chemistry, 154, 190, 198, 232
Child, 82, 109, 121, 127, 138, 142, 148,
    157, 177, 179, 180
Child birth, 9, 10, 72, 88
Child psychologist, 137
Child labour, 168
Child welfare, 27
Childhood, 48, 79, 137, 141, 183, 256,
    261
Chimpanzees, 230, 232
China, 58
Chlorine, 215
Chlorophyll, 217
Christ, 17, 18, 25, 26, 140, 165, 166
Christian, 15, 25, 28, 30, 31, 149, 157,
    160, 161, 165, 166, 171
Christianity, 15, 18, 21, 25–7, 30, 153,
    165, 166, 258, 259, 266
Christmas, 25, 41

Chromosomes, 212, 214, 216, 217, 235
Church, 27, 29, 30, 151
Church Christian, 25, 26
Church Roman Catholic, 140, 141, 152
Church Bells, 28
Cinemas, 56
Circumcision, 7, 12, 13, 83, 86, 167,
    252
Claustrophobia, 56
Clitoris, 12, 14
Cobalt, 215
Coelenterates, 220, 224, 225
Coeliac plexus, 240
Coitus, 54, 55
Constantine the Great, 27
Copernicus, 29, 142
Copper, 215
Coprophilia, 40
Corals, 224
Cosmic energy, 233, 267
Cosmic rays, 195, 196
Cosmos, 35, 191, 205, 266
Cosmogonies, 20, 21, 23, 24, 156, 157,
    160, 187, 191, 192, 203
Cosmology, 69
Cosmosphere, 246
Crabs, 228
Creation, 156, 157, 158
Cricket, 98
Crime, 50, 130, 135, 136, 185, 265
Criminal, 67, 94, 126, 128, 134, 138,
    159, 163, 166
Crucifixion, 18, 25
Crusades, 162, 168
Cytoplasm, 213, 217

Darwin, C., 30, 236
Darwinian, 231, 235
Darwinism, neo, 237
Death instinct, 249, 250, 251, 264
Death penalty, 69
Deity, 129
Delinquents, 133
Diabetis, 231
Diana, 26
Dietetics, 40
Dionysus, 26
Divorce, 67
Dreams, 31, 34, 42, 45, 47, 78, 79, 96,
    99, 125, 259
Druids, 23, 24
Drug addiction, 134, 266
Dupeyrat, Father, 10, 11, 18, 29

Earth goddess, 17
Earthworm, 240, 267
Easter, 25, 26
Eddas, 23
Eddington, 192
Eden, Garden of, 156, 158, 161, 165

Education, 83, 90, 93, 94
Ego, 4, 5, 9, 23, 24, 27, 29, 31, 42, 43, 46, 50, 51, 53, 55, 57, 63, 64, 66, 69, 70, 71, 76, 78, 82, 91, 92, 93, 102, 104, 107, 109, 110, 121, 124, 125, 130–6, 150, 173–8, 229, 244, 246, 247, 249, 251, 252, 257, 265
Egypt, 26
Egyptians, 26, 161
Einstein, 193, 194
Eisteddfod, 24
Electron, 193–8, 203, 205, 208
Elements, 196
Ellis, Havelock, 48
Elysium, 122
Embryology, 79, 230, 231
Encyclopaedia Biblica, 160, 166
Endocrinology, 71
Enzymes, 209, 211, 212
Eovertebrate ocean, 233
Eroticism, 30, 95, 96, 97
Eskimo, 11
Essenes, 165
Eucharist, 27
Eunuch, 84
Europe, 131
Eve, 156, 157, 158
Excommunication, 28
Excrement, 9
Exhibitionism, 47
Exogamy, 63

Fairy tales, 79, 171
Fascist, 259
Fenichel, Otto, 31, 46
Fetish, 38
Fiji, 15
Fish, 221
Flagellates, 218, 219
Flugel, J.C., 47, 48, 108, 109, 111, 168, 258, 259, 262
Flugel, Ingeborg, 100, 101, 166
Folklore, 7, 24, 25, 79, 80, 158, 163, 171, 189
Foetus, 230, 231
Forsyth, Dr. David, 23, 26, 30, 31, 161, 234, 235, 238
Fox hunting, 99
Frazer, Sir James, 7, 8, 15, 18, 21, 25, 26, 29, 79, 101, 148, 164
Freemasonry, 51, 86
Freud, Sigmund, 14, 15, 31, 42, 46, 50, 51, 78, 82, 109, 137–40, 151, 171, 177, 181, 236, 252, 264, 267
Frigid, 59, 63
Frigidity, 67, 92, 158
Funeral rites, 124, 125

Galaxy, 199–204, 235
Gale, E. F., 212
Galileo, 29, 141, 142, 236

Games, 95, 96, 97, 98, 101
Gametophyte, 219
Gas, intergalactic, 201
Gastric ulcer, 35, 231
Gautama, 22
Gene, 212–17, 234, 235, 237
Genesis, 24, 30, 157, 158
Gill clefts, 231, 238
Girl Guides, 140
Glover, Dr. E., 75, 109
Glycocolle, 209
God, 34, 60–2, 116, 151–7, 160, 163, 164, 166, 190
Gore, Bishop, 154, 158, 159, 166
Gorilla, 230
Gospel, 25, 165
Greece, 18, 149, 150
Greeks, 21, 150

Hair, 8, 48
Haldane, 231
Hallow Eve, 23
Hand washing, 38, 39
Hanging, 134
Harrer, Heinrich, 22
Heaven, 160, 162, 165
Hebrew, 156, 160, 164
Heimann, Paula, 78, 104
Helium, 201, 203
Henson, Bishop, 154
Hephaestos, 160
Hereditary characteristics, 212
Heterosexual, 56, 85, 86, 128, 139
Hindu religion, 153, 156
Hindus, 21, 22, 58
Hindustan, 21, 58
Hitler, A., 259
Holophytic nutrition, 218
Holozoic nutrition, 218
Homosexual, 51, 56, 94, 129
Hormones, 209
Hoskin's Test, 28
House of Commons, 123
Hoyle, F., 204
Huguenots, 29
Huitzilopochtli, 26
Hume, David, 154
Huxley, J., 232, 236
Hyaloplasm, 214
Hydra, 220, 224, 225
Hydrogen, 203, 208, 209, 215, 261
Hysteria, 264
Hysteric, 31
Hysterical Conversion Symptoms, 244

Ice Age, 230
Id, 3, 14, 16, 17, 19, 23, 25, 29, 37, 42, 43, 45, 52, 53, 54, 58, 62, 65, 66, 67, 69, 70, 76, 93, 94, 103, 104, 109, 110, 113, 117, 119, 121–39, 158, 163, 169, 173–8, 244, 249–252, 257, 268

Impotence, 34, 59, 66, 67, 158
Imprisonment, 131, 134
Incest, 7, 15–19, 43, 62, 63, 129, 137, 149, 150, 153, 159, 169, 170, 185, 252
India, 21, 71, 263
Indian, Red, 161
Inge, Dean, 154, 159
Inquisition, 28, 35, 168
Insects, 228, 246, 247, 267
Iodine, 215
Iron, 215
Isotopes, 207
Israel, 158

Jacques, Elliott, 106, 116
Japanese, 24
Jelly fish, 224, 227
Jesus, 165
Jew, 10, 165
Jonah, 129
Jones, Ernest, 111, 171, 172
Josephus, 165

Kant, Immanuel, 154
Kerman, 21
Khnoumou, 21
Kinsey, A.C., 130
Klein, Melanie, 7, 77, 78, 80, 95, 106, 114, 127, 138, 249

Lamarckian, 236, 237, 239
Lamas, 22
Las Cases, 28
Law, 109, 128, 129, 134, 143, 191, 253
Laye, Camara, 12, 13
Lemur, 232
Leucin, 209
Libidinal, 41, 43, 51, 58, 88, 101, 106, 114, 119, 121, 125, 129, 130, 134, 135, 169, 177–9, 180, 244, 250
Libido, 37, 40, 41, 44, 51, 56, 60, 76, 84, 169, 177, 249
Lizards, 231
Lister, 71
Llorente, 28
Lowell Observatory, 200
Lowie, 29

Macallum, 233
Macrocosm, 198
Magi, 21
Magic, 7, 8, 11, 27, 28, 31–3, 129, 164, 166, 232, 255
Magnesium, 215
Mahomet, 23
Mahometan power, 21
Malinke tribe, 12
Malinowski, Prof., 27
Mana, 33, 147, 148, 256

Manganese, 215
Mammals, 76, 221, 226, 227, 230, 232
Maoris, New Zealand, 24
Marmion, 264
Marriage, 57, 58, 60, 66, 67, 68, 70
Masochism, 136
Masochist, 133, 153, 162
Masonic feast, 43
Masturbate, 93, 97, 179, 258
Matrimony, 58, 59, 62, 63, 64, 65, 66, 67, 253
Mendelian laws, 251
Menstruation, 9, 10, 64
Metazoans, 220, 233
Methane, 208, 209
Messiah, 163, 164, 165, 166
Mexico, 26, 28
Microcosm, 198
Middle Ages, 27
Middlemore, Merell, 75
Milky Way, 199
Miller, 208
Milton, 162
Miocene epoch, 230
Mithra, 25
Mitosis, 218, 219, 238
Molecules, 196–8, 206–10, 213, 233
Molluscs, 220, 221, 225
Moloch, 11, 190
Momerie, Rev. A. W., 157
Money-Kyrle, 7, 10, 14, 128
Monkey, 230, 232
Monotheism, 150, 151, 154
Montaigne, 58
Moses, 157
Moslem, 58, 161
Murder, 9, 13, 14, 16, 17, 19, 22, 86, 120–2, 130, 137, 149, 150, 159, 177, 185
Muskhogeans, 24
Mussolini, 259
Mutations, 220, 235, 237
Myers, C. S., 237
Mysticism, 30, 31
Mythology, 7, 18, 20, 24–7, 85, 149, 150, 153, 154, 155, 157, 160, 162, 163, 166, 171, 189, 203, 266, 267
Mythology, Christian, 21, 23, 25
Mythology, Greek, 26, 160, 166
Mythology, Hebrew, 23, 25
Mythology, India, 21
Mythology, Northern, 23
Mythology, Roman, 166
Myths, 20, 150, 171

Nativity, 25, 26
Natural Selection, 235, 237
Nazi, 115, 259
Neolithic man, 161
Neuromotor apparatus, 223, 224
Neutrons, 203

New Guinea, 10, 18, 29
Nitrogen, 215
Nuclear bomb, 263, 264
Nucleic acid, 211
Nucleoproteins, 211
Nucleotides, 212
Nucleus, 196, 197, 212, 217
Nursery Schools, 81

Obsession, 14
Obsessional, 10, 39, 40, 79, 166
Observatory, Mount Wilson, 201
Oedipus, 15, 16, 21, 43, 62, 99, 122, 151, 152, 158, 159, 160, 163, 164, 165, 169, 170, 171, 183, 252, 253
Old Testament, 21, 24, 157
Olympic Elk, 128
Omnipotence, 32-4, 88, 122, 146-8, 153, 156, 181, 191, 248, 250
Omnipotent, 61, 191
Ontogenetical, 38
Ontogeny, 4, 80, 163, 240
Ontology, 79
Ophthalmology, 88
Orgasm, 68
Orgy, 16, 42, 86
Oxygen, 215, 217

Pacific Islands, 75
Pagan, 28, 165, 166
Paley, 154
Palthorpe, Dr., 131
Pantheism, 154
Paralyses, 244
Paralysis agitans, 226
Paramecium, 223
Paranoia, 115
Paranoid, 106, 116, 189
Parricide, 7, 17, 19
Parsees, 21
Parthenogenesis, 156
Parties, 54, 55, 57
Penicillin, 238
Penis, 14, 46
Penrose, 131
Persia, 21
Peru, 28
Perversions, 19, 61, 84, 85, 129, 258
Phallic symbol, 156, 160
Phallus, 41
Phobias, 14, 56, 78, 79, 90
Phosphorus, 215
Photosynthesis, 217
Phylogenetical, 38
Phylogeny, 4, 80, 163, 240
Physics, 154, 190, 232
Plague of London, 263
Pleasure principle, 82, 85, 90, 181, 190, 229, 246, 265
Planarian, 225, 226
Planets, 204

Plasma genes, 213
Platyhelminthes, 225
Political, 107, 123
Politics, 253
Polytheism, 155
Pope, The, 30, 140
Potassium, 215
Potency, 41, 45, 47
Prayer, 8, 30
Prayer Book, 16, 252
Pregnancy, 71, 91
Pregnant, 90
Prison, 60, 131, 132
Prohibitionism, 41
Projection, 106, 116, 129, 132, 147, 250, 261
Promiscuity, 265
Prostitutes, 68, 126
Proteins, 198, 207, 208, 209, 211, 212, 213, 215, 217, 266
Protein molecule, 209, 211
Protein synthesis, 211, 212, 213
Protestants, 171
Protons, 195, 196, 203, 205, 207, 208
Protoplasm, 198, 207, 208, 210, 215-7, 223, 224, 233, 246, 266
Protozoa, 219, 222-4
Puberty, 9, 12, 30, 88, 186, 251
Punishment, 23, 108, 129-37, 159, 162, 163, 170, 177, 185

Quantum mechanics, 195
Quantum theory, 193, 194, 197

Rabies, 214
Rape, 19, 91, 99, 121
Reflex arc, 240, 243
Regicide, 7, 17, 148, 149
Relativity, principle of, 195, 235
Religion, 7, 8, 23, 25-8, 44, 147, 148, 153, 162, 167-71, 189, 252, 262, 266, 267
Religions, 69, 103, 141, 145, 148, 149
Religious belief, 151, 166-8, 171, 172, 255
Religious ceremonies, 160
Religious concepts, 158
Religious dogma, 30
Religious Ecstasy, 170
Religious ideals, 258
Religious practices, 165
Religious ritual, 39, 148
Repression, 4, 49, 51, 88-90, 131-3, 170, 175, 252, 260
Reptiles, 221, 222, 230, 262
Resurrection, 27
Ribonucleic acid, 210, 211
Ribose, 211
Riviere, Joan, 31
Robertson, Archibald, 154, 165
Rome, 149, 150

Romans, 21
Roman Catholics, 58, 151
Roman Church, 28, 30
Roman Empire, 27
Rousseau, Jean Jacques, 93, 258
Russia, 10

Sacrifice, 7, 17, 18, 35, 100, 105, 108, 148, 151, 164, 167
Sadism, 23, 25, 29, 85, 86, 88, 131, 132, 136, 138, 162, 175, 250
Sadistic, 100, 107, 116, 123, 129, 130, 132, 133, 135, 157, 178
Santa Claus, 150
Saracens, 162
Satan, 160
Savage, 9, 15, 17, 26, 34, 79–83, 105, 109, 171
Savagery, 12, 175
Schizoid, 106
Schizophrenia, 35, 79, 181, 265
Schizophrenics, 80, 87, 106, 190, 265
Schmideberg, Melitta, 79, 80
Scouts, Boy, 140
Sex, 39, 64, 88, 89, 90, 92, 93, 113, 118, 152, 158, 159, 160, 176, 184
Sex education, 88–93
Shaw, Bernard, 131, 236
Siam, King of, 8
Siberia, Bedel Tartars, 24
Siblings, 53, 77, 143–8, 153, 256
Sinker, Rev. R., 157
Slaten, Rev. A. Wakefield, 161
Slipher, Dr., 200
Sodium, 215
Solar radiation, 233
Solar system, 197, 199, 203, 204
Soma, 238
Spain, 28
Spaniards, 26
Spanish Inquisition, 130
Spencer, Herbert, 235
Spencer-Jones, Sir Harold, 202
Spiders, 228
Spinal cord, 227
Spinoza, 153, 154
Spirogyra, 219
Sponges, 220, 224
Spongeoplasm, 214
Sporophyte generation, 219
Stag hunting, 100
Stanley, 214
Staphylocci, 238
Stebbing, Rev. T. R., 158, 162
St. John the Baptist, 26
Stone Age, 85
Strachey, Alix, 87, 109, 110, 115, 116, 124, 125, 140, 141
Stokes, Adrian, 97, 98
Streeter, Canon B. H., 162
Suicide, 59, 133, 134, 170

Sulphur, 25
Superego, 4, 14, 16, 17, 19, 23, 24, 25, 29, 37, 39, 40, 42, 43, 45, 53–5, 57–69, 70, 76, 88, 89, 93–5, 101, 103, 107, 109, 110, 113, 121-7, 129, 130, 132, 133, 135, 137, 139, 141, 142, 149, 150, 158, 159, 163, 168–170, 174–80, 185, 243, 249, 251, 252, 257, 258, 261, 268
Supernatural world, 8, 31, 192
Supernaturalism, 232
Superstition, 7, 10, 19, 32, 35, 69, 71, 105, 128, 147, 166, 171, 181, 187, 255
Suttie, Dr. Ian, 115, 142, 166
Switzerland, 28
Sympathetic Nervous System, 227
Symptom formation, 244
Symptomatic behaviour, 55, 163, 251, 253, 257, 258, 265
Symptomatology, 15, 162, 163, 189, 255, 264, 268
Syria, 26

Taboos, 7, 8, 9, 10, 15, 16, 17, 19, 24, 31, 40, 41, 55, 59, 60, 62, 63, 69, 118, 127, 170, 252, 253
Tarsier, 230
Television, 56
Testament, New, 163, 166
Theatres, 56
Theism, 153, 154
Thyrotoxicosis, 231
Tibet, 22
Torture, 130
Totem, 15, 41, 148
Totemism, 14, 15, 100, 149, 151, 153
Totems, 7, 14, 15, 41, 44, 60, 62, 101, 127
Trade Unions, 140
Transference, 6, 66, 81, 92, 119, 120, 125, 182
Transvestism, 46
Tuberculosis, 134
Turks, 162
Tyburn Tree, 134

Uganda, 9
Ultra violet light, 217
Unconscious, 9, 15, 17, 19, 35, 39, 40, 41, 42, 47, 48, 49, 51, 52, 54, 56, 63, 70, 73, 77, 81, 85, 88, 89, 91, 93, 94, 97, 99, 101, 107, 111, 112, 115, 116, 120, 122, 124, 127, 132, 133, 135, 136, 138, 139, 142, 144, 146, 149, 157, 158, 159, 160, 161, 171, 172, 174, 176, 184, 185, 186, 187, 244, 252, 255, 259, 260, 266
Unemployment, 108
Unicellular animalcules, 230, 231, 233, 240

United Nations, 259
Universe, 203, 232
Urethra, 12
Uterus, 32, 66, 73, 231
Utopia, 256, 257

Vaginismus, 68
Valin, 209
Vatican Council, 30
Vedas, 21, 22
Vertebrates, 220, 221, 225, 227, 229, 233
Victorian times, 76
Virgin, 26, 27, 91, 152, 164, 166, 167
Virginity, 41, 46
Viruses, 211, 213–6, 234, 242, 246
Vitzilipuztli, 26
Volcano, 121

Wales, 24
War, 50, 52, 75, 79, 99, 102, 103, 107–9, 111, 112, 114, 116, 117, 118, 120, 123, 124, 126, 127, 130, 150, 168, 176, 177, 260, 262–6, 268
Weston la Barre, 50, 53
Whit Sunday, 23
Witch, 23, 28, 29, 35, 130, 168
Womb, 156
Worms, 225, 239

Yellow fever, 214

Zeus, 29
Zinc, 215
Zoroaster, 21
Zuckermann, 52
Zug, 29
Zygote, 216

GEORGE ALLEN & UNWIN LTD
London: 40 Museum Street, W.C.1
Auckland: 24 Wyndham Street
Bombay: 15 Graham Road, Ballard Estate, Bombay 1
Buenos Aires: Escritorio 454-459, Florida 165
Calcutta: 17 Chittaranjan Avenue, Calcutta 13
Cape Town: 109 Long Street
Hong Kong: F1/12 Mirador Mansions, Kowloon
Ibadan: P.O. Box 62
Karachi: Karachi Chambers, McLeod Road
Madras: Mohan Mansion, 38c Mount Road, Madras 6
Mexico: Villalongin 32-10, Piso, Mexico 5, D.F.
Nairobi: P.O. Box 12446
New Delhi: 13-14 Ajmeri Gate Extension, New Delhi 1
São Paulo: Avenida 9 de Julho 1138-Ap. 51
Singapore: 36c Prinsep Street, Singapore 7
Sydney, N.S.W.: Bradbury House, 55 York Street
Toronto: 91 Wellington Street West